# THE MOST
# FAMOUS WOMAN
# IN BASEBALL

RELATED TITLES FROM POTOMAC BOOKS, INC.

Jack Johnson and Christopher Rivers, *My Life and Battles*

Gene Carney, *Burying the Black Sox: How Baseball's Cover-Up of the 1919 World Series Fix Almost Succeeded*

Curt Smith, *Pull Up a Chair: The Vin Scully Story*

Steven Travers, *A Tale of Three Cities: The 1962 Baseball Season in New York, Los Angeles, and San Francisco*

# THE MOST FAMOUS WOMAN IN BASEBALL

## *Effa Manley and the Negro Leagues*

## BOB LUKE

Potomac Books, Inc.
Washington, D.C.

Library of Congress Cataloging-in-Publication Data
Luke, Bob.
 The most famous woman in baseball : Effa Manley and the Negro Leagues /
Bob Luke. — 1st ed.
      p. cm.
 Includes bibliographical references and index.
 ISBN 978-1-59797-546-9 (hardcover : alk. paper)
 1.  Manley, Effa, 1897-1981. 2.  Baseball team owners—United
States—Biography. 3.  Women baseball team owners—United States—Biography.
4.  Newark Eagles (Baseball team)—History. 5.  African American business
enterprises. I. Title.
 GV865.M325L85 2011
 796.357092—dc22
 [B]
                                                            2010050944

Printed in the United States of America on acid-free paper that meets the American National Standards Institute Z39-48 Standard.

Potomac Books, Inc.
22841 Quicksilver Drive
Dulles, Virginia 20166

First Edition

10 9 8 7 6 5 4 3 2 1

In memory of Barbara

# CONTENTS

*Introduction*                                             ix

1   The Lady Makes a Splash                                 1
2   The Manleys Come to Baseball                            9
3   Abe Trades Brooklyn for Newark                         17
4   Effa Steps Up                                          31
5   Effa Comes Into Her Own                                41
6   Fireworks                                              55
7   Cobbling Together a Lineup                             69
8   War Comes to Newark                                    81
9   The Eagles Adapt to the War                            95
10  Branch Rickey Drops the Color Bar                     115
11  A Reunited Team                                       121
12  Striving for Respectability                           133
13  Effa's Life After the Eagles                          149

*Epilogue*                                                165
*Appendix*                                                169
*Acknowledgments*                                         173
*Notes*                                                   175
*Index*                                                   213
*Suggested Readings*                                      225
*About the Author*                                        227

# INTRODUCTION

Effa Louise Brooks Manley grew up in a black neighborhood in Philadelphia, worked in New York City's fashion industry, and gained prominence in Harlem's civil rights movement before becoming the best-known and most controversial executive in black baseball. With the benefit of a high school education, good looks, a passion for advancing the rights of African Americans, street smarts, compassion, a confident tongue, and a wealthy husband, Effa Manley kept the Newark Eagles together from 1936 to 1948.[1]

She mothered, disciplined, and cajoled young black players in their prime; traded barbs and insults with sportswriters; pleaded with assemblymen, senators, and U.S. officials to stop players from deserting the Eagles for Latin America; and fought with Branch Rickey, president and general manager of the Brooklyn Dodgers, as he stole her players during the early days of integration—all the while juggling the details essential to keeping the team in operation.

While they didn't always agree with her, sportswriters on the Negro weeklies agreed on her good looks. They referred to her as "attractive," "charming," and "effervescent," and as a "hula-hipped Harlem beauty." Her acid tongue, on the other hand, prompted A. S. "Doc" Young, sportswriter for the *Los Angeles Sentinel*, to characterize Effa as "vitriolic."[2]

As the only wife to attend the owners' meetings—generally comprising of middle-aged black men, most of whom ran numbers and operated clubs—Effa pressed the owners to make changes that would make the leagues run more like a business. She envisioned a future for Negro league baseball as an institution that would be a source of pride and employment for blacks by providing increasing salaries for players, more jobs for stadium personnel, modern ballparks in big cities, minor leagues where young players could hone their skills, and a regular schedule of games that would not be beholden to the whims of booking agents and their fees. Her vision, she knew from the start, was at odds with the status quo, but she relished the challenge.[3]

Effa did not suffer fools easily and did not hesitate to say so. Her self-confidence and belief in her ideals could at times show a self-serving side that worked to her disadvantage. Although she was a sharp businesswoman, she had a warm spot for children, including the players' children as well as her own nieces and nephews (she had no children of her own). Effa helped players find jobs during and after their playing days. She made no secret of her attraction to men, as evidenced by romantic relationships with several players, as well as four marriages. She was, in her own words, "soft on music."[4]

She tended to lie about her age, shaving off three years whenever possible. While her birth certificate could not be found, the 1910 Census and her high school records show her year of birth as 1897. In 1977, however, she told interviewer William Marshall that she was born in 1900, and she used 1900 as her birth date on her application for a marriage license in 1956.[5]

Her husband, Abraham Lincoln Manley, owned the Eagles. His success in numbers and in real estate in Camden, New Jersey, during the 1920s allowed him both to underwrite the team and to show Effa the good life. He helped out by deciding what trades to make, scouting for new players, and hiring and firing managers. If Effa was energetic and ambitious, Abe was laid back and "genial."[6] Abe liked to hang with the players. He rode the bus with them to games and to spring training, even though his weight and swollen ankles made the trips, at times, unbearable. He let players know he was the boss by handing each one of them their dollar-a-day meal money. He licked his thumb and finger before handing out each bill to be sure no one got two by mistake. In Newark Abe drank beer and played poker with the players at Dan's Tavern, just around the corner from the Grand Hotel, at 78 West Market Street, where fans and players mingled after games. Abe took his poker seriously and played well. Opponents nicknamed him "Old Squirrel" for his ability to end up with most of the chips. If one played a hand well, it was likely to be said, "You played that hand just like Old Squirrel."[7]

Monte Irvin, an Eagle from 1937 to 1948 (except for the three years he served in the military) and a Hall of Fame outfielder for the New York Giants, remembered, "Sometimes Abe won all the guys' money. He had deep pockets so he could bluff them out. . . . He'd loan the money back to them and expect to be paid on payday. Guys would lose their entire paycheck. One time, after a game had ended, Abe counted his money and found he had a dollar and thirteen cents. Mule [Mule Suttles—a Hall of Fame first baseman for the Eagles] dug in his pocket and said, 'All I've got is two cents, Cap.' Abe said, 'Give it to me so I can make it $1.15.' And Mules did. I couldn't believe what I was seeing."[8]

Both Manleys advised the players on matters of conduct. Abe told them, "No girls, no drinking, no smoking. I don't want any lovers on my ball club. You can sacrifice for five months." Larry Doby, who played for the Eagles from 1942 to 1947 with three years off during World War II and who later joined the Cleveland Indians for a Hall of Fame career, remembered Abe checking to see if the guys were patronizing the Newark bars. "He knew Newark," Doby said, "so he'd just walk into a bar. He'd never say anything. Just his appearance was enough."[9] Effa told the players, "Don't do too much carousing or you'll apt to be in weak, bad shape to show up on the field." Unlike Abe, Effa was not opposed to players having girlfriends, but she did think pitchers should abstain from sex the night before a game because "that is something that I feel takes too much away from a guy."[10]

Effa and Abe provided black Newarkers with a sanctuary where they could, for several hours, escape the segregation and discrimination that dominated the lives of most African Americans. In 1939 fans paid eighty-five cents for a box seat, sixty cents for a grandstand seat, and fifteen cents for a seat in the bleachers. Many arrived at the stadium on the number 31 bus, which ran the length of South Orange Avenue, for a fare of a nickel.[11] Once inside, people did not have to worry about where they sat, where they walked, what they said, or whom they looked at. Decked out in their finest clothes, men, women, and children picnicked, socialized, drank, gambled, cheered, and strutted to their hearts' content. Amiri Baraka, a Newark native and American poet, playwright, essayist, and music critic, remembered attending Eagles games with his father: "The hot dogs and root beers! . . . A little big-eyed boy holding his father's hand. . . . It was like we all communicated with each other at a more human level than was usually possible out in cold whitey land. . . . All that love and noise and color and excitement surrounded me like a garment of feeling. I know I thought that's the way life's supposed to be."[12]

In addition to hot dogs and root beers, fans could buy Cracker Jack, peanuts, and candy, or patronize the bar. Those who preferred home cooking brought picnic baskets overflowing with chicken, potato salad, barbeque, and cornbread to the disappointment of the stadium vendors.[13]

Besides baseball, Effa had a passion for civil rights. She sponsored protest marches, benefit games, and collected money for the National Association for the Advancement of Colored People (NAACP). She served as treasurer and board member of the Newark chapter. During the Eagles' tenure in Newark, some advances toward integration in education, employment, housing, and health care did occur, but major improvements wouldn't happen until the civil rights legislation of the 1960s and the city's recovery from the 1967 riots.

○

This book draws on primary sources, including the files Effa kept from 1938 to 1946. Her letters reveal spats with sportswriters, admonishments to players and owners, and pleadings with government officials. Effa left the files behind when she moved out of her house at 71 Crawford Street in Newark. "I just left them there," she told interviewer William Marshall years later. "And I had two steel file cases of the five-drawer kind, drawers full of all kinds of records and information."[14] Fortunately, a contractor discovered them while renovating the basement for the new owner and donated them to the Newark Public Library, where they remain today. Her scrapbook, preserved at the National Baseball Hall of Fame and Museum, contains newspaper clippings, photographs, poems, awards, certificates, and letters. The papers of Jackie Robinson, Branch Rickey, the NAACP, African American sportswriter Art Carter, and Philadelphia Stars owner Ed Bolden added depth. Black weeklies of the time provided information about the Eagles fortunes as well as conditions in Newark. My interviews with the three surviving Eagles—Monte Irvin, James "Red" Moore, and Willie C. "Curly" Williams—added additional perspective as did my interview with Jerry Izenberg, longtime sportswriter for Newark's *Star Ledger* daily newspaper. Interviews with Effa Manley, Larry Doby, Bill Veeck, and Monte Irvin by William Marshall for the University of Kentucky Libraries A. B. Chandler Oral History Project, and interviews with Effa Manley and Eagles player Fran Mathews by Allen Richardson for his graduate work at San Diego State University contributed invaluable information.

# CHAPTER ONE

## The Lady Makes a Splash

She had worked eleven years for this day. On Sunday afternoon, September 29, 1946, under partly cloudy skies with temperatures in the midsixties, Effa Manley, age forty-nine, sat head down, eyes closed, arms crossed, unable to watch the scene unfolding in front of her at Ruppert Stadium in the ninth inning of the seventh and final game of the Negro Leagues World Series. The Kansas City Monarchs, champions of the Negro American League (NAL), had the tying and winning runs on second and third with two outs. She heard what she described as "the sickening sound of a bat hitting a ball." Monarch third baseman Herb Souell had popped Eagles pitcher Rufus Lewis's offering high above first base, where Lennie Pearson squeezed the ball into his glove, making the Eagles world champs. She eased back in her seat, drained and too numb to move. Well-wishers crowded around her with congratulations in what she described as "this hour of triumph."[1]

○

Effa was born on March 27, 1897, through an extramarital union between her African American seamstress mother, Bertha Ford Brooks, and her white employer, Philadelphia stockbroker John Marcus Bishop. "My mother," Effa said, "was a beautiful seamstress. She sewed only for wealthy white people. In the course of her sewing she met my father, and I was born as a result."[2] Her mother's husband, Benjamin Brooks, successfully sued Bishop for $10,000 for alienation of affection and divorced Bertha. Several years later, Bertha married Benjamin A. Cole, an African American nine years her junior.

1

Effa was a light-skinned African American woman who could pass for white (as she did on more than one occasion), yet she always maintained that she was, in fact, white. She told interviewer William Marshall in 1977, "I am white." As she explained her ancestry to Marshall, her mother's father was American Indian and her mother's mother was of German descent, and her mother, Bertha Ford, was white. She noted that she had olive skin "if you look close," which she attributed to her mother's father.[3] Her mother reinforced to her the idea that she was white. One day the principal of her integrated elementary school asked Effa why she always played with the white children. Not knowing how to respond, she asked her mother what she should say to the principal. Her mother told her, "You go back and tell her you're just as white as she is."[4]

Not everyone agreed that she was white. Monte Irvin said, "When she got older it became more apparent she was black; she got darker. Any African American person can see the difference. Don Newcombe [who pitched ten years in the majors after two years with the Eagles] and I stopped by to see her after she'd moved to Los Angeles [when Effa was in her sixties], and you could tell then this lady is African American."[5]

U.S. Census records for 1900 and 1910 support Irvin's account. Both censuses describe Effa and her mother as black. Instructions to the 1900 enumerators told them to describe as black only "those persons who have three-fourths or more black blood." The 1910 instructions reserved the designation black for "all persons who are full-blooded negroes [sic]." Curiously enough, while her mother appeared to the enumerators to meet the criteria for being described as black in both instances, Effa would have been more appropriately described as mulatto, "all other persons having some proportion or perceptible trace of negro [sic] blood."[6]

Regardless of her heritage, as a child Effa lived in a black family, the Cole household with her stepfather, mother, three black stepbrothers (Jacob, John, and Alphonso), and two black stepsisters (Ruth and Elizabeth). While she was growing up from 1897 to 1915, "passing" reached its peak, but most blacks like Effa, who could have passed for white, chose not to for a combination of reasons— fear of being condemned by their family and friends, a wariness of whites, and not wanting to forsake the security of the black community.[7] Family considerations probably led her to live life as a black woman, as she maintained close relationships with her family throughout her life.

During Effa's formative years, the family lived at 105 South 34th Street, four blocks west of where Philadelphia's 30th Street Amtrak station sits today. By the fall of 1914 the family had moved a mile and a half east toward downtown Philadelphia to a house in another black neighborhood at 1700 Bainbridge Street. She graduated from Newton Grammar School in the spring of 1911 and entered Penn Central High School that fall. She pursued a vocational program that included courses in cooking, oral expression, and sewing. She graduated in 1916. She would make good use of the lessons she learned in her oral expression classes.[8]

After graduation she moved to Harlem. Following in her mother's footsteps and using her light complexion to her advantage, she landed a job in a millinery shop in Manhattan that would have barred her if the owner had thought her to be black. There she "spent quite a few years [about sixteen] in the millinery business, making hats and taking a little additional training in designing." Not satisfied with the solitary and arduous business of making hats and dresses, she added modeling to her repertoire by participating in Harlem fashion shows conducted by "society women" at the Manhattan Casino, an elaborate hall at 280 West 155th Street and Eighth Avenue that could accommodate six thousand people. Each night she took the A train from Manhattan back to her apartment. The A train, made famous by Duke Ellington, ran as an express between the 59th and the 110th Street stations, the first stop in Harlem. During this time she met her first husband via the assertive style that would be her trademark throughout her life. "I went after him and I got him," she said of Charles Bush, whom she met on the beaches of Atlantic City. The marriage lasted only a few months.[9]

O

Abe Manley, the son of William and Rebecca Manley, was born on December 20, 1884, in the town of Hertford, in North Carolina's Perquimans County. William, known by family members as "Grandpa Bill," was born in Virginia in about 1844. He owned a tract of land where he farmed and raised horses, one of which, Sailor Boy, he raced at local tracks. By 1900 seven children lived in the Manley household. William and Rebecca raised them in the Quaker tradition, which brought with it demands about how one should behave. When a boy came to the house to court one of the Manley girls, Rebecca Manley placed an alarm clock on the mantel. When the alarm went off at 11:00 p.m., the visitor said his good-byes and went home. William expected the children to work once they were old enough.

Abe's brother Nathan took up bricklaying in his teenage years. As a high school student Abe had no plans for his future, so his father told him to get a job in the sawmill. Abe did not like it but had no choice. One day he pushed a piece of wood too close to the blade and lost the index finger on his right hand. After stopping the bleeding, he went home and told his mother he was leaving before his father got home.[10]

Abe traveled to Norfolk, Virginia, where he lived until 1916, when he moved to Brooklyn and took a room at 57 Fleet Place. By 1921 he was back in Norfolk, this time at 919 Falkland Street in the home of Lois Spavey. He listed his occupation as chauffeur in 1921 and as laborer for the next three years. By 1925 he had moved to Camden, New Jersey, where he initially lived at 1013 Francis Street before moving to 1068 Francis Street in 1930. He gave his occupation as a laborer for three of those years, and in one year he reported being a barber.[11] While Abe may have at times been a chauffeur, a laborer, and a barber, at some point he started running numbers and buying real estate. Despite his many moves, he stayed close to his brothers, who took summer jobs on a ship and visited Abe when they docked in whatever city he was in. Abe gave them spending money, and on one occasion, for unknown reasons, told them they should be circumcised, an operation that he paid for.[12]

In Camden Abe ran his businesses and amassed his fortune out of the Rest-A-While Club, housed in a building he owned. Many considered the club, located at 822 Kaighn Avenue, Camden's most prominent Negro political and social club. Physicians, attorneys, and schoolteachers were among its members. Poker pots reportedly ran as high as $20,000. Luxuriously furnished, the club boasted a private bar, a steward, sleeping apartments, a billiard and game room, and a piano valued at $ 8,000.

Robert Bumbrey, reported to be Camden's political king and most prominent philanthropist, owned the club. Abe served as the club's treasurer. Bumbrey's wife, Clara, spent her time with the children of the neighborhood. Each Christmas "Aunt Clara" piled gifts under a decorated tree for them to open.

On Easter Sunday, April 5, 1931, four armed and masked men broke into the club at 4:00 a.m. and robbed two members of $160. One member, twenty-eight-year-old Leroy Atkins, who had purchased the piano with money from his numbers "hits," suffered a fatal shot to the stomach from a sawed-off shotgun as the robbers were leaving. Bumbrey, asleep on the second floor, jumped out of his bedroom window and broke his leg. Abe was not present.

Atkins received what a *Philadelphia Tribune* reporter described as "a regular Al Capone funeral . . . with the proverbial metal casket, a room full of designs valued at five hundred dollars, mobs of curiosity seekers, and the long cortege to the cemetery." The cortege went a mile out of its way so Bumbrey could view it from his hospital window. The men responsible pleaded guilty to the charges, which saved them from the "hot squat," or electric chair.

A bombing of the club a year and a half later drove Abe to Harlem. In the early hours of September 12, 1932, an explosion blew away the front of the two-story brick house, ripped up the stone front porch, broke windows half a mile away, and woke hundreds of citizens. Police suspected rival numbers bankers from Philadelphia to be behind the bombing. A report by an undercover policeman had named Bumbrey as one of Camden's two top numbers men. The blast threw Bumbrey, again asleep in his bed on the second floor, onto the floor.[13] Camden's district attorney, a personal friend of Abe's, told him, "You'd better get out of town."[14] Abe took his friend's advice.

O

Abe and Effa both loved baseball. Effa walked from her apartment to Yankee Stadium, where she rooted for Babe Ruth.[15] "I was crazy about Babe Ruth," she said. "I used to go see all the Yankee games hoping he'd hit the ball out of the park."[16] Abe played baseball as a boy and attended games of the Negro league Hilldale Giants at Hilldale Stadium in Darby, Pennsylvania. Abe made friends with the players, including a future Eagle, catcher and manager Raleigh "Biz" Mackey. Abe took his first business interest in baseball when he bought a team, the Camden Leafs, in August 1929. The Leafs faced off against such other clubs as the Germantown Black Sox, the Italian Americans, and the Twelfth Ward Club of Camden at the ballpark of the Crescent Country Club in Fairview, New Jersey. The Leafs folded after the 1929 season.[17]

Previous accounts report that Effa and Abe met for the first time at Yankee Stadium during the 1932 World Series between the New York Yankees and the Chicago Cubs. However, they had actually met sometime before as evidenced by the fact that Effa and Abe, along with the Bumbreys, sponsored the Charity Ball for fifteen hundred people at Camden's Convention Hall, located at Haddon

Avenue and Line Street on a Friday evening, January 29, 1932. Although they had not yet been married, news coverage of the ball had referred to the couple as Mr. and Mrs. Abe Manley. Her outfit included "flowing black lace and pearls." Other women wore long white gowns. Men dressed in tuxedos. Proceeds went to Camden Mayor R. R. Stewart's Relief Committee.[18]

After a courtship of more than a year, Effa and Abe married on June 15, 1933, and settled into an apartment at 741 St. Nicholas Avenue, in the Sugar Hill area of Harlem, home to many of Harlem's upscale residents, including Thurgood Marshall, an attorney in the landmark *Brown vs. Board of Education* case decided by the Supreme Court in 1954 and later the Court's first African American associate justice.[19] Effa listed her race as black on the marriage license application.[20]

Abe, who had also been married once before, introduced Effa to Lincoln Continental automobiles, mink coats, Oriental rugs, and diamond rings. Both generous and possessive, he bought his bride-to-be a five-carat diamond ring from Tiffany's, but only after he made her sell the jewelry she'd received from former boyfriends.[21] When they returned to pick up the ring, Effa "got a kick" out of the salesgirls making sure they got a look at the couple. "They heard," Effa said, "this old Negro man had bought a ring for this pretty young white woman."[22] Later that year Abe bought Effa a mink coat, the first of four mink items she owned during their marriage, which she insured for $700, and a Hudson seal coat that she insured for $60. Effa told an interviewer, "My husband liked to see me dressed up in furs and look real expensive so the players would have confidence that their checks would be coming." That may have been more rationalization than fact. Abe's fondness for diamond rings for himself and Lincoln Continentals made no secret of his wealth.[23]

Abe's family had reservations about the marriage. To them it appeared that Abe had married a white woman. Abe's relatives lived in segregated communities in North Carolina, where whites were feared. Joel Manley, a great-nephew of Abe, remembers his father telling him how scared he was when Joel, at age twelve, disregarded the "whites only" sign over a drinking fountain on the ferry between Norfolk, Virginia, and southern Maryland. "I didn't know what they [whites] might do to you," his father told him. Fortunately, nothing happened. Abe's relatives gradually came to accept the marriage. Many of the family visited the couple during their years in Newark, and Abe took Effa with him on trips to Hertford.[24]

They differed in appearance as well as temperament. Light-skinned Effa was taller and more slender than Abe, who stood about five feet, seven inches with a gingerbread complexion and a portly stature. During Sunday gatherings of Abe's brothers, sisters, and their children at the Manleys' Newark residence, Effa talked all the time, usually about her baseball dealings and some of the players. Abe was more pensive, talked little about himself, and had the reputation in the family for being a deep thinker and a welcome dispenser of financial advice. Sunday visits always included piano recitals by one or more of the children, followed by cake and cookies, which Effa had baked, accompanied by a scoop of ice cream.[25]

○

What Abe did immediately following their marriage is not known, but Effa plunged into social and civil rights ventures. In June she arranged for her mentor, Cora Rollins, to stay two nights at the Manleys' home before both saw Rollins off to Europe for a four-month vacation. Rollins played a prominent role in Chicago's civic and political circles in her position as the first Negro member of the board of the Illinois Women's Democratic Club. She held leadership positions in hospital associations, auxiliary clubs, and the League of Women Voters.[26]

While Rollins was in Europe, Effa led boycotts against white merchants on 125th Street in Harlem, who prospered by selling to blacks but refusing to hire them in any position other than as elevator operators. At a dinner for Joe Louis, who would win the world heavyweight boxing championship crown in 1937, Effa and William Davis, editor of the *New Amsterdam News*, a black weekly, struck up a conversation about how hard it was for Negroes to find jobs in Harlem. Davis suggested Effa approach Blumstein department stores because Mrs. Blumstein "was a nice person and would hire a black person if you asked her." After mulling the idea over with several women friends "and getting nowhere," Effa approached Rev. John H. Johnson, rector of Saint Martin's Episcopal Church at Lenox Avenue and 122nd Street in the heart of Harlem. He changed the group's name from the Harlem Women's Club to the Citizens League for Fair Play. Effa collected $75 in donations to pay the incorporation charges.

With the help of other ministers, the Citizens League collected two weeks worth of sales slips from Blumstein's to show the department store's owners that blacks made up a majority of their trade. Confronted by Johnson and Effa with the slips, the Blumsteins still refused to hire blacks as sales clerks. League members, including Effa, then picketed the store for several weeks in midsummer, when the temperatures exceeded the 100 degree mark, carrying signs that read, "We Won't Shop Where We Can't Work," and using loudspeakers to broadcast their demands that the Blumsteins hire black sales clerks. Johnson took Effa and a lawyer with him for a second meeting. The Blumsteins and their lawyer refused to budge at first.

Effa introduced a personal note in the talks when she said, "You know, we think just as much of our young colored girls as you do your young white girls but there's just no work for them. The only thing they can find to do is work in someone's home as a maid or become prostitutes." Her statement, she said, so shocked the Blumsteins that they agreed to hire Negro women as sales clerks.[27] On Monday, July 26, 1934, William Blumstein issued a statement, prefaced by a disclaimer that the store had never practiced any form of discrimination, saying the store would, "in recognition of the principles asserted by the Rev. Dr. John H. Johnson," employ fifteen colored sales clerks within two weeks, twenty more in September, and more in the future as dictated by business conditions.

Johnson and Effa celebrated their accomplishment the following Saturday. After waiting three hours for a downpour to stop, fifteen hundred people, led by the Jenkins Orphanage Band, paraded down Lenox Avenue to 110th Street, then up 7th Avenue to 145th Street, past the Manleys' apartment on St. Nicholas Avenue, and then to Dorrance Brooks Square, where Johnson and others delivered victory speeches.[28]

Harlem, especially the commercial corridor of 125th Street, would see more protests and boycotts before blacks gained an economic footing close to that of whites, but the first step had been taken. By June 1936, three hundred blacks had found "gainful, clean, and decent" employment on 125th Street. Effa took these developments to be an example of the fine things her race, which she felt did not know its own strength, could accomplish.[29] At the same time, Abe decided to get into baseball.

# CHAPTER TWO

## The Manleys Come to Baseball

At their meeting in Pittsburgh on Tuesday, November 13, 1934, the National Negro League (NNL) owners granted Abe a franchise to operate the Brooklyn Eagles. The Eagles joined the New York Cubans as Gotham City's second Negro league team.

Abe brought to the table a gambling spirit and a prodigious bankroll—without either of which he would not have survived the precarious financial and organizational venture that was Negro league baseball. The Great Depression had pushed the NNL to fold at the end of the 1931 season. Its replacement, the East-West League, did not complete the 1932 season. The year 1933 saw the emergence of a second NNL and the first Negro league All-Star game, known as the East-West Classic, which was played in Chicago's Comiskey Park. The game attracted over nineteen thousand fans and was the financial highlight of the season. The nation's sagging economy, however, resulted in sparse attendance at regular games in 1933 and 1934, forcing the owners to dig deep into their own pockets to meet expenses.

The league suffered a lack of organization as well. Owners raided players from other teams; players left, or "jumped," their teams for more attractive opportunities elsewhere; and umpires received little support. The league did not maintain a central office or even a central filing cabinet.

Mindful of complaints from fans and sportswriters over the league's uneven performance in 1933 and 1934, owners addressed both the financial and organizational issues at their January 1935 meeting, held at the West 135th Street YMCA in Harlem. They passed a resolution calling for most of the monies from subsequent East-West games, and other all-star promotions, to go to the league's treasury instead of being parceled out among owners and teams. The moguls called for fines and a ten-day suspension for any player slugging an umpire and a fine for any owner who failed to report such an incident.

The owners also adopted a constitution, written by Abe and Robert Cole, owner of the Chicago American Giants. Three owners—Alejandro "Alex" Pompez of the Cubans, Cumberland Willis "Cum" Posey of the Homestead Grays, and Edward "Chief" Bolden of the Philadelphia Stars—drew up rules regulating the selection, hiring, and jurisdiction of umpires. The group elected William Augustus "Gus" Greenlee of the Pittsburgh Crawfords as chairman; Thomas T. "Smiling Tom" Wilson, owner of the Nashville Elite Giants as vice chairman; and Cole as treasurer. As often happens to the best-laid plans, the constitution and related rules soon fell into disuse. Sportswriter W. Rollo Wilson, in his final year as NNL commissioner, had the unenviable and impossible task of ruling over eight strongly minded owners.[1]

Smiling Tom Wilson ran numbers, owned the Paradise Club, and served one term as president of the Elks Club in Nashville, Tennessee. He organized his first black baseball team, the Nashville Elite Giants, in 1921 and shuttled them from Nashville to Detroit, to Columbus, Ohio, and to Washington, D.C., before settling in Baltimore in 1938. The pockets of his pinstriped suits held wads of cash. His fondness for the ladies resulted in four marriages. As is remembered in Neil Lanctot's *Negro Leauge Baseball*, his tendency to disappear in times of crisis led *Pittsburgh Courier* sportswriter Wendell Smith to complain, "Tom was often harder to find than a snowball in the tropics."

Alex Pompez promoted the Cuban Stars in New York City during the 1920s and owned the New York Cubans from 1935 to 1950. By 1935 he was running numbers and performing chores for New York mobster Dutch Schultz. After he was indicted in 1936 on racketeering charges by New York County District Attorney Thomas E. Dewey, Pompez slipped away to Mexico. He returned to New York under an agreement to turn state's evidence on Schultz's operation and managed to escape retribution, perhaps because Schultz, born as Arthur Flegenheimer, was no longer around. A single shot from a sawed-off shotgun to his stomach, administered by one of four assassins who cornered him in a booth at Newark's Palace Chop House and Tavern, ended his life on October 23, 1935.

Cum Posey, the only NNL owner to have played in the Negro leagues, built a reputation as a successful and innovative manager-owner. He, along with James L. "J. L." Wilkinson, owner of the Kansas City Monarchs in the rival NAL, introduced night baseball before the majors played under the lights. Posey directed the Grays to eight NLL pennants from 1937 to 1945. Rufus "Sonneyman" Jackson, who ran numbers and rented jukeboxes to clubs and restaurants in Pittsburgh, financed the Grays. Posey wrote a regular column, "Posey's Points," for the *Pittsburgh Courier,* reputedly had a woman in every city, and served on the Homestead, Pennsylvania School Board.

Ed Bolden, a forty-year veteran of the post office, owned, in partnership with white booking agent Ed Gottlieb, the Philadelphia Stars. A shy and modest man, Bolden preferred to operate behind the scenes.

Gus Greenlee managed several boxers including John Henry Lewis, the first black light-heavyweight champion, and operated his Crawford Grill—a center for jazz, booze, gambling, and women—in Pittsburgh. He initiated the re-emergence of the NNL in 1933and served as its president for five years.

Robert Cole, a Chicago undertaker, owned Cole's American Giants from 1932 to 1935. The Giants won the NNL pennant in 1933 and 1934 and narrowly lost the 1935 pennant to the Stars. Finding the distance between Chicago and the eastern cities to be too great, Cole dropped out of the NNL.

Charles H. Tyler, a chicken farmer and owner of the Chicken Shack Restaurant and Tavern in Avenel, New Jersey, owned the Newark Dodgers from 1934 to 1935.[2]

The press liked this meeting. One scribe enthused over the results, comparing them to those of the Continental Congress, "when state jealousies were forgotten as the sacred document became greater than the petty interests of the states." The meeting also pleased Abe to the extent that he and Effa hosted a Saturday night bash at the posh Small's Paradise in Harlem for more than a hundred people, including the owners, their guests, and reporters. The press, not surprisingly, praised Abe for developing close ties between owners and the journalists.[3]

Prior to the meeting Abe had negotiated the use of Ebbets Field, home to the Brooklyn Dodgers, directly with the Dodgers' management, thereby avoiding booking agents and their fees for scheduling playing dates. He hired Ben Taylor, age forty-seven, to manage the team.[4] Taylor, one of four brothers who starred in the Negro leagues, began his player-manager career in 1924 and continued managing until his retirement from baseball in 1941.[5]

On the following Monday, Manley and Taylor met at Abe's office in the Democratic Club on 7th Avenue in Harlem to select players from the pool made available to them by the other teams.[6] *New York Amsterdam News* sportswriter Romeo Dougherty praised Abe for his choice of office, as it gave the game a healthier image than did choosing a tavern in which to conduct business—a not too subtle slap at Greenlee.[7]

Abe and Taylor ordered the players to report to spring training in Jacksonville, Florida, where Abe allowed the team the luxury of three weeks to get into shape. Most Negro league teams spent only a week or ten days in camp before hitting the exhibition trail to hone their skills while generating revenue. With several exceptions, the players who came north "on a big, blue, new Eagle bus," were an undistinguished lot, making the Eagles the question mark of the league.[8]

As has been the case with major league expansion teams, the existing teams did not make their best players available to the newcomer. The Eagles, nevertheless, boasted three stars: Ted "Double Duty" Radcliffe, George Giles, and Leon Day. New York writer Damon Runyon gave Radcliffe his nickname because he was in the practice of pitching the first game of a doubleheader and catching the second. Abe recruited Duty from an independent team. His stay with Abe lasted only a few months. He jumped the Eagles in June to play for a white semipro team in Bismarck, North Dakota, that offered him more money.[9] Twenty-six-year-old George Giles's defensive skills made him an asset to any team, as did his ability to manage younger players. Giles became a free agent when the Baltimore Black Sox folded in 1934. Eighteen-year-old Leon Day, who played his rookie year with the Baltimore Black Sox in 1934, came to the Eagles with Giles and proved to be Abe and Taylor's best pick. Day holds the strikeout records in the NNL, the Puerto Rican League, and the East-West game. Throughout his career, he hit for an average and played every position, except catcher, well. He never took a windup as a pitcher but started his motion with the ball close to his ear, much as a third baseman does in making the throw to first. At five feet, nine inches tall and weighing 170 pounds, Day was one of the smaller, but most feared, pitchers in the Negro leagues.[10]

After the team returned from Florida, Abe made his most important personnel decision, asking Effa to "do many little things that he had to have taken care of." She assumed the title of business manager and hired Carrie Jacobs, office secretary; Edison Thomas, bus driver; and Eric Ellidge, road secretary.[11]

Brooklyn's fans got their first look at the NNL's newest team on May 17, not at Ebbets Field, but at the Harlem Opera House, located on the same stretch of 125th Street, between 7th and 8th Avenues, as the Victoria and Apollo Theaters. A musical revue that featured heavyweight contender Joe Louis served as the main attraction, but Addison Carey, who sponsored the revue, introduced the Eagles and the Grays onstage the day before their opening game. Dougherty, not wanting to raise fans' expectations to unrealistic levels, warned in his April 27 column, "Abe Manley and Ben Taylor will have their work cut out for them when they send the Eagles against the Pittsburgh outfit [the Grays] for Posey's teams on occasions of lesser importance have seldom lost."[12]

Effa made her presence known by staging a gala on opening day, Saturday, May 11. Both teams, "led by a drum major with a white fur shako two inches shorter than the Chrysler tower," marched from home plate to the centerfield flagpole "while a hot colored band itched to break into a blues number instead of the military march it was playing."[13] Effa recruited New York's Mayor Fiorello LaGuardia to throw out the first ball.[14] Other celebrities in the mayor's box included Rev. Johnson, who enclosed two tickets for a reception at his church in his letter thanking Effa for inviting him to the game; George W. Harris, editor of the *New York News*, a black weekly; radio commentator Lowell Thomas; and *New York Daily News* sportswriter Jimmy Powers.[15]

The Grays manhandled the Eagles 21–7 behind a barrage of twenty-three hits given up by four Eagles pitchers. Played under sunny skies with the temperature in the sixties, "It was," said Effa, "a terrible game. I never saw so many home runs before in my life. I went home in the third inning and had my first drink of whiskey."[16] The Eagles, however, came back to split Sunday's doubleheader, winning the first game 18–9 and losing the second, 4–2. The Eagles evened the series by winning Monday's game, 4–3.[17]

By splitting the series, the Eagles exceeded Dougherty's expectations. Abe, however, aspired to better things and continued his search for new players. He signed several without Taylor's involvement, but the newly signed players had no impact. The Eagles' losses over the next two weeks led Abe to fire Taylor at the end of May and replace him with Giles as the team's player-manager.[18] The team's last place position at the end of the first half of the season, with a 3–16 record, proved to Abe the difficulty of bringing a newly formed team up to competitive level in the NNL. Appearing unruffled, he said, "I never fool myself by thinking we can develop a crackerjack club in less than a year. We are building and I am satisfied."[19]

Taylor was not. He resented Abe for firing him only a month into the season and sued him. Taylor complained the firing came too late for him to find a position with another team, and he charged that Manley fired him only to save a few bucks. Manley did save the salary of one person by asking Giles to be both player and manager. Taylor said if he had known Manley was going to use his own judgment on players and not the manager's, he never would have signed with the Eagles.[20] Taylor lost his suit.[21]

Abe's newly acquired players finally gave the Eagles a lift in early July, when the team took three out of four games from the Chicago American Giants. Spectators at the fourth game, which the Eagles won 5–3, included "a yardful of screaming females."[22]

Among the players Abe signed was an outfielder with the Atlantic City Bacharach Giants, Christopher "Crush" Holloway, thirty-eight, who was nearing the end of his twenty-year career in the Negro leagues. Holloway, as his nickname implied, hit with power. He excelled in the outfield. His speed made him a dangerous bunter and base runner. He kept his cleats filed and slid into bases with them held high, looking to "undress" an inattentive infielder.

Abe also bought right-handed pitcher Terris McDuffie, twenty-five, from the Newark Dodgers. McDuffie baffled batters with his control of a variety of pitches rather than with blazing speed. In his first league start for the Eagles he gave up only five hits to beat the defending champion Philadelphia Stars 4–1 at their home stadium, Parkside Field, which the Pennsylvania Railroad originally built in the 1920s as a field for its YMCA team. Large letters across the back of McDuffie's warm-up jacket read, "Terrance the Great." Off the field, the flamboyant McDuffie fancied diamond rings and gold watches. He considered himself a ladies' man and quickly became Effa's favorite paramour. She ordered Giles to start McDuffie for games when she wanted to show him off to her lady friends.[23]

Abe maintained an interest in sports other than baseball and liked being in the company of celebrities. In between acquiring Holloway and McDuffie, Abe helped a committee sponsor a testimonial dinner for three black track and field superstars: Jesse Owens, from Ohio State University, who would win four gold medals at the Berlin Olympics the following year; Eulace Peacock, a sprinter from Temple University who beat Owens in seven out of ten races in 1935 but missed the '36 Olympics because of a torn right hamstring that ended his career;

and Cornelius Johnson, a high school graduate and winner of the gold medal for high jumping at the 1936 Olympics. Johnson would earn a snub from Adolf Hitler as well as a gold medal. As Johnson and fellow African American and silver medalist winner Dave Albritton walked toward the awards platform, Hitler left the stadium.[24]

The committee held the dinner at Small's Paradise in Harlem, where Abe had feted the NNL owners and reporters earlier in the year. This time the committee paid the bill. The predominantly male committee numbered more than sixty and included assemblymen, lawyers, Eunice Carter (the first black U.S. assistant district attorney in New York City), Roy Wilkins (NAACP assistant secretary), Rev. Adam Clayton Powell Jr. (an ordained minister and member of the New York City Council), Romeo Dougherty, and many more.[25]

O

The Eagles ended their maiden season two places higher in the standings than they were when Abe fired Taylor, sixth place in the eight-team league. Buoyed by that progress, Abe said he would field the team next year, 1936. "Some of my contemporaries," he said, "operated for fifteen years before their clubs won 75 percent of their games or won a profit." The Dodgers assured him that the Eagles could again play at Ebbets Field.[26]

Pitching had been a bright spot for Abe as the season ended. Following the McDuffie win over the Stars, Leon Day and Bill "Cannonball" Jackman, a thirty-eight-year-old journeyman pitcher, combined for a doubleheader win over the second-place Cubans, 5–1 and 5–0 on August 24. Jackman beat the last-place Newark Dodgers 19–8 and contributed a homer and two singles the following Sunday in the first game of a doubleheader. Dougherty noted that the club had made good progress and predicted the team's following would grow by leaps and bounds the next year. [27]

One who enjoyed the Eagles' play, as evidenced by his attendance at every game at Ebbets Field, was eighty-year-old Judge Stephen W. McKeever, majority stockholder and president of the Brooklyn Dodgers. Steve, with his brother Edward and Charlie Ebbets, had financed the field's construction in 1912 and 1913. Jovial and outgoing, Judge McKeever sat with a bottle of milk in a specially con-structed cushioned armchair in the last row of the grandstand. He showed off his colostomy, a novel operation at the time, to anyone who cared to look. "I like this ball team," Judge McKeever said. "They're classy. I'd like to see them here more often."[28]

The Judge got his wish. Abe scheduled two weeks of postseason exhibition games at Ebbets Field, including one with the House of David, a baseball team sponsored by a religious colony of the same name based in Benton Harbor, Michigan, whose members sported long beards. The bearded nine featured fifty-two-year-old ex-major leaguer and Hall of Famer, Grover Cleveland Alexander. A charity doubleheader on September 8 featured the Cubans against the Stars and the Eagles taking on the Crawfords, who featured Satchel Paige, Josh Gibson, Oscar Charleston (considered by many to be the greatest Negro league player of all time), and "Cool Papa" Bell, the speediest of all Negro leaguers. Cubans' player-manager Martin Dihigo played all nine positions. It was one of the Eagles' first benefit games that Effa arranged, and the Crispus Attucks Council received a portion of the gate to support its charitable work of funding playground activities for Brooklyn youngsters.[29] A week later the Eagles split a Sunday doubleheader against a team of white minor league all-stars picked from the clubs in the International League to close out their season at Ebbets Field.[30]

Monday evening found Abe and Effa at a banquet sponsored by Gus Greenlee, whose Crawfords had won the championship of the National Association of Negro Baseball Clubs, as the NNL was formally known, and Alex Pompez, owner of the runner-up Cubans at the latter's home field, the Dyckman Oval at 204th Street and Nagle Avenue in Harlem. A newspaper photograph of the banquet showed Effa, the only one with a smile, and eight dour-looking male moguls around a table with empty dishes and wine bottles.[31]

Not only did the Eagles' pitching success at the end of the season give fans hope for a better 1936, but Abe's eye for talent had brought a number of strong players to the team. In addition to Giles, Day, McDuffie, and Holloway, Abe had signed outfielders Clarence "Fats" Jenkins and Ed Stone. Jenkins, age thirty-seven, stole bases with abandon and hit .321. Stone, twenty-six, was best known for his superb arm and had his best year-to-date batting average of .323.[32] Giles, Day, Jenkins, and Stone all earned spots on the 1935 East-West Classic's East squad.

While the Eagles wrapped up the season, Effa continued her civic activities. She chaired a twenty-seven-person committee that included Rev. Johnson and four physicians. The committee planned the entertainment at a dance to benefit the Edgecombe Sanitarium on November 12 at the Renaissance Casino in Harlem. The sanitarium offered moderately priced medical treatment to Harlem residents. The reporter who covered the dance referred to Effa as a "well-known socialite."[33] She would soon become well known in the world of Negro league baseball.

# CHAPTER THREE

## *Abe Trades Brooklyn for Newark*

At the end of the season Abe changed his mind about returning to Brooklyn. He had lost $30,000 in the New York baseball market.[1] Those who could afford the price of a ticket had their choice of three major league teams—the New York Yankees, the New York Giants, and the Brooklyn Dodgers—two other professional black teams—the New York Cubans and the New York Black Yankees (which played as an independent team at the time); and numerous semipro teams such as the Bushwicks, the Bay Parkways of Brooklyn, and the Farmers of Glendale. Nat Strong, a Brooklyn booking agent who found himself without his accustomed cut of the gate at Ebbets Field, had retaliated against Abe by charging half-price for games at nearby fields.[2] Abe looked to Newark, New Jersey, fifteen miles to the west across the Hudson River, for a fresh start. He knew Tyler was willing to sell his Newark Dodgers, so Abe bought him out, combined the rosters of the Eagles and the Dodgers into the Newark Eagles, and returned all unwanted players back to the NNL as free agents.[3]

The Eagles could not avoid black baseball competition altogether in New Jersey. The New York Black Yankees played their home games in Hinchliffe Stadium, located fifteen miles to the north of Newark in Paterson, New Jersey, in 1936–1937 and, again, from 1939 to 1945.[4] Both teams, however, would be close enough to the New York area that blacks from Harlem and other New York communities could attend the games of both teams. Unlike Ebbets Field, the Eagles' new home field, Ruppert Stadium, was equipped with lights, so Abe's team could play both day and night games. Abe hoped to build on the black baseball foundation

Oliver Brown had fashioned with his Newark Browns, who played for a time in 1932 in the ill-fated East-West League, and by Tyler's Newark Dodgers in 1934 and 1935.[5] Abe also knew that the Newark Bears, a farm club of the New York Yankees, had defeated the Minneapolis Millers, the American Association champions, to win the Junior World Series in 1932; finished in first place in 1933 and 1934; and "was competitive if not spectacular" in 1935 and 1936.[6] Perhaps some of the Bears' fans, mostly white, would come out for the Eagles.

O

The Newark that greeted Abe and Effa was 90 percent white. Residents lived in neighborhoods of Irish, Germans, Jews, Italians, Russians, Poles, and blacks, who made up 8 percent of the population. Manufacturing and financial businesses dominated Newark's center of commerce, which was connected by railways to the rest of the country and by its extensive seaport to the world. Theaters, clubs, and taverns flourished in Newark during the 1920s. Many had remained open during Prohibition, which ended in 1933. For a membership fee, one gained access to Newark's speakeasies and to any of its thousand saloons (about one for every 429 residents, the most per capita of any American city). Newark's five breweries—Ballantine, Hensler, Kruger, Feigenspan, and Weidenmeyer—slaked the thirst of many a partygoer. Top jazz entertainers and comedians—Ella Fitzgerald, Billy Eckstine, Sarah Vaughan, Jackie Gleason, Redd Foxx, and Duke Ellington—regularly made the rounds of Newark's segregated clubs and theaters. Black artists were permitted to perform in the white theaters, but black patrons were relegated to the balconies.[7]

Jim Crow ruled not only Newark, but all of Essex County, which included Newark, and the state of New Jersey, even though the state had laws on the books dating back to 1883 that prohibited segregation in hotels, restaurants, and public schools. Some citizens of Newark, both black and white, nevertheless fought for equal rights. Essex County's sheriff, James McRell, made a dent in the practice of having only whites serve on grand juries when he appointed the Rev. James Hughes to a panel in May. Prominent civil rights leaders, including former assemblyman J. Mercer Burrell, the state legislature's only black member in the 1932–34 sessions, held a ceremony in the sheriff's office commending him for selecting Hughes. Burrell himself had advanced the cause of equal rights the year before by sponsoring and shepherding through the New Jersey Assembly a bill that guaranteed payment of attorney fees and court costs "of about $125" to a plaintiff who won a suit claiming he or she had been deprived of his or her legal rights. Previously, plaintiffs were lucky to be awarded five or six dollars toward their court costs, which discouraged many from bringing suit even if they thought they could win. Statewide discrimination in hiring practices for federally funded building projects prompted representatives from Newark and six other New Jersey cities, under the sponsorship of the National Urban League, to ask Interior Secretary Harold L. Ickes to fine contractors who violated the Work Progress Administration's nondiscrimination provisions. The tensions between the two groups surfaced toward the end of the meeting in Ickes's office in Washington, D.C., when one federal government official said it was not the government's place "to force white men to work with Negroes when whites strenuously object to it." Lester B. Granger, chairman of the league's delegation, responded, "[I]t is not the duty of the federal government to cater to the ignorant, personal prejudices of every illiterate who comes out of the backwoods and wishes to express his ego on a relief job."[8]

Confrontation, however, was the exception. Newark's black community put more energy into building institutions to help blacks cope with the racism than into combatting it. Black businessmen opened the Peoples Finance Corporation. Professional societies, such as the Negro Funeral Directors of New Jersey, the Newark Barbers' Protective Association, and the Modern Beauticians, served as support groups for black entrepreneurs. Black fraternal groups and lodges, such as Negro Masons and the Alpha Lodge, provided social and self-help networks for Newark's upwardly mobile and civic-minded blacks.[9]

Discrimination pushed most of Newark's black population, roughly forty thousand people in 1936, west of downtown and into the Hill area, so named for its hilly terrain, of the Third Ward. Most belonged to one of four social classes—a small group of professionals (doctors, dentists, undertakers, and attorneys) who entertained at home and rarely went to clubs and taverns; working people who attended church regularly; working people on the younger side looking for a good time at the clubs; and the "sports," people whose lives revolved around illicit activities such as gambling, prostitution, and bootlegging. Sports were also known as "upper shadies," a term signifying one whose wealth came from illegal means and who lacked a formal education. Abe was a "sport." His money did, however, make it possible for Effa to dress in the style of a professional woman, which helped her gain entry into their clubs and associations. Her association with Abe, however, barred her from full acceptance by the professionals.

Newark's blacks of all classes felt the effects of the Great Depression, which had been in place for more than six years when Abe bought Tyler out. Women in the Third Ward worked largely in the garment trade while many men sought jobs in meatpacking, tanning, and tool- and dye-making trades. For many, cleaning was the only type of work available. The Third Ward was home to some entrepreneurs such as women beauty parlor owners and others who ran small grocery and candy stores. Many Third Ward residents said they relied on "mother wit"—inborn instincts—in order to survive.[10]

O

Abe's first order of business was to secure a ballpark. He made a deal with the Newark Bears' vice president, George Weiss, age forty-one, for an annual lease of Ruppert Stadium, the Bears' home. The Bears, a minor league affiliate of the New York Yankees, got 20 percent of gross ticket revenue, which came out of Manley's 50 percent share of the total proceeds. Abe had to pay for all services—police, ticket sellers, ushers, etc.—which cost about $100 a game, plus $65 for use of lights during night games. Ticket prices ranged from fifteen cents for a bleacher seat for children under twelve, to eighty-five cents for a box seat.[11]

The arrangement pleased Abe as he again had laid claim to a stadium without having to pay booking agents' fees. First known as David's Stadium, Ruppert Stadium was built out of steel and concrete in 1926 at the intersection of Wilson Avenue and Delancy Street on the eastern edge of Newark, bordering the Passaic River in the Ironbound section of town, near what is now the New Jersey Turnpike. New York Yankees owner Jacob R. Ruppert changed the name to Ruppert Stadium when he bought the Bears in 1932. Ruppert wanted a top-flight minor league team near enough to New York so that players could be brought up on a moment's notice. A U.S. Congressman from 1899 to 1907 and a beer baron of the first order, he owned the Yankees from 1915 to 1939. He bought Babe Ruth from the Boston Red Sox in 1919 for the then unheard sum of $100,000, plus a $300,000 loan against the mortgage on Fenway Park, thereby tagging Beantown with the Curse of the Bambino.[12] On paper the stadium held twelve thousand people, but putting a rope across a portion of deep centerfield created a standing-room area that could accommodate more. Pull hitters liked the short porches in right and left field, 305 feet from home plate to each. Deep center field presented more of a challenge at 410 feet. Smoke from the nearby city dump often caused game delays and sometimes cancellations.[13]

With the stadium issue settled, Abe arranged for the team to stay at the Grand Hotel, a large, two-story, redbrick building at 78 West Market Street. People gathered at the Grand after an afternoon game to socialize around the bar and enjoy the food, which Irvin described as "outstanding." Effa, Irvin said, never had to pay for a drink when she put in an appearance. "Women," he said, "sought out their favorite player at these gatherings and, if they didn't know the player's name, would ask for them by their number." Then the two could dance to the music of bandleaders such as Fletcher Henderson, Charles Johnson, and Count Basie, and performers like Cab Calloway, Earl "Fatha" Hines, Lionel Hampton, and Fats Waller. Poet Amiri Baraka frequented the Grand with his father after games and remembered "everybody highlifin', glasses jingling with ice, black people's eyes sparkling and showing their teeth in the hippest way possible . . . seeing Doby and Lennie Pearson and Pat Patterson . . . and wearin' my eyes and ears out drinking a Coca-Cola, checking everything out." Baraka's biggest thrill was the time his father pushed him forward for an introduction to Monte Irvin, who "would bend down and take my little hand in his."[14]

The league's business began during the owners' January 28–29, 1936, gathering at the Citizen's Club at 15th and Lombard Street in Philadelphia. The meeting showed the strains of the league's weak governance. Greenlee, the league's president, left the meeting early to attend to one of his boxers, John Henry Lewis, during a bout in Denver on January 29 against Emilo Martinez.[15] Greenlee's departure led several to question his commitment to the league, and they discussed voting him out of office at the next meeting. Commissioner Ferdinand Morton failed to appear on Saturday and spent only an hour and a half at Sunday's meeting, leading to rumors that a new executive structure without a commissioner might soon appear. John Clark, league secretary, was absent on Saturday but responded to the group's telegram asking him to catch the next train from Pittsburgh to join them on Sunday. Horace Greeley Hall, an official at Cole's Metropolitan Mutual Insurance Company, represented Cole at the meeting. Citing the lengthy travel required of the Chicago team to play the eastern-based teams, Hall proposed withdrawing the Giants from the league to form a western circuit. The owners tabled Hall's proposal until the March meeting. They also tabled James "Soldier Boy" Semler's application for his New York Black Yankees to join the league as a full member.[16]

Born in Texas, Semler allegedly earned his nickname by baking bread for soldiers in France during World War I. A numbers banker, Semler operated the Black Yankees as an independent team that put out the welcome mat for players dissatisfied with their NNL team. The Cubans and the Eagles returned the favor by enticing some of Semler's players to leave him. Upset about not gaining membership in the NNL, he sued Pompez and Manley in an attempt to reclaim the players that the two had recently taken from him.[17]

While the owners met in Philadelphia, a combination team of Brooklyn Eagles and Homestead Grays played in the Puerto Rican Winter League, thanks to Effa's interest in finding winter employment for players. "I was very unhappy about the boys not having any work . . . so I proceeded to make us contacts in Puerto Rico."[18] Using the Eagles' name and uniforms, the team handily won the championship by beating the Newark Bears in six straight games at the end of the season.[19]

That series marked the only meeting between the Eagles and the Bears. Effa later tried to arrange a winner-take-all game at Ruppert Stadium against the Bears, but Weiss turned her down. He also rebuffed her offer to split the proceeds. Pride outweighed financial gain for Weiss. An Eagles win would embarrass the Bears and all of organized baseball. Weiss no doubt knew that the Eagles had beaten the Bears in Puerto Rico, and that the Cincinnati Reds, who were also training in Puerto Rico, had lost two games out of three to the Eagles.[20] The Reds finished the 1936 season with a 74–80 record—good for fifth place. Weiss also knew some Negro league teams had beaten major league teams on continental U.S. soil. The Baltimore Black Sox beat Connie Mack's Philadelphia Athletics on one occasion, embarrassing baseball commissioner Kenesaw Mountain Landis so that he ruled only three major leaguers could play on any team that played a Negro league team. "That way," Irvin said, "you couldn't say you beat a major league team. You could just say you beat a group of guys that included some major leaguers."[21]

The owners reconvened in March 1936 at the YMCA in Harlem to make final plans for the upcoming campaign. Seeing the handwriting on the wall, Greenlee resigned the presidency. The owners replaced him with Ed Bolden and elected Abe as vice president. They "rejected outright" Semler's application for NNL membership, a clear indication they were not pleased with his style of doing business. Abe announced he had signed Ray Dandridge, twenty-three, a member of the Newark Dodgers during the previous season and the leagues' best third baseman, and Willie Wells, thirty, from the Chicago American Giants, the Negro leagues' premier shortstop.[22]

Wells came to the Eagles only because of a dispute between himself and Cole. Cole had told Wells he would put Wells's salary in a protected account if Wells would urge his teammates to complete the 1935 season without pay. Wells refused, saying, "I never went for anything crooked. . . . I'm not worried about me because I know I can play." Cole called a meeting so that Wells could ask the players to forgo their salaries, but Wells surprised Cole by saying "I appreciate it that you fellows look to me as your leader, but you had better find another team to join because I'm not going to be here."[23]

Abe signed other players during the winter, including George "Mule" Suttles, thirty-five, also from the Giants, a free-swinging, homerun-hitting first baseman who drove the ball over five hundred feet on occasion. Giles ended up with the Black Yankees. Abe chose William Bell Sr. to manage the team. Bell, a pitcher, had his greatest success on the mound with the Kansas City Monarchs from 1923 to 1930 and was known as a manager with a knack for developing young players.[24]

Calvin Service, sports editor of the *Chicago Defender* called Abe's team, with a pitching staff led by Day and McDuffie, the league's most improved and predicted the Eagles would win the pennant. The Eagles responded with a mixed showing against the semipro Springfield Grays during their first game in Ruppert Stadium—a Sunday doubleheader played on May 3. After clobbering the Grays 21–1 in the first game, Manley's men took it easy in the second game and lost it 2–1.[25]

The Newark Eagles played their first NNL game against Tom Wilson's Washington Elite Giants in Washington's Griffith Stadium on Saturday afternoon, May 16, under partly cloudy skies with the temperature in the high sixties. U.S. Senator Sherman Morton, a Democrat from Indiana, threw out the ceremonial first ball after the teams returned from their march to the centerfield flagpole. The Negro leagues never succeeded in attracting the president to an opening day game. Wilson had invited Franklin Roosevelt to throw out the first ball but received a reply that he was too busy.[26] FDR did, however, make the ceremonial toss at Griffith Stadium to start the Washington Senators' 1936 season, as he did for each and every Senators' opening day for the first eight years of his presidency. The Eagles, with McDuffie pitching, lost 5–1, and were limited to four hits and shut out until the ninth inning, when Wells scored the Eagles' lone run.[27]

Service's prediction notwithstanding, the Eagles had lost so many games by the end of May that they had been nearly eliminated from the first-half flag race. (That year the owners had voted to divide the season into two halves and hold a playoff if different teams prevailed at the end of the first and second half.) Three losses to the Homestead Grays over Memorial Day weekend at Forbes Field, home of the Pittsburgh Pirates, removed any doubt. The Eagles finished the first half in fourth place.[28]

Abe remained upbeat. Described by the press as "the magnate who has invested more cash money than any other," he ordered Bell to "give the players their heads." "Our policy," he added, "is anything goes. . . . I'm going to capitalize on the natural color my team has and by the second half you'll see our club going full steam ahead." At the same time, Effa caught the attention of one sportswriter who referred to her as "charming."[29]

Abe got some unexpected good news at the owners' June meeting in New York City. Commissioner Morton, whom most owners considered a do-nothing commissioner, brokered an agreement between Semler and the other owners that resulted in the Black Yankees gaining full membership in the league. In return, Semler withdrew his suit against Abe and Pompez.[30]

More good news came the Manleys' way in June, when heavyweight contender Joe Louis agreed to throw out the first ball at the Eagles June 19 night game against the Stars at Ruppert Stadium, despite his bout the previous night with German heavyweight Max Schmeling. Louis, about whom Damon Runyon once said, "more has been written about Joe Louis than any other living man except for Lindbergh," evidently felt confident about the bout's outcome. The lead-up to the fight held the world's attention. The two combatants symbolized the growing conflict between Hitler and the English-speaking world. Effa, capitalizing on the pre-fight publicity and with the help of a committee chaired by Newark physician W. T. Darden, promoted the game as one of many Eagles games played for a charity, in this case the Newark Camp for Underprivileged Children. Heavy rains, however, postponed the fight until Friday night, when Schmeling, in an upset, knocked Louis out in the twelfth round. The Eagles and Stars played the scheduled game before a smaller-than-anticipated crowd, and without Louis.[31]

While Bell was giving the players their heads, Abe kept recruiting players with an emphasis on young talent. He sponsored tryouts for high school and college players and kept in touch with his contacts who served as scouts throughout the country. His most promising acquisition came from the Mohawk Giants of Schenectady, New York—first baseman James "Red" Moore, age eighteen. Moore had attracted Effa's attention with his play in a postseason all-star game, after which she asked him if he'd like to play for the Eagles. "I told her, 'sure thing,'" Moore said, "but she never sent for me. The Mohawk Giants picked me up and I played with them until she sent a driver to pick me up in June after a game in Schenectady." Asked if he had any trouble breaking his contract with the Giants, he said, "Nah, those contracts didn't mean a thing."[32] Moore brought smooth fielding but light hitting, which allowed Suttles, whose fielding prowess did not match his prowess at the plate, to keep his bat in the game by playing right field. Bell resigned as manager in June, saying his managerial duties interfered with his pitching. Now in need of a manager, Abe took the job himself, becoming the only owner-manager in the league.[33] The Eagles finished second behind the Crawfords.

O

Until now Effa had toiled in obscurity, overseeing the team's administration and logistics. She stepped out of the shadows at her first owners meeting in January 1937 in Philadelphia, where she took a seat at the table and offered her assessment of the league's state of affairs. She announced that the league was in a state of disarray and made suggestions for improvement. Her comments impressed Posey, who said that Effa was quickly learning the business and that she, "in no uncertain terms, expressed her disapproval of the way the members conducted league business and the wonderful future possible if they conducted themselves in a business-like manner."[34] Shortly after her comments, Bolden failed to win re-election as president. Candidates to replace him included Ira Lewis, sports editor of the *Pittsburgh Courier*; Leonard "Big Bill" Williams, an underground figure from Pittsburgh; and Lemuel Williams, a Cleveland-based promoter.[35] All three offered a measure of independence, as none owned a team, a fact that pleased Effa. Lewis and Leonard Williams declined the offer. Lemuel Williams could not garner enough votes, so the owners turned once again to Greenlee to be their president. Wilson emerged as the vice president and Abe as treasurer. The owners elected William Nunn, a sportswriter for the *Pittsburgh Courier*, as secretary, replacing John Clark, who had close ties to the Crawfords. Morton won reelection as commissioner.[36]

While the owners coped with the league's structure, or lack thereof, Abe forged ahead in his efforts to improve the Eagles. He struck a trade with Greenlee in which Greenlee gave up second baseman Dick Seay, thirty-two, and outfielder Jimmy Crutchfield, twenty-six, in return for Harry Williams, a journeyman ballplayer whose performance at second base had not pleased Abe, and moderately talented outfielder Thadist Christopher. Abe got the best of the deal. In Seay he acquired the best defensive second baseman of the 1930s, who always delighted fans with his glove work. Crutchfield, a 150-pound speed merchant, entertained fans by catching fly balls behind his back. With Seay at second, the Eagles had what became known as the "million-dollar infield": Dandridge at the hot corner, Wells at short, and Suttles at first—except when Abe inserted Moore for defensive purposes. Sportswriters hailed the infield "as comparing favorably . . . with many of the famous combinations who have written their names in 'Baseball's Hall O' Fame.'" Christopher never reported to the Crawfords, instead preferring the warmer climate and better pay in Santo Domingo.[37]

Not content to rely on trades to build the Eagles roster, Abe formed a farm club, the Winston Salem Eagles, which operated out of Winston-Salem, North Carolina and played its home games at Piedmont League Park. Spencer "Babe" Davis, a shortstop of modest abilities, managed the team. Davis's Eagles played throughout the 1937 and 1938 season without developing anyone of note for the parent club.[38]

O

Abe took time out from recruiting to rub elbows with members of the black community's elite on March 12 during amateur boxing night at Harlem's Salem-Crescent Club. Sugar Ray Robinson, who held the world's welterweight and middleweight titles during his career, had started his career at the Salem. Abe watched the fights in the company of aldermen, sheriffs, and doctors. The previous evening Abe had joined a number of "luminaries" in attendance at amateur bouts at Harlem's Rockland Palace, 280 West 155th Street, Harlem's leading fight club in the '30s and '40s.[39]

Effa continued her civic and social activities. In February she took an active role in organizing a relief committee to aid those whose lives had been shattered by the great floods of 1937. Damage from flooding throughout the Ohio and Mississippi River valleys had left more than 270,000 people homeless. The devastation exceeded the combined effects of the floods of 1926–27 and the Dust Bowl drought of 1930–31.[40] Bertha Cotton, a well-known Harlem socialite and the wife of Dr. Norman Cotton, chaired the committee's planning from her home on fashionable West 139th Street. The committee sponsored a dance at Harlem's Savoy Ballroom in early March. The Savoy, one of the earliest integrated facilities in Harlem, carried a reputation as the "World's Finest Ballroom." It featured large, luxurious, carpeted lounges and mirrored walls and could handle five thousand people.[41] A month after the dance, Effa's name appeared on a list of "prominent Harlemites" who had attended a piano recital at the Town Hall in New York City. Names of doctors, attorneys, and socialites completed the list. The recital attracted "a huge outpouring . . . who were jubilant at the new spirit manifested by supporting Negro artists in their downtown appearances." Effa and Dr. Darden organized another benefit game to support the Newark Student Camp Fund, this one against the Baltimore Elite Giants on June 10, the first night game of the season at Ruppert Stadium. The committee used the Eagles' proceeds to send underprivileged children from the Third Ward to summer camp.[42]

O

The million-dollar infield, a strengthened outfield, and a strong pitching staff led by Day and McDuffie made Newark look like the team to beat in the '37 campaign, which by a vote of the owners, would be played as one season and not divided into halves. Stone, Wells, and Suttles hit the ball so well in spring training that Assistant Manager Tex Burnett, who served as player, manager, and coach for thirteen teams during his twenty-five-year career, had to curtail their batting practice because they hit too many balls over the fence, losing them to the clutches of youngsters waiting beyond. Abe looked most to McDuffie to lead the Eagles. McDuffie's stomach problems, which had required the care of a physician in Puerto Rico over the winter, had disappeared. Abe hoped McDuffie would improve on his 1936 performance, which included two victories over Satchel Paige in three matchups, as part of his seventeen wins against eight defeats in league play. His record for the past four years stood at 107–25.[43]

Neither McDuffie, "the Dizzy Dean of colored baseball," nor any of his fellow players led the Eagles to the pennant. Three straight losses to an improved Homestead Grays team, bolstered by the addition of Josh Gibson, the "black Babe Ruth," in late June, knocked the Eagles out of first place. The Eagles made another run at the top spot, only to be thwarted by the same Grays who took another three games from them in mid-August. Abe's charges finished the season in second place behind the Grays. A bit of good news reached the Manleys when Suttles amassed the most votes—27,502—in a poll conducted by twenty black newspapers to determine the starters in the East-West Classic. Five other Eagles—Day, Stone, Wells, Dandridge, and Seay—joined Suttles in Chicago for the game as members of the East squad.[44]

Effa also attended the game. Four of the NNL owners voted for her to represent the league's financial interests at the Classic. After the game, Posey said Effa "handled the affairs in a capable manner and gave each member an intelligent financial report of the game."[45] Greenlee, who had never been a fan of Effa's, disagreed, saying, "the proper place for women is by the fireside and not functioning in positions to which their husbands have been elected."[46]

The relationship between Greenlee and Effa ruptured further when Greenlee learned to his embarrassment and anger that Effa, along with Abe and Posey, had scheduled a "World Series" between the NNL pennant winner, Posey's Grays, and the pennant winner for the newly formed Negro American League, established in the spring at Cole's urging. Greenlee said that he did not sanction the series; "that it is nothing more than a personal promotion staged by Mrs. Effa Manley, Mr. Abraham Manley, and Cumberland Posey" (the three opted for the series take to be split among the teams rather than be put into the league treasury as Greenlee preferred); and that "next year all teams will abide by the rules . . . and will not endeavor to usurp the authority or ignore the position of this office." He noted there had been several instances in which Effa and Abe "had overstepped their bounds," including changing the location of an owners meeting from Philadelphia to New York without consulting him. He closed, "You may rest assured there will be a reorganization of the league . . . in 1938."[47]

Greenlee's objections aside, the series took place, though the leadup to it was unorthodox. Because the Chicago Giants objected to the Kansas City Monarchs being awarded first place by one-half a game in the first half of the season, the NAL moguls decided on a best of seven games playoff to determine the NAL pennant winner. The series went down to the seventh game, which the umpires called on account of rain at the end of the seventeenth inning with the score tied 2–2. Representatives of the two leagues then decided the team representing the NAL in the World Series would include players from both the Giants and the

Monarchs. To be fair to the NNL, the representatives said the Grays could use players from the Eagles, who had finished second. Dandridge, McDuffie, and Wells represented the Eagles in the nine-game series that the East (i.e., the Grays plus Eagles) won eight games to one. The final two games took place on September 27—a doubleheader in Baltimore's Oriole Park. Baltimore's black weekly newspaper, the *Afro-American,* ran two photographs on its sports page the following day, one of play on the field and one of Effa, whose reputation had reached such prominence that the paper incorrectly identified her as the Eagles' owner.[48]

O

Prior to the World Series, Effa had sponsored a dance, both to thank the residents of Newark for their support and to raise money for the team. On September 10 New Jersey Governor Harold G. Hoffman led a group of city and county officials to Krueger Auditorium in Newark, where Chick Webb, a popular bandleader in Harlem, with his band and a teenage singer by the name of Ella Fitzgerald, were scheduled to provide the music.[49] Effa's contract with their agent called for the band to perform between 10:00 p.m. and 3:00 a.m. They did not appear until 2:00 a.m. Effa, miffed at their lateness and the fact that over one thousand people had left the dance hall when they learned another band was playing, refused to let them perform and promised to sue them, though it is not clear that she did. Those who stayed partied on, and what proceeds were raised went to the team.[50] In spite of the confusion, John M. Dabney, owner of a local chain, John M. Dabney Funeral Parlors,[51] pointed to the Eagles' "fine record and good fellowship" as "helping in a big way to make this interracial goodwill a living reality."[52]

Perhaps with an eye toward fostering international goodwill, Effa and Abe hosted at their home African-American Joseph Roan, a 1931 graduate of Virginia State University with a degree in agriculture who had taken a job in Tashkent, Russia, to find ways to produce better crossbreeds of plants from India, America, and Africa. "Being a Negro," Roan said during a 1936 interview in Moscow, "one feels more like a man and a human being living in the free socialist society. Living in Soviet Russia plays a tremendous role in my life, in my wife's life (she also graduated from Virginia State and taught English to a group of collective farmers in Russia), and my son's life."[53] Effa, to her consternation, would soon find many of her players expressing similar sentiments about playing ball south of the border.

# CHAPTER FOUR

## *Effa Steps Up*

While Abe continued to recruit players, oversee spring training, hold the title of league treasurer, and bask in the company of his players, in 1938 Effa took charge of the Eagles' day-to-day operations and finances. Tom Wilson adopted a more cordial stance toward Effa's financial role in the league than had Greenlee. In a letter in which he enclosed signed blank checks for Effa to use to pay league bills, Wilson wrote: "Your letter was nice and kind and I do hope I will be able to keep every ones confidence as long as I am connected with the League in any manner."[1] Wilson's letter would be the high point of their relationship. Effa directed the team's marketing activities by hiring people to post placards around Newark announcing upcoming games, sponsoring Ladies' Days, hiring publicity agents to place stories about the team in local papers, writing letters of protest to sportswriters whose articles about the Eagles she disagreed with, and inviting prominent individuals from as far away as Washington, D.C., to be her guests on opening day. She started giving interviews to the press, an activity formerly handled by Abe. Effa explained to the press in February 1938 that she and Abe were pretty well satisfied with the current lineup, but that "there are two or three players in the league whom we have our eye on."[2] A reporter from the *Pittsburgh Courier* contacted Effa to ask if Abe's failure to get a seat on a Trans World Airlines flight to Pittsburgh for an owners meeting amounted to discrimination. She held the airline blameless, saying Abe did not arrive at the Newark airport until thirty minutes before the flight and his reservation had probably expired. She pointed out that he got a seat on the next flight.[3]

Effa's notoriety spread beyond Newark when weeklies throughout the country published a picture of her perched on the dugout steps in an Eagles jacket and cap. She at first refused the *New York Post* photographer's request, saying he should be taking pictures of Abe, not her. She relented when the photographer, a "young boy who was in tears," told her he'd "be in the doghouse" if he did not get the shot. Effa remembered the photograph for the rest of her life. In 1978 she claimed, "Every paper in the country ran the picture." While it was an overstatement, her claim did carry with it a well-founded sense of pride. "At that time," she continued, "women wouldn't dream of that sort of thing. In fact until today they're not running ball clubs."[4]

For a change, the Pittsburgh meeting was devoid of discord among the owners. They agreed to changes in the league's governance and finance structures as Greenlee made good on his promise that 1938 would be a year of changes. The owners replaced Commissioner Morton with an advisory board consisting of Manley, Greenlee, and Wilson. The trio had full power to "settle disputes and frame legislation for the league," thus putting control of league matters in the hands of three owners. No account of Effa objecting to this decision could be found—perhaps because Abe was one of the three—but the move did not square with her commitment to install a non-team owner as league president. Effa would pursue this cause for the next ten years. The owners reduced players' salaries and limited each team's roster to sixteen players. They selected Greenlee to attend the NAL's upcoming meeting in Chicago. The NAL now consisted of the Kansas City Monarchs, Memphis Red Sox, Chicago American Giants,[5] Cincinnati Tigers, Detroit Stars, Birmingham Black Barons, Indianapolis Athletics, and the St. Louis Stars.[6]

Conflict did erupt, however, between the owners and several players. In an effort to discipline a contingent of star players, led by Satchel Paige, who had jumped their teams last spring for more lucrative pastures in Santo Domingo, the owners levied $200 fines against each offending player. Upon hearing about the fine, Paige threatened to form his own team with the "rebel" players, as the owners referred to them, and barnstorm around the country. Abe shot back, saying, "If the rebel group will not return to the league and accept the rather mild penalties levied, they can go to the devil." Abe said any team that played outside of the league organization should be blackballed from playing NNL and NAL teams. After the meeting, Abe faced a rebellion of his own. Four of his starters—Leon Day,

Ed Stone, Ray Dandridge, and Bob "Glasseye" Evans (a twenty-seven-year-old right-handed pitcher who, like his good friend Dandridge, had made the transition from the Newark Dodgers to the Newark Eagles)—were holding out for more money.[7] Abe admitted being disturbed by the holdouts but expressed his belief that things would be worked out shortly, which they were. While the details could not be found, it would not have been out of character for Effa to instigate a come-to-Jesus session with the men, either in person or through one of her many letters. All four reported to spring training by the April 1 deadline. Raises, if any, would have been on the small side.[8]

The best news Abe received about the Eagles roster that year did not make the papers. On one of his tours of semipro games in nearby New Jersey towns in his chauffeur-driven black Lincoln Continental, a player with the Orange Triangles, an amateur team in Orange, New Jersey, caught his eye—a high school senior named Monford "Monte" Irvin, age eighteen. Abe wrote Irvin's mother asking permission to meet the boy. Irvin replied suggesting they meet at the YMCA across the street from his house on a Saturday at 1:00 p.m. "I thought the Y with its motto of 'clean body, mind, and spirit' would make a good impression on him," Irvin said. "He offered me $125 a month and when I asked for a bonus he told me 'no bonus.' I told him other teams were interested in me, but he said, 'You should be happy and proud to play with the guys you know.' [Abe knew that Irvin knew Stone, Pearson, and Day.] 'Plus,' he told me, 'you live at home.'"

Irvin signed without a bonus. A standout in all sports, Irvin liked baseball the most. He had met future Major League Hall of Famers Lefty Grove, Jimmie Foxx, and Lou Gehrig when they visited his high school at the invitation of his gym teacher. Irvin remembered them as "great looking athletes, clean cut. I watched their every move and saw how they conducted themselves. So I said right away that if this is what baseball can do to a person, then I want to become a baseball player."[9]

The money also appealed to the eighteen-year-old. Players made more money than the average person. "If you made $25 a week," Irvin said, "that was a lot of money. My father never made more than $15 a week. [Irvin came from a family of eleven children.] Many guys started at a dollar a day, then you might get a little raise up to $10 a week. At $15 you're doing pretty good. Potatoes only cost ten cents for five pounds. We ate a lot of spaghetti and secondhand meats. My mother and sisters were such great cooks. They doctored that meat up so it tasted pretty good and added lots of vegetables and fish. A quarter bought enough fish at the fish market to feed five people."

The Irvins were not the only family that kept a close eye on their budget. "We had all kinds of people in Orange," Irvin said. "Jews, Blacks, Italians, Irish. We [African Americans] were a minority—maybe 5 to 10 percent in high school but with more coming up from the South every day. [The Irvins had moved to Orange from Halesburg, Alabama.] But the point was everyone was struggling with menial jobs in places like Westinghouse, Monroe Calculating Machines, and the foundry."

During a short tryout under the eye of former Eagles' manager William Bell at Hinchliffe Stadium, Irvin, who hit .666 his senior year in high school, blasted a dozen balls over the four-hundred-foot fence in left field and pegged balls on a line to Bell at home plate from deep center field. Irvin impressed not only Bell but also two members of the Homestead Grays, whom the Eagles would play later in the day. Buck Leonard and Josh Gibson asked to meet the youngster. The meeting started a friendship among the three superstars, who "killed each other on the field" but met afterward "to talk a little trash and drink a little mash."[10]

Irvin started with the Eagles in June 1937 but played only in away games in places where no one would recognize him. He played under the name Jimmy Nelson to preserve his amateur status at Lincoln University in Oxford, Pennsylvania. He borrowed the name from the catcher for the Triangles. "He was a great catcher," Irvin said. "A great physique, great arm; he was just what I wanted to be."[11] Midway into the season, Abe gave William Bell his unconditional release from the team. Abe explained that one player had to be released for the Eagles to meet the league's player limit rule and that he chose Bell because the team needed a younger pitcher. Bell left on "cordial terms" and devoted himself to semipro ball in his hometown of El Campo, Texas.[12]

Abe made his boldest personnel move when he approached Greenlee about purchasing Satchel Paige from the Crawfords. Abe knew Paige, rebel or not, would give the Eagles the leagues' best starting pitching rotation—Paige, Day, and McDuffie. Before his meeting with Greenlee, Manley said, "If we can agree on a price, the purchase will be made."[13]

Paige, in an irrepressible style all his own, was meanwhile working on his own price, even as the black weeklies were reporting that Abe had paid Greenlee "several thousand dollars" for the league's best self-promoter and one of its top two or three pitchers. Paige, who let it be known he was for sale to anyone who had $2,000, drove east from Pittsburgh to New York to confer with Abe. Not realizing the Manleys had moved from New York to Newark, Paige showed up at their former New York residence to learn that not only had they moved into Apartment 3 at 55 Somerset Street and opened an office at 101 Montgomery Street, both in Newark's Third Ward, but that Abe was on his way to Jacksonville, Florida, with the team for spring training. Paige found New York more appealing than a drive to Jacksonville. He put himself up at Harlem's Woodside Hotel; bought a gray, tailor-made Easter suit; and took boogie-woogie dancing lessons. Asked by a reporter about his baseball future, he admitted that there "was plenty going on in New York about forming a team to play in Argentina," but that his only immediate interest in the matter was seeing his former teammate, Anthony Cooper, "off when the ship sails" for Argentina. He said he would not make a final decision on joining Cooper in Argentina until he met once more with Greenlee, whom he hoped would waive the $200 fine. He justified thinking about jumping by telling a reporter, "Say you are getting a salary of six hundred dollars a month and somebody comes along and offers you three times that amount. Wouldn't you take it?" He said he was in no hurry to make a decision about his baseball future, because Joe DiMaggio, a holdout from the New York Yankees at the time, advised him to "keep on holding out until I got results." He wanted to talk with Effa, who agreed to talk with him "on general matters but not about business because we don't have Greenlee's permission to talk with Mr. Paige."[14]

Upon hearing Paige was in New York, Abe feared the pitcher was closer to going to South America than he was letting on. From Jacksonville, Abe hired New York attorney Richard E. Carey, a former assistant district attorney, to serve Paige with an injunction that would prevent him from leaving the country.[15] On Thursday morning, April 28, after Paige failed to appear in court for a hearing, New York Supreme Court Justice Ferdinand Pecora signed a restraining order that barred Paige from leaving the country. A week later Effa issued a terse statement, saying only, "Paige belongs to us. No further action has been taken since last week's court action." Restraining order or not, Paige went missing. A clerk at the Woodside said he was back in Pittsburgh but would be returning to New York any day. Effa refused to confirm or deny a report he was on his way to join the Eagles in Jacksonville. She did confirm that Abe had paid over $5,000 for the footloose Paige.[16]

Paige did not go to Jacksonville. The Eagles returned to Newark to start the season with an exhibition doubleheader on May 8 against the Bay Parkways, a semipro team based in Brooklyn. The pitching staff consisted of Day, McDuffie, Bob Evans, John Wright, and Homer Craig. A Pittsburgh sheriff, Abe, and Greenlee continued to look for the pitcher. The sheriff wanted to see Paige because Greenlee held a bond on Paige stemming from an earlier court case in which Alderman Harry Fitzgerald had found the pitcher guilty of "fraudulent conversion" for possessing two Crawford uniforms and $200 of Greenlee's money. Abe wanted Greenlee to return the $5,000. The spectacle delighted the press. Sportswriters called for Sherlock Holmes and Scotland Yard to join the hunt.[17]

The Manleys and Greenlee met at Ruppert Stadium on Sunday, May 15, for the Eagles opening league game against the Crawfords amid chilly winds and cloudy skies. The Greater Newark Elks Band and a group from the Emmett Guyton Post of the American Legion, under the leadership of J. Mercer Burrell, led players from both teams on a high-stepping parade to the centerfield flagpole, where Burrell raised the Stars and Stripes. Newark Deputy Mayor William Fox shed his suit jacket to throw out the first pitch. The Eagles beat a strong Crawford club 6–3 behind the seven-hit pitching of McDuffie.

The Eagles had a promising team even without Paige. The million-dollar infield was still intact. Day and McDuffie were among the league's best pitchers. Outfielders Stone, Crutchfield, Irvin, and Lennie Pearson—age twenty, a handsome and broad-shouldered slugger whom Effa would correspond with in the off-seasons when he played in Latin America—brought speed to the field and lively bats to the plate.[18]

○

As the Eagles were starting the baseball season, Newarkers witnessed another form of sepia entertainment—namely the showing in white-owned theaters of three motion pictures with African American stars during the last two weeks of May and the first week of June. Just as Negro league baseball teams in the New York–Newark area had no stadium to call their own, Newark had no theaters that featured blacks in movies and stage shows. *Bargain with Bullets* played at the Empire for a week and starred Ralph Cooper. Cooper, a dancer and emcee as well as an actor, hosted weekly amateur contests at the Apollo Theater, where he spoke in hip show-biz lingo and emceed the Apollo debuts of Ella Fitzgerald, Sarah Vaughan, and James Brown. A week after *Bargain with Bullets* closed, Louise Beavers, who appeared in more than 160 movies during her forty-year career, starred in *Life Goes On* at the same Washington Street theater for eight days. Both played to capacity audiences, but the biggest draw was the premier showing of Joe Louis's *Spirit of Youth*, in which the famous boxer made his screen debut, at the National Theater. The movie played to standing room only audiences for five days.[19]

In addition to limited entertainment, Newark's black population suffered disadvantages in medical services, employment, and housing. The number of blacks contracting tuberculosis more than doubled between 1932 and 1938. As the result of a quota system, only the most severe cases from Newark's African American community gained admission to the Essex Mountain Sanatorium at Caldwell, twelve miles away.[20] New Jersey's Civil Service came under attack by Burrell, now chairman of Pride of Newark Lodge No. 93, an Elks organization, and others for "gross discrimination" in hiring practices. Cases in point included two men, Walter G. Shouse of Princeton and William E. Griffin of Englewood, who both passed the state's automobile mechanics examination but were passed over for appointments while 140 whites with lower scores won appointments. Blacks and whites took opposite sides in a federal housing program initiated in Montclair, New Jersey, eight miles from Newark. The proposed housing project, which would replace slums with apartment buildings, met stiff opposition from "the silk-stocking element," who were afraid the project would "entice an unwarranted influx of out-of-town Negroes to the city."

Amid the discrimination, however, signs of progress could be found. Four merchants, with stores adjacent to the F. W. Grand Silver five-and-ten-cent store at 192 Springfield Avenue, which had been the target of pickets for four weeks, claimed in court the pickets interfered with their business. The court noted in its opinion supporting the picketers that employment opportunity for Newarks' "40,000 to 50,000" blacks was "pitifully small," and that "they can obtain work as common laborers, as janitors, as domestic servants, but very little beyond that." In another sign of progress, the city commissioners appointed Harold Lett to the five-member Newark Housing Authority. Lett, executive secretary of New Jersey's Urban League, became the first black to serve on the Housing Authority, which had several million dollars at its disposal for slum clearance.[21]

O

The same Newarkers had little to cheer about at Ruppert Stadium. By the end of June 1938 the team had managed to move from fifth to fourth place in the now seven-team league by taking two games from the hapless Black Yankees, who finished the first half in last place, by the scores of 11–6 and 4–3. The Stars doused that winning streak by beating the Eagles three games out of four, dumping the team back into fifth place.[22]

The team's problems continued when Semler, who had found it more profitable to play a doubleheader at Yankee Stadium than to play a single game at Ruppert, cancelled a scheduled league game against the Eagles in late July, leaving eagle without the time to schedule a game against another team. Effa bypassed the league officials and complained directly to Semler in a letter. Yet, in a similar move, Effa notified the Crawfords in mid-July that the Eagles did not want to play a scheduled game against the Craws on August 7 in order to extend a westward trip against NAL opponents. The Craws, she felt, had plenty of time to reschedule as none of the other NNL teams had a game on August 7, and, therefore, she insisted, her decision did not constitute a cancellation. A cancellation forced the canceling team to pay a forfeiture fee to the other team. The Craws' business manager, John Clark, saw it differently and told Effa so in a letter. Not one to take being disagreed with lightly, she took three, single-spaced paragraphs to defend herself to Clark and concluded, "[O]ne can only do right when he is dealing with people who will do right. This office stands ready to do everything right under any circumstance, live up to all agreements, pay all bills, etc., but to have a worthwhile organization everyone must do the same thing." She sent copies of both of letters to Abe as to leave no doubt in his mind about how she felt. She implored Abe, "Please don't make any concessions to those niggers. Just think of the dirty deal they gave us when they cancelled out on the 26th to play in Yankee Stadium. Remind them that they started the whole mess." She signed her letter "Your Baby." [23]

Effa's letters did little to improve the Eagles' profits, and they finished the season in fifth place. Heavy rains kept the Eagles and other eastern teams idle for two weeks in August. Abe estimated the rains cost the league $25,000 in lost gate receipts.[24]

Abe's attempted purchase of Satchel Paige had also lightened his wallet. Paige, still a fugitive at the end of the season, ended up in Mexico after playing in Venezuela. Wilson had given Paige a deadline of June 15 to report to the Eagles or be banished from the league. He initially ignored the deadline but later reconsidered and wrote Effa to say he'd like to play for the Eagles. In an undated 1938 typewritten letter he wrote, "Daer Mrs Manley . . . Listen Mrs Manley, I Thought I Heard Some One Say That I Belonged To You Why Do You Take So Lound To Send For Me I Have Ben Wating and Wating For You To Write Me But It Look Like Something Is Wrong . . . So I Am Going To See Just Wheat You Have To Say About Me. So If You Get This Letter Please Answer It at Once." A response from Effa was not found, but in an interview forty years later she said she received another letter from Satchel in which he promised to play for the Eagles if she'd be his girlfriend. "Oh murder," she said to William Marshall in recounting the story years later. "Butch Bell was my publicity man, and I showed the letter to Butch and said, 'Butch, what do you do in a case like this?' I was kind of cute then too. . . . So of course, I didn't even answer his letter because it was one of those things."[25]

In the midst of these developments, Abe turned the manager's job over to forty-year-old Dick Lundy, whom he had acquired from the Atlanta Black Crackers. Lundy, known by his nickname, "King Richard," was the best Negro league shortstop in the 1920s. He also managed the Newark Dodgers in 1934–35 and played as a utility player for the Eagles during their last year.[26]

Shortly after Lundy's arrival, Abe learned that Effa had been romantically involved with McDuffie in the past, and that McDuffie had knocked her down and kicked her in a lover's quarrel in New York City's Pennsylvania Railroad Station. Later, Eric Illidge, the Newark Eagles' traveling secretary, overheard Abe say on a bus ride to Pittsburgh, "When I get there I'm gonna trade that son-of-a-bitch McDuffie to Posey." Abe did not make the deal with Posey but did get rid of McDuffie through a trade to Semler's Black Yankees for rookie pitcher Jimmy "Slim" Johnson, noted as an underrated pitcher who had pitched the Yankees to impressive wins over the Grays. The press gave McDuffie's temper as the reason for the trade.[27]

Following McDuffie's departure, Effa started seeing Ham Jones, a tall, handsome detective on the Orange, New Jersey, police force. "I hated to see that happen," Irvin said, "because Abe was such a nice guy." The scuttlebutt among the Eagles was that all was well during the early years of their marriage but that Abe developed an illness that prevented him from performing sexually, so Effa looked elsewhere.[28]

Abe wasn't the only one who had a problem with McDuffie. In a letter to Abe, Newark physician W. W. Wolfe wrote, "I want to commend you for letting Mr. McDuffie out. . . . He put too much emphasis on his socializing. His arrogant way on the ball field was disgusting to the fans and I dare say had a bad effect on the players." Wendell Smith said McDuffie deserved the trade as he was the only player for either the Eagles or the Grays at the Grays' Silver Jubilee anniversary game "who squawked at the umpire."[29]

McDuffie's departure left a hole in the starting pitching rotation that a young Jimmy Hill, age twenty, stepped in to fill. Hill lived in Lakeland, Florida, where he threw batting practice for the Detroit Tigers during spring training and drew rave reviews from eventual Hall of Famer and Tiger first baseman, Hank Greenberg. Abe, alerted to Hill by a friend, signed him to an Eagle contract after seeing him throw only a few pitches.[30] Lundy gave Hill his first starting assignment on Sunday, August 28 in an exhibition game against the Bushwicks—a team that featured major leaguers either on their way up or on the way down. Hill pitched shutout ball for eight innings against former New York Yankee Waite Hoyt, thirty-nine, who had just been released from the Brooklyn Dodgers after a Hall of Fame career with the Yankees, to lead the Eagles to a 5–1 victory.[31]

Hill's performance buoyed the Manleys' spirits as they looked to next year. They hadn't had much to celebrate since McDuffie had left. Day had been unavailable since June owing to an arm injury, and Paige wasn't an option. An exasperated Abe Manley announced in December that he would never have Paige on his club. "There is no question," Abe said, "but that Satchel is a great pitcher and would help our club materially but we cannot let even a twirler so good as Paige run our league." Greenlee was also fed up with Paige, saying, "I have gone along with Paige for a number of years and have always had trouble."[32] As 1938 drew to a close, Abe was left holding $5,000 while Paige explored employment options elsewhere.

# CHAPTER FIVE

## Effa Comes Into Her Own

By 1939 Effa was calling shots that, in organized baseball and most other organizations of the time, were the purview of male executives. However, she did not need an executive title in order to take executive actions. "I am not writing you this letter as an official of Negro National League baseball," she wrote to NAL Commissioner R. R. Jackson on April 28, "but simply as one of the teams who is very anxious to see organized baseball properly conducted." A veteran of the Spanish-American War, a three-term Republican Chicago alderman, and a former postal employee, Jackson had prior black baseball experience with the Columbia Giants and the Leland Giants, and had been part owner of the Chicago American Giants. From her opening line to Jackson Effa went on to point out that NAL teams acted too quickly in signing players from the NNL's Crawfords before all NNL teams had waived their interest in the players. Greenlee had resigned from the NNL to concentrate on his boxing interests and pulled the Crawfords from the league to play as an independent team in Toledo, Ohio, making free agents of the Crawfords' players. While she assured Jackson that the NNL could win any "war over players," she said such a war "should be out of the question so far as we people of intelligence are concerned." Such a war, she rightfully thought, would further diminish the image of Negro league baseball in the eyes of the public and weaken the already fragile structure of the leagues. She asked Jackson to return the players to the NNL and to "please look at this thing morally, financially, and as a race issue, as well as technically."[1] Jackson refused to return the players. The owners resolved the issue by transferring the Toledo team to the NAL at a joint

NNL/NAL meeting in June, giving the NAL jurisdiction over those Crawford players that the NNL teams, who also wanted some of Greenlee's players, had not yet signed.[2]

A week later Effa received a letter from Grays pitcher Raymond Brown, Cum Posey's son-in-law and one of the top NNL pitchers, in which he offered to play for the Eagles for $215 a month. Some would have considered Brown's offer a windfall and signed him. Effa did not. She immediately wrote to Posey and his business manager, Rufus Jackson, saying emphatically, "Gentlemen it is ridiculous to refer him to some other club, as we are all in one Organization, and should try to strengthen the Organization." She advised them to offer Brown what they could and "leave it for him to accept it, or else stay out of baseball so far as organized Negro baseball is concerned." They may have made Brown an offer, but he pitched in Mexico, assembling a 15–8 record before returning to the Grays late in the season.[3]

At the same time that she was trying to foster an ethical and moral base of operations, Effa wanted teams to report the results of their games in a timely manner to the black weeklies—something they were not doing, which led to confusion over the standings. In a letter to Wilson, Greenlees' successor as NNL president, Effa said she was writing to Ed Gottlieb, as league secretary, to ask the teams to send the results to Gottlieb, but if that was inconvenient, she offered to have someone available in the Eagles' office every Sunday night to receive game results over the phone. She added, "I wish you, as Chairman, would order the teams to do this and stipulate a fine for the first one who fails to do so."[4] Wilson rarely issued any order to his fellow owners. Effa's plea went unanswered.

The inconsistent reporting continued. Effa took her case to Chester Washington of the *Pittsburgh Courier*, telling him that the Eagles' record as published in the *Courier* was incorrect and that Posey was not reporting the Grays' results on a regular basis. She offered as a possible explanation for Posey's recalcitrance: "[H]e may be able to do a little juggling if the race is close."[5] While no record could be found of Posey having done any data juggling, Effa's instincts proved to be on target in 1944. Posey claimed the second game of a Labor Day doubleheader in Detroit, which the Grays lost to the New York Cubans, was an exhibition game, not a league game as had been scheduled. Had the second game been counted as a league game, the Stars, and not the Grays, would have won the 1944 flag. Effa fared no better with Washington than she had with Wilson.[6]

Lack of reporting and Effa's innuendo about Posey's motives prompted Wendell Smith, who had been keeping his criticisms of the Negro leagues' foibles under wraps, to take the varnish off his commentary in his June 3 column. "By refusing to run the league in a business-like manner," Smith wrote, "it has misrepresented itself to the public and in general has been a putrid character and a very bad actor. . . . It is controlled mainly by a group of hard-headed, desperate, and incapable individuals who are far from worthy of their positions." Posey reacted to Smith's column in a letter to Effa by defending the standings as reported in the *Courier* as accurate.[7] As Effa pushed her one-woman reform campaign, the ill will among the owners and between the owners and the press continued. Remarkably, so too did the games.

While Effa freely dispensed advice and criticism, often wrapped in appeals for racial progress, unity, and morale imperatives, her response to criticism of herself took on a more personal flavor. Posey took Effa to task for allowing two Eagles, Suttles and pitcher John Wright, to play for the Atlanta Black Crackers in a 1939 spring training exhibition game against the Grays. The Grays won the game, but had they not, the press, Posey complained, would have made a big deal out of a semipro team like the Crackers beating the NNL champion Grays. "How would you like it," Posey said, "if I had sent [Ray] Brown, [Josh] Gibson, [Buck] Leonard to one of these Southern clubs to try to beat the Eagles so they could print it all over the World as they do?" Effa responded, "You can dish it out but you can't take it. How do you think I felt when you brought Bankhead and Harry Williams in addition to your 1938 pennant winning strong Club, to play my weak team in Daytona Beach with two of my men still in Puerto Rico. Put yourself in the other fellows' place, and see how it feels."[8]

○

NNL owners elected Wilson to succeed Gus Greenlee as president at their February 1939 meeting in Gottlieb's Philadelphia office. Greenlee's resignation was accepted "with regret," and the owners unanimously passed a resolution making him honorary league president. Wilson's election met with mixed reactions. Posey thought well of Wilson, saying the new president is a "rough and ready fellow, who probably controls more votes than any Negro in America . . . and is probably the best liked man in baseball by players, owners, and the public." Sportswriter Sam Lacy offered no opinion on Wilson's affability, but did think the election of another owner as president posed an impartiality challenge to the administration of league affairs. Effa thought little of Wilson as the league's president. She saw him as a playboy who put "having a little drink and a little fun" ahead of his base-ball responsibilities.[9] They would be at loggerheads for the duration of Wilson's tenure as president.

The owners' meeting concluded with well-intentioned agreements to im-prove the league's image and speed up play. Club owners and secretaries were now subject to the same penalties that players faced for criticizing umpires: any team walking off the field in protest of an umpire's decision would forfeit the game and their franchise. Also an umpire could no longer be discharged without a hearing and the agreement of four of the six owners. In the interests of speeding up the games, infielders could no longer throw the ball around the infield between innings. Members closed the meeting by observing a moment of silence out of respect for Philadelphia Stars pitcher Stuart "Slim" Jones, who was found dead at age twenty-five on a street in Baltimore in December. Jones pawned his overcoat for $20 to buy a bottle of whiskey and had caught double pneumonia.[10]

Though the moguls had taken some steps forward, Effa thought more should be done. She said so after the meeting adjourned, in three letters to Wilson none of which he answered. Finally, on May 16, 1939, in a pique of frustration, she wrote once more to Wilson, who was in Nashville tending to his ventures there while the team's business manager, Vernon Green, oversaw Wilson's Baltimore Elite Giants. "This," she wrote, "is the fourth letter I have written to you and re-ceived no answer to. I certainly hope you get this one and answer it right away." She laid out her concerns and suggestions about scheduling, publicity, and play-ers jumping contracts. Two weeks later she received a telegram from Wilson that read, "Meet me in Gottlieb's office tonight to get things straightened out."[11] Effa decided against the eighty-five-mile trip from Newark to Philadelphia at such a moment's notice and her concerns went unaddressed.

O

Six weeks before the owners met to deliberate the future of NNL baseball, forty-two-year-old Marian Anderson, a world-renowned Negro contralto signer, gave a concert for five thousand people jammed into Newark's Mosque Theatre. As hap-pened during her concerts in Paris, South America, Europe, and Carnegie Hall, the crowd "reluctantly permitted the great contralto to end her appearance here with three encores and five curtain calls." However, the Daughters of the American Revolution (DAR), with no reluctance, barred Ms. Anderson from singing at Constitution Hall on April 9 in Washington, D.C. At first the DAR claimed the hall was booked for the date in question but later said, even had it been available, Anderson could not have used it because "the hall is leased in accordance with rules applying to most theatres, halls, hotels, and restaurants in the capital which call for segregation of the races." The District of Columbia's Board of Education followed suit by barring Ms. Anderson from using the city's largest high school, Central High (now Cardoza)—a school for whites in the city's segregated education system. Following Eleanor Roosevelt's resignation from the DAR in protest of its decision to bar Ms. Anderson from their hall and an invitation from Harold Ickes to perform outdoors at the Lincoln Memorial, she sang for a diverse crowd of 75,000 people on April 9, Easter Sunday afternoon.[12]

The decision of the DAR spawned many protests, including the formation of a planning group for the Carol Brice Concert for Human Rights, scheduled for Carnegie Hall. Effa joined with a group of nineteen women and one man from New York, New Jersey, and Pennsylvania to plan the concert. Brice, age twenty-two, also a black contralto, was a student at the Julliard School of Music in New York. She first gained national fame by performing with Bill "Bojangles" Robinson in the musical *The Hot Mikado* at the 1939–40 New York World's Fair, and she also sang at FDR's third inauguration. A photograph of the planning group shows the women dressed in their finery with most wearing fashionable hats. Among them was Mrs. Dorothy Height, who went on to be the long-serving president of the National Council of Negro Women, to receive the Presidential Medal of Freedom, and to become known for her stylish taste in hats of all colors and shapes. The only man in the group, Neil Scott, stood to Effa's right.[13] A search of the Carnegie Hall archives failed to turn up a record of the concert.

The fact that Marian Anderson could perform in Newark but not in Constitution Hall did not mean that discrimination was no longer a problem in Newark. A study financed by the New Jersey State Legislature reported what everyone knew: employers routinely discriminated against blacks. City Hospital had no black nurses, physicians, or interns; Newark's African American population was "shockingly deprived of representation on policy-fixing boards"; and blacks in Newark had the largest percentage of houses unfit to live in of any city in the state.[14]

One place where discrimination did not impinge on Newark's black residents was at Ruppert Stadium. The ballpark offered blacks a sanctuary free of slurs, insults, or rejection for a couple of hours. "Negro league baseball," said Stanley Glenn, a catcher for the Philadelphia Stars from 1944 to 1950,

> was a great happening. The ballpark was one place you could vent. There were so few places to go. Only black-owned restaurants could you go to. Philadelphia, Newark, Baltimore, it didn't matter. Black folk had so little to do that they went to the ballpark. It was the number one place to go after church. And we had open seating. At least 20 percent of the fans were white. They sat anywhere. We never had that crap. Ladies came dressed in their Sunday best—high-heeled shoes, silk stockings, long-sleeved gloves, and hats on their heads. They'd sit there in the 90-degree heat. Men came in their Sunday suits complete with tie, hat, and shined shoes."[15] Effa would make the same point in a letter to F. W. Martin of the *Herald*. In complaining that Martin had not covered the Eagles' 1943 home opener, she said, "I know people like you and your brother are glad Negroes have the baseball to go to. It means they spend that much time in healthy, outdoor environment, of which they have so few places to go.[16]

O

Abe's recruiting efforts led him this year to the New Jersey State Prison Farm in Bordentown, New Jersey, where one Obadiah Brewer had been incarcerated. Abe wrote to J. Russell Lacy, an official at the prison, on March 20, inquiring about Brewer. Lacy answered, saying Brewer was the best colored player on the prison's team, but he had been transferred to the Trenton State Prison after the baseball season ended. Lacy suggested Abe contact R. William Lagay, the Trenton prison's principal keeper, for information about Brewer. Nothing came of Abe's inquiry, and Brewer never played for a Negro league team.

Another prison contact did work out for the Eagles in 1939. Fred "Sardo" Wilson wrote Abe from prison in Miami asking for a job with the Eagles. Abe signed Wilson after his release and found himself rewarded with Wilson's .327 average at the plate and solid defensive work in the outfield. A talented baseball player, Wilson's personal demeanor kept his teammates on edge. "Wilson," Irvin said, "was the meanest man I have ever known." Wilson argued with almost everyone and often threatened to "stick" somebody. Irvin recalled Wilson complaining to him about Wells in 1939. "Every time something comes up," Irvin remembered Wilson saying, "that son-of-a-bitch knows more than anybody else.

I just want to stick him. I just want to see what color his blood is." Wilson never did stick Wells or anyone else on the Eagles, but he did shove his switchblade between the ribs of Ethiopian Clowns pitcher Dave Barnhill after an argument. Barnhill recovered. (Years after he left Negro league baseball in 1945, a patron of a Miami bar fatally stabbed Wilson during a brawl.)[17]

Wilson replaced Crutchfield, whom Abe had released based on Eagles' manager Dick Lundy's report from the Eagles' spring training camp in Daytona Beach, Florida, saying that "if this Wilson is not a natural hitter, I will be sadly disappointed." Lundy also reported to Abe that rookie pitcher James Brown, from Laurenberg, North Carolina, "With his blinding speed is expected to be a great asset to the Eagles mound staff." Brown soon proved Lundy right. Dandridge signed with Martin Dihigo to play in Venezuela, breaking up the million-dollar infield and starting a competition among four rookies for the hot corner position. Leon Day, who spent most of 1938 on the bench with a sore arm, reassumed his place in the starting rotation. Irvin, the papers reported, would join the team in early summer after classes let out at Lincoln University.[18] With the other starters returning from last year, the Eagles promised to field a strong team on opening day.

Abe could have strengthened the Eagles even further had he taken Satchel Paige up on his March request to return to the Negro leagues. But Abe had meant what he said the previous December about Paige's negative impact on the league and made no reply to Paige. The free-spirited pitcher spent 1939 barnstorming the country with the Satchel Paige All-Stars.[19]

As Abe readied the team for its upcoming campaign, Effa prepared for her opening day gala. She hired Jerry Kessler, a white law student at the University of Newark, as the team's advertising man. Effa wanted to attract more whites to the games in general, and to opening day in particular. She thought Kessler could distribute Eagles schedule cards to whites in Newark and ask other whites to distribute the cards in return for game passes. She engaged Murray Halpern of the Adler Show Company in Newark to print the cards "because this should be a good means of Adlers getting their advertisement in a lot of places they might not otherwise go." She rented a thirty-seven passenger bus for $39 from the Trenton Transit Company to transport the marching band from the Manual Training Industrial School for Colored Youth in Bordentown, New Jersey, to Ruppert Stadium, and offered to reserve box seats behind the band for as many officials from the school as would like to attend. The Manual Training School served as New Jersey's state-operated, coeducational vocational school for African Americans from 1886 to 1946.[20]

On Sunday afternoon, May 14, 1939, at 2:00 p.m. under sunny skies and before a sold-out, spiffily dressed Ruppert Stadium crowd that included a greater number of whites than usual, Burrell again led the Emmitt Guyton American Legion Color Guard to the centerfield flagpole accompanied by music from the Bordentown school band in crisp, khaki uniforms. Indoor track star John Borican donned an Eagles hat on the mound for the ceremonial first pitch. His fastball hit the batter in the left thigh. Fortunately for the batter, it was a "looping" fastball. Borican had had his best season in 1939 when he won eleven of fifteen races and set world indoor records in the 800 meters, 880 yards, and 1,000 yards. A month earlier, the North New Jersey sportswriters had honored him with a dinner at the Grand Hotel to celebrate his world-record 1,000-yard performance. Effa chaired the dinner's sponsoring committee. A portrait artist by profession, Borican died four years later at age thirty from of a mysterious form of pernicious anemia.[21]

Once the game began, the Eagles struggled in a 7–5 loss to the Stars. One Eagle who distinguished himself was "Cracker" Nelson, who, the *Chicago Defender* said, "handled himself like a veteran. His throwing is good, fielding steady, and he is fast at coming in on bunts." "Cracker" was, of course, Monte Irvin. The *Defender* had not received word that Irvin had withdrawn from Lincoln University to play baseball full time.[22]

The Eagles didn't struggle for long, and won four in a row over the last two weeks in May at Ruppert Stadium, taking both ends of a doubleheader from the Baltimore Elite Giants and the Stars. Pitchers made the difference. Young Jimmy Hill shut out the Giants 4–0 in a two-hitter. James Brown and Jesse Brown held the Giants to two runs in the second game to prevail 4–3. Jesse Brown set the Stars down by a score 5–2 in game three and helped his own cause with a single that drove in two runs. Leon Day, making his first start in a year, shut out the Stars 1–0 in the nightcap.[23]

Now in first place, the Eagles followed up with a doubleheader sweep of the Grays by the lopsided scores of 20–3 and 14–6 before an appreciative crowd in Buffalo, New York. Suttles treated the fans to four round-trippers, and in an unusual burst of speed for a man his size (he stood 6' 3" and weighed 215 pounds), he stole home. Effa, who was attending a four-team doubleheader at Yankee Stadium that Sunday, "jumped up out of her box seat and rushed up into the shade of the grandstand to cool off—so excited was she when she heard the results over the loud speaker." Bill "Bojangles" Robinson and Rev. John Johnson, seated in nearby boxes, applauded the news. Effa would have preferred to be at the Eagles' game, but she went on only one bus trip with the team—to a game in Trenton, New Jersey in 1936. "I definitely curbed their style," she said. "Abe said they liked to sing and joke . . . and I was definitely out of place. So that was the only bus trip I ever made."[24]

By June 17 the Eagles had completed a twelve-game winning streak, putting them well ahead of the Grays. Prospects for a first-half flag looked bright. Irvin, now playing under his own name, rounded into form with a five-for-five day at the plate in support of an Eagles 15–7 win over the Stars on June 24 in the first game of a twin bill. Max Manning, age twenty-one, and from Atlantic City, was in his sophomore year with the Eagles and made his first start of the year. He limited the Elite Giants to four hits in the second game. Manning carried the nickname "Dr. Cyclops" because of his thick glasses.

The Grays fashioned a winning streak of their own, so that by the first of July the Eagles were "clinging" to the NNL lead. The Eagles helped their case by beating the Stars 8–1 in the first game of four-team, Sunday doubleheader in Yankee Stadium behind home runs by Suttles, Stone, and Wells. McDuffie gave up 12 hits to the Elite Giants, and the Black Yankees lost the second game 4–0, no doubt putting a smile on Abe's face. When the first half ended, however, neither Abe nor Effa had much to smile about. The Grays claimed the flag while the Eagles finished in second place.[25]

A four-page handwritten letter to Effa from actor-poet Earl Sydnor did cause Effa to smile. Sydnor, who lived on Harlem's fashionable 139th Street and whose poems appeared in the *Saturday Review* and *Vanity Fair*, reminded Effa that they'd played cards at a party at the Orange, New Jersey, YWCA the previous winter, that she'd given him passes to Eagles games and asked him to read one of his poems. He chose one Walter Winchell had published in his *New York Daily Mirror* column. She liked it, he noted; so had others. He told her the poem had been well received during his readings in such places as Richmond, Atlanta, Alabama, Texas, and now California, where he was appearing in Clare Boothe Luce's hit Broadway comedy *Kiss the Boys Good-bye* in San Francisco. After each reading of the poem, Sydnor wrote Effa, "I thought of you." He closed by saying "Will call you sometime in June to at least say 'Hello.'" The poem read,

> *As dawn creeps through the window lace*
> *And paints a pattern on your face*
> *I kiss each sleeping eyelid closed*
> *And hold you in my arms repose.*
> *I curse myself that I could bring*
> *Such tire to a lovely thing.*[26]

Whether Sydnor called or not is not known, but June found Abe continuing to seek players to bolster the Eagles. He bought Raleigh "Biz" Mackey from Wilson's Baltimore Elite Giants. Mackey, an eventual Cooperstown legend from Eagle Pass, Texas, at age forty-two could still catch every day, hit over .300, and throw aspiring base stealers out from a squatting position. He quickly showed Abe his skill at handling pitchers. Twenty-year old James Brown had to be relieved on June 29 after throwing fifteen balls and only one strike against the Black Yankees. The next night, in a game played at Belmar on the Jersey shore, Mackey caught Brown and his control was perfect.[27]

Mackey's addition helped the Eagles to again finish in second place behind the Grays as the second half ended. While the Manleys would have been happier with first place, they took pride in the fact that three of their number—Day, Suttles, and Wells—were elected by fans to starting positions for the East squad at the East-West Classic. Effa attended the game and came away with two suggestions on how to improve the gate receipts: reduce both ticket prices and publicity costs for future Classic games. The owners' responses to her suggestions are not known, but sportswriter Frank A. Young's reactions are on the record. He said in the *Chicago Defender*, "She opposed every move that helped put 32,000 paid admissions in Comiskey Park. . . . Her arguments are, as Bassinno said to Antonio in Shakespeare's *Merchant of Venice*, 'like two grains of wheat lost in two bushels of chaff, you may seek all day ere you find them—and when you have found them they are not worth their search.'" Another of Effa's proposals, in which she questioned the benefits of monies paid to Posey for his work on the game, not surprisingly struck a sour note with Posey. In his pique, he bypassed Effa and wrote to Abe, saying "I do not like Mrs. Manley to take the attitude that I am to get something for nothing just because I was allowed something for work on each East-West game. I did not ask to do this work."[28] Once again, Effa's proposals met resistance.

During the same meeting at which Effa made these suggestions, the owners decided, for reasons unknown, to hold a four-team, best-of-five game play-off series based on won-lost records for the entire season to determine the NLL pennant winner. The first-place Grays faced the fourth-place Stars while the second-place Eagles met the third-place Elite Giants. The Grays and the Giants prevailed. The Giants beat the Grays three games to two to clinch the flag.

○

Abe was as cost conscious as his wife. He supported Effa's decisions to deny players' requests for raises, bonuses, and advances, and to charge players $25 if they failed to return a uniform borrowed for winter play. Foul balls gave Abe opportunities to save money. He could be seen running after them in Ruppert Stadium while wearing a hundred-dollar suit. When an opposing batter had fouled off seven or eight balls into the stands, Abe leaned over the roof of the Eagles' dugout from his seat in the first row and yelled at Biz Mackey, the team's manager, "Tell that dick-licker [McDuffie, the pitcher] to walk him [the batter] or strike him out." Two pitches later the batter walked to first base. Reflecting on his association with the Manleys, Irvin said of Abe, "I wouldn't say he was cheap, but let's just say he was super thrifty." Abe's "super thrifty" attitude came through in a non-baseball setting. In an exchange of letters in October with Craig Vail, the landlord for the Manley's Montgomery Street office, Abe requested a rent reduction. Vail replied, "At the present time we are increasing rents and not reducing them . . . and regret exceedingly that we are unable to comply with your request. . . . Your rent for this month is still outstanding, and we would greatly appreciate your forwarding same to us by return mail."[29] Shortly afterward the return address on Effa's letters read "55 Somerset Street," the Manley's residence in Newark.

While taking a thrifty stance in his business dealings, Abe showed a generous side to his family. He saw to it that eight of his nieces and nephews graduated from college; he supported those who chose to pursue graduate or professional degrees, and he made sure they had money for expenses. Abe helped pay for dental school for one of Nathan's sons, Langston Manley, and supported the opening of a nursery school by his wife, Ivory, in Brooklyn. He paid for family trips back to the family homestead in Hertford, and those who went were chauffeured with him and Effa in his black Lincoln Continental. Abe, whose wealth amounted to at least $1 million by the late 1930s, liked to tell relatives, "You'll be in good shape when I go."[30]

Abe extended his generosity to Effa in her real estate endeavors, even in instances when she went against his wishes. Effa found herself $6,500 in debt owing to a mortgage and repairs on an apartment house, the Elm Apartments, that she bought in Germantown, Pennsylvania, six miles northwest of Philadelphia. She had expected to spend "about a thousand dollars." Support from Abe had not, for once, been forthcoming. Effa told her stepbrother, Jacob, "No one would believe how much money Abe has spent since he has known me, and he has made up his mind he is not going to spend any more and I cannot blame him." She turned to Jacob for help, asking him to solicit his friends at the post office for potential renters so that if white tenants were not found by Christmas, to "keep the block white, we will have tenants lined up." After Jacob failed to turn up enough tenants, Effa finally turned to Abe who made up the difference because, Effa believed, "he did not want to fall out with me."[31]

O

If Effa's real estate investments worried her, she had to be pleased with the financial results for the 1939 NNL season. Favorable weather, a large turnout for the East-West Classic, and increased attendance for all teams but two, the Grays and the Stars, put the league's treasury in the black. Attendance rose by 50 percent at Ruppert Stadium from what it had been in 1938.

The Eagles' bottom line would have looked even better had they won the pennant, which many observers believed would have happened had Hill not missed the last month because of an unspecified illness. Hill's absence diluted the unexpected contributions of Manning, another strong performance by Irvin, and Mackey's play and coaching. Hill did not let his illness stop him from asking Effa for a $20 advance a month after the season ended. Effa, knowing his talents, sent the money order reluctantly, saying "I do not like sending you money so soon. . . . I do not like to think you are in need." She counseled him to collect his unemployment insurance. "Now James," she said, "I want you to take care of the matter right away. There is no reason in the world why you should not be receiving it."[32]

In addition to finding renters for her apartments and helping Hill with his finances, Effa had her eye on the NAL owners meeting scheduled for December 9 and 10 in Chicago. Posey, Wilson, and the Manleys would be attending as NNL representatives. Before the meeting, Effa wrote owners in both leagues proposing that William Hastie, thirty-five, a Harvard Law School graduate, ex-federal judge, and current dean of Howard University's Law School in Washington, D.C., be elected as commissioner of Negro league baseball. "I have talked with him," Effa wrote, "and feel certain he will accept the office if it is the desire of all members." Hastie did not attend the meeting, leaving Effa to make the case for him. Though Effa carried proxies from Semler and Pompez, NAL owners said such a decision could not be voted on unless both leagues were in joint session.[33] The owners scheduled a joint session for February 24, 1940, in Chicago.

# CHAPTER SIX

## *Fireworks*

Players jumping contracts, booking agents, race issues, Effa's demands for a non-baseball person to preside over Negro league baseball, and sportswriters' criticism of the moguls all collided during the February 2, 1940, meeting, making it the most contentious of all the NNL owners' meetings.

Before the meeting started, however, Effa wrote a rarely seen personal letter, to Thelma Wells, Willie's wife, at their Jacksonville, Florida, home. She brought Thelma up to date on her activities and shared some baseball news with her. With an inkling that Wells would choose Mexico over Newark this year, she told Thelma, "We have decided we must take steps against those players who jump their contracts" but went on to say, "Don't take it personal." Effa wrote also that she had been corresponding with Satchel for a month or so because he now "wants to play with us this year." She closed with, "Now Thelma dear, no matter what Wells does, and where you go, please write me sometime. I hope to always be in touch with you, aside from the baseball I have a very warm spot in my heart for you." Thelma replied four months later from the Hotel Lafayette in Mexico City saying that she'd read about the Eagles' opening day and that "it must have been swell. I only wish I had been there instead of here." She said Wells liked Mexico City, but she had seen all the sights and, feeling handicapped by not knowing Spanish, looked forward to coming home in a few weeks. She closed with "Give my love to Mr. Manley and say hello to Carrie" (the Manleys' secretary).[1]

In late January Abe busied himself obtaining some much-needed capital from one of his scouts, Percy Simon, forty-four, a black sports promoter in Norfolk,

Virginia. Percy and Abe may have known each other for some time as both lived in Norfolk and Camden during the same years before Abe moved to Harlem in 1932. Simon co-owned the Big Track Club in Norfolk, a supper club that offered meals and entertainment. Blues singer Irene Batteaste performed there. Simon, like Abe, enjoyed the fights and could be found at ringside in Norfolk and well as New York, especially when Joe Louis took to the ring in the Big Apple.

In the process of arranging the financing, Abe tied up some loose strings. He changed the team's legal name to the Newark Eagles Baseball Club from the Brooklyn Eagles Baseball Club. He also filed a form with the Unemployment Compensation Commission of New Jersey asking permission to discontinue filing required reports for Brooklyn Eagles players. In the papers Abe said Simon had acquired the team, now called the "Newark Eagles Baseball Club at 155 Spruce Street, Newark, N. J." The filing made it sound as if Abe had sold the team to Simon, but no other evidence of a sale could be found. Abe may have taken out a loan from Percy with the team as collateral. In any event, the Manleys used the proceeds to continue operations while paying Simon a monthly salary.[2]

O

Prospects for the Eagles' 1940 season brightened in January when Abe, in a dramatic change of heart, announced that he had signed Satchel Paige to a contract and that Dandridge would return to Newark from Mexico. The combination of Paige and Dandridge joining the Eagles would more than make up for Wells's decision to play in Mexico.[3]

Pleased by Paige's signing, Effa also looked forward to seeing William Hastie in the role of commissioner for both leagues. Hastie dashed those hopes when he wrote Effa on February 1 to say his current commitments, including chairing the National Legal Committee of the NAACP, would prevent him from devoting the time necessary "to carry out the large task of guidance, direction, and publicity." Hastie's letter did not dampen Effa's desire to remove Tom Wilson as NNL president. Wilson's support for Gottlieb's practice of booking games in Yankee Stadium and taking 10 percent of the gross angered Effa to no end. Along with Semler and Pompez, Effa and Abe resented not only the 10 percent fee, but what they took to be an invasion of their New York territory by an outsider—and a white one at that.[4]

Abe quickly recruited Clilan Betnany "C. B." Powell to stand for election as NNL president. Powell, age fifty-six, was publisher of the *New York Amsterdam*

*News*, a graduate of Howard University's Medical School, and one of the first black doctors to specialize in X-ray treatments. His business experience came from cofounding the Victory Mutual Life Insurance Company in 1922.[5]

Posey opposed removing Wilson. The Grays' owner lauded Wilson's first-year performance. "Wilson has been," Posey said, "a success as president of the Negro National League during his first year and should be re-elected. He has brought order out of chaos."[6]

The February 2 meeting showed how other owners reacted to Abe and Effa's proposals and how Effa responded to their reactions. Abe nominated Powell. He spoke highly of Powell, saying his affiliation with the *News* would be good for baseball in New York. Posey promptly nominated Wilson. Posey, Bolden, and Wilson voted for Wilson while Abe, Semler, and Pompez cast their votes for Powell. The normally laid-back Wilson said he was "infuriated by the secretive manner in which a few of the members attempted to oust me." He came close to tears when Semler cast a vote against him. Discussion of Gottlieb's booking activity became so heated that sportswriters waiting outside Gottlieb's office heard shouting. They heard Effa's voice above the din yelling, "We are fighting for something bigger than a little money! We are fighting for a race issue. In other words what we are doing here has become more important than we." At that, Posey jumped up and left the meeting, vowing not to return until "Abe could keep his wife at home where she belonged." With tempers flaring, the group postponed the election until the day before the interleague meeting scheduled for February 24. The moguls did manage to agree on a three-year ban for players who jumped their contracts and to relieve Greenlee of his status of honorary president because he owed the league $787 from games played in Yankee Stadium. The *Afro-American* ran a group photograph of the men in attendance and a separate photograph of a smiling Effa captioned "Stormy Petrel."[7]

Art Carter's and Posey's coverage of the meeting infuriated Effa. Carter, who did not attend the meeting, reported that Effa "hurled epithets" at Cum Posey, whom Carter quoted as saying that Effa took advantage of her sex in the deliberations, though he did not say how. Clearly, though, her gender was an issue for Carter. He characterized Effa as "a female fanfaron" doing all the talking while Abe said barely a word. (Webster's defines "fanfaron" as "a bully; a hector; a swaggerer; an empty boaster.") Carter added, "Baseball is replete with failures where women have been involved," although he gave no examples.[8]

Carter downplayed the booking conflict by pointing out that Gottlieb's booking role at Yankee Stadium had been approved the year before by a vote of 5–1 with the Manleys present, though Abe likely cast the one nay vote. Carter added that the matter could be easily worked out with Wilson in the president's chair. He suggested, to no avail, that the owners reduce Gottlieb's take from 10 to 5 percent.[9]

Effa delivered a swift and detailed response. In a two-page, single-spaced, typed letter written the day she read Carter's column, she reminded Carter he was not at the meeting so he could "only write what someone told you . . . which is unfortunate when important issues are at stake." She pointed out errors Carter made, such as referring to Posey as secretary and treasurer when "Mr. Abe Manley was elected treasurer of the league by a unanimous vote." She excused Carter "this error as it is just another point on which you have been misinformed." She took exception to Carter's statement that she opposed Wilson only because he supported Gottlieb's booking efforts. She said the league's present status "has resulted in small salaries for players and meager profits for owners. The public and the ball players are entitled to a better break. The only way this is possible is through the adoption of sound business practices and an impartial staff of officers. This is my position and I shall continue to take such a stand." She closed by saying she hoped they could soon meet, "not because I am a woman and will be taking advantage of that fact as you said I did at the league meeting, but I would like to tell you a lot of things you should know about baseball."[10]

Effa, who had heard before Posey's complaint that the man knew she proposed for leadership roles nothing about baseball, liked to remind him and others that when the 1919 Black Sox scandal forced major league owners to hire a commissioner to restore integrity to the game, they chose a non-baseball person, Kenesaw Mountain Landis. Landis, a fan of the Chicago Cubs, had made his living for fifteen years as a federal judge in the District Court of Northern Illinois in Chicago before becoming commissioner.

While Effa's commitment to finding an outside executive to run the NNL brought howls and admonishments from Carter and Posey, Lem Graves Jr., a sportswriter for the *Norfolk Journal and Guide* who often visited with the Manleys on their trips to Norfolk, saw Effa's work in a more positive light. "She is not," he wrote, "the usual, know-it-all, busy-body woman delving into men's affairs. Rather, she is an intensely interested, well-informed, capable, efficient, and strong-willed woman who runs a man's business better than most of the men."[11]

Posey, Greenlee, and Wilson did not share Graves's opinion, and tensions stayed high between Wilson and the New York moguls. Wilson unilaterally changed the location of the February 24 meeting from Chicago to Pittsburgh, bringing expected yelps from Semler, Pompez, and Effa. Semler suspected Wilson of laying a trap for him in Pittsburgh, where Posey, Wilson, and Greenlee, the latter still residing in Pittsburgh, would use good fellowship and whiskey to change his mind. "They figure they'll get me down there and after we kill two or three bottles of whiskey," Semler said, "I'll be on their side. It'll never happen. I'm going to see this thing through."[12] Wilson lost that round. The owners met in Chicago.

Before they got there, Effa received a fan letter from Oliva Mamie Rodolph of Charleston, South Carolina. In her letter addressed "Dear Stormy Petrel," Rodolph said she hoped Effa remembered the "little lady from Charleston who took breakfast with you at Mrs. Cora Rollins'" in Chicago in 1934. She asked Effa to "accept my congratulations on the stand you took at the Philly meeting. It takes real courage to hold your own against such strong men. You are a real pro at it."[13]

It did not take Effa long to step forward again and offer another challenge. At the NNL moguls' next meeting held at Chicago's Grand Hotel on February 24, Effa, joined by Abe, Pompez, and Semler, threatened to form a new league minus the Giants, Grays, and Stars, if that's what it would take to make the league run more like a business. Nothing came of the challenge, and the moguls finally resolved the leadership crisis when Pompez, "in the interest of peace," changed his vote, ensuring that the league officers for 1940 remained as they had been in 1939.

Thinking his change of vote may have engendered some political capital for him, Semler, along with the Manleys and Pompez, proposed that owners do their own booking so that they could put the money previously set aside for Gottlieb toward players' salaries. Without increasing salaries, the New York bloc argued, fans had little chance of always seeing the best Negro leaguers. Bans on players jumping to teams south of the border were often winked at because they were surefire gate attractions when they did return. Semler miscalculated. Gottlieb, with Wilson's, Posey's, and Bolden's support, kept his booking responsibilities and his 10 percent. Both leagues held a joint session the following day and accomplished nothing of significance.

The meetings ended, but the tension between the owners did not. Posey's account of the meeting in his *Pittsburgh Courier* column Posey's Points created another sore spot for Effa. He had, she said, shortchanged her views and those expressed by Pompez and Semler. "It is only fair," she wrote to Posey, "for us to give our ideas of administration a chance as you have given yours." This time she went public in her fight with Posey by sending a copy of her letter to him to all the weeklies. Her letter struck a sympathetic chord with Frank Young, sportswriter for the *Chicago Defender.* Young, who the previous year had criticized Effa for her East-West game cost-cutting suggestions, replied that he now found Effa to be "very gracious and ladylike and knowing more about baseball than some of our colored experts." He promised her "whatever tirade our Homestead Gray friend [Posey] writes . . . will not find any space in my columns." Young sent his "kindest regards to Mr. Manley who so graciously holds his wife's fur coat."[14]

O

With the meetings behind them and no damage done to the status quo, the Manleys turned their attention to the action on the field. They did not like what they saw. Three of the Eagles' best players—Wells, Dandridge, and Day—were in Mexico when spring training opened in Savannah, Georgia. Abe, who, Dandridge said, "always treated us good," expected Dandridge to sign with Newark, but that was before Dandridge and Effa talked contract terms. "I was making $150 a month and asked for twenty-five dollars more," he said. Effa, whom Dandridge characterized as "pushy-pushy," said no. "Mexican League President Jorge Pasquel offered me $350 a month plus expenses for me and my family. She knew about the offer. That's why Wells and I caught the plane together." Effa remembered Dandridge's request and its outcome differently. She remembered the star third sacker saying that if she met the Mexico offer, he'd stay in Newark. But, she told him she did not want to get into a bidding war with the Pasquels because "they were millionaires. . . . I'm sure they could have outbid me." She later said that she advised Dandridge to go.[15]

In another disappointment, Abe learned that while he thought he had an agreement with Paige, Paige thought otherwise and remained in Puerto Rico, where he had played winter ball. Abe and Effa filled the gaps left by the jumpers with younger players, including Francis Mathews, who starred as the first black captain of French Technical High School's baseball team in Cambridge, Massachusetts. Other youngsters Abe signed included Vernon Riddick, who had attended Morgan State College in Baltimore, Maryland; Clarence "Pint" Israel from Rockville, Maryland; and pitcher Lenial Hooker, whose North Carolina probation officer gave him permission to play for the Eagles until September 6.

While the replacements got into shape, Effa continued her campaign to stanch the flow of players to Latin America. She wrote to Tom Wilson and J. B. Martin, president of the NAL, soliciting both "if you feel inclined . . . to take any official steps." Adopting a conciliatory tone this time she said, "[P]lease do not misinterpret the tone of this letter. . . . I am not trying to dictate to the Chairman what his duties are. I hesitate to take the first steps . . . but I can not sit idly by any longer and not put forth an effort to protect myself." She also made a specific request of Martin to prevent Paige, who she said "belongs to me," from again barnstorming the country with the support of Kansas City Monarchs owner, J. L. Wilkinson. Anticipating that neither president felt so inclined, Effa engaged the services of attorney Richard Carey a week before she wrote the letters to Martin and Wilson to ask the U.S. State Department to deny Pearson, who was preparing to travel to South America, a passport. The State Department's response was not documented, but Pearson did not go south. Effa said she "was willing and able to talk him out of it."[16] Why Effa singled Pearson out for special attention and what inducements, if any, she offered, is not known.

Even with Wells, Dandridge, and Day in Mexico, the Eagles had a solid core of players, notably Irvin, Stone, and Pearson in the outfield; Mackey behind the plate; Hill and Manning on the mound; Suttles at first; and Seay at second.

As usual, Effa made elaborate plans for the Eagles opening day game on May 5, 1940, against the Black Yankees. Invited celebrities included two women: Cora Rollins and Elsie LaMoine. LaMoine lived in Harlem's Sugar Hill District, not far from the Manleys' former residence, and ran a ready-to-wear shop in Harlem on Lenox Avenue near 135th Street. Other notable guests included Jocko Maxwell, a famous black sportscaster for WWRL in Woodside, Long Island, and WLTH in New York City who called many an Eagles game and who asked Effa for season passes for himself, his brother, and his father; Andy Razaf, the Harlem-based lyricist for such songs as "Ain't Misbehaving" and "Honeysuckle Rose"; John Borican; Henry Armstrong, world welterweight boxing champion who threw out the first ball with his suit jacket buttoned; ex-New Jersey Governor Harold G. Hoffman; J. Mercer Burrell; and State Senator Robert C. Hendrickson, who would serve in the U.S. Senate from 1949 to 1955. Effa's stepsister, Ruth, a nurse in the Harlem Hospital, accepted Effa's invitation to attend the game with her two children and husband. Overlooking no detail, Effa wrote to A. Phailstock, whose band would be performing, telling him to please get busy learning the National Anthem, which is played "with a certain tempo," if he did not know it and to include "Take Me Out to the Ball Game," and "Happy Days Are Here Again" among his selections.[17]

Fans enjoyed themselves at the game. Spirits of all types ran high—some in bottles both in and under the stands. For many, opening day marked the real beginning of summer, and most were in a celebratory mood. After the game, some continued partying at the Grand Hotel or the Afro Club, where singing, eating, and drinking continued late into the night.[18]

On the field, pint-sized Jimmy Hill stole the opening day show before thirteen thousand spectators under partly sunny skies and temperatures in the low sixties. He held the Black Yankees to three hits in seven innings and hit a three-run homer to lead the Eagles to a 5–2 win. For hitting the season's first home run at Ruppert Stadium, Hill received jewelry from a local company, $40 in cash, four hats, a pair of shoes, and complete barber services for one year from fans whose names announced over the loud speaker system for their generosity. Pearson, to Effa's delight, went three for four at the plate. Both teams left the next day for a twelve-day barnstorming tour of the South. Upon their return, the Eagles split a doubleheader with the Stars at Ruppert Stadium. Hill kept his standing as the Eagles' number one pitcher by throwing a complete game to beat the Stars 6–1. His performances so pleased Effa that she agreed to his request for his girlfriend Mary Irvin (no relation to Monte) to join him in violation of Abe's professed code of conduct. In her letter to Mary's mother Maggie, Effa said she's "afraid if she [Mary] does not come here, he will come back home to her." Effa told Maggie, "I will see to it she is comfortable . . . will send her home if she does not like it . . . and that I am pleased to know James is only interested in her. So many of the Boys are a little wild." Since Hill stayed with the team, it's likely Maggie took Effa up on her offer to pay Mary's way to Newark.[19]

Hill was not the only pitcher on Effa's mind. She received a telegram from Satchel Paige on May 31 inviting her to come see him in Richmond, Virginia. This she did, accompanied by Abe and Mule Suttles. There she found the Satchel Paige All-Stars, along with J. L. Wilkinson, who told her no one had offered Paige a contract, so "I picked him up." Wilkinson bankrolled Paige's team, which had been doing nicely barnstorming the country with the Brooklyn Royal Giants and playing occasional games against NAL teams. Not quite believing what she saw, Effa cut off further conversation, returned to Newark, and again wrote Wilson and Martin, but this time she dropped the conciliatory tone. Citing her and Abe's need to make a profit, noting she had agreed to pay Paige $1,000 a month, and saying that Paige's situation showed how weak the league was, she wrote, "I expect each of you to order Wilkinson to send Paige to Newark immediately this week." Martin did not go that far, but he did order all NAL clubs to cancel all games with Paige's club. Unsatisfied with Martin's response and getting no response from Wilson, Effa threatened to pull the Eagles out of the league if Paige did not report to Newark. Abe, who believed some NAL owners had befriended fellow owner Wilkinson by persuading Paige to stay with his All-Stars, retaliated by using two NAL players—Buzz Clarkson, a shortstop, and Ernest "Spoon" Carter, a pitcher, from the NAL Toledo Crawfords—in a doubleheader against the Grays on June 16, despite orders from Wilson not to use the two.

The owners finally resolved the Paige matter at another rough and tumble joint league meeting, this one at Harlem's Woodside Hotel on June 18 and 19, where "the fur flew." The owners eked out a late-night compromise that ended two years of recriminations. The Manleys, Wilson, and the other NNL owners allowed the NAL to claim the rights to Paige in return for the Eagles being allowed to keep Clarkson and Carter. The NAL got the best of the deal as Clarkson and Carter, while both were players of above-average talent, were no match for Paige's ability to fill seats, regardless of what team he played with. Effa withdrew her threat to leave the league.

Paige, who evidently did not hear of or care about the compromise and thought he could negotiate his own deal, dropped Effa a line a month later from the Angelus Hotel in Vancouver, British Columbia, on July 24. In it he talked about wanting to pitch in the East-West game and finish the season with the Eagles. "Now don't be angry with me," he wrote. "Just tell me what you will give me to Finish the Season with you and Send me a ticket on the Plane and I will come and finish the Season with you." Paige did not pitch in the East-West game, nor did he join the Eagles. He signed with Wilkinson's Kansas City Monarchs, where he played until 1948, when Bill Veeck signed him to a Cleveland Indians contract.[20]

Effa's efforts to sign Paige did not sit well with Hazel M. Wigden, an employee of the State of New York Department of Law, whose favorite team was the Eagles, for, as she put it in a letter to the *New York Amsterdam News*, "some inexplicable reason." She said fans were tired of and disgusted with the Eagles' halfhearted play in exhibition games against white teams. "They can break your heart as they slouch out to their positions as though if they had to step once more, they would flop." She asked Effa, "So who is Satchel Paige that you should desire him as though he were God himself?" Suggesting that Effa pay more attention to showing fans a good baseball game than to pursuing Paige, Wigden asked, "Aren't there other pitchers in this whole wide United States of America, even maybe in South America?"[21]

If there were such pitchers, they did not come to Abe's attention. The Eagles would have welcomed such pitchers after winning two of their first four league games but struggling to a third-place finish for the first half of the season. Eagles manager Lundy generated some excitement as the first half was drawing to a close when he provoked home plate umpire "Bulldog" Turner, an ex-football player, into knocking him out. Lundy, who had a drinking problem, disputed Turner's call that an Eagles player was out at first in an 8–1 losing cause against the Grays on June 20. Eagles first baseman Fran Mathews recalled hearing the crowd go, "Wow!" behind him as he was throwing the ball around the infield (the owners' earlier resolve to stop such throwing to speed games up had dissipated), as the Eagles took the field. "I looked around, and the man [Lundy] was flat on his back. He had jumped at Turner and Turner had knocked him cold. . . . I thought he was dead. His eyes was flopping." The police accompanied Lundy into the Eagles' dugout on their way to the locker room. In the dugout the police discovered a bottle of wine that Lundy had hidden behind the water cooler.[22]

○

As the second half of the season opened, the Eagles, for the second consecutive year, advanced the cause of integration a bit with a Saturday game on July 6 to benefit Newark's Knot Hole Gang, a group of twelve thousand children sponsored by the Board of Education's recreation department. Previously, only the Newark Bears had played benefit games for the Knot Hole Gang, which provided tickets to youngsters who could not afford them.[23] On August 6 the Eagles played another benefit game, this one against the Stars, to benefit the Newark Community Hospital, New Jersey's only "colored" hospital. Effa served on the Committee to Benefit the Community Hospital and wrote letters soliciting purchases of tickets from the state's "colored" physicians and morticians. Those who responded found their name listed as patrons of the game on the scorecard.[24]

O

While Effa organized benefit games, Jim Crow made several appearances in Newark. He showed up in the form of a ticket clerk at Penn Station who called the train station's reservation service to ask about a reservation for "a colored lady." The lady, Mrs. Letteria May Dalton, of Lima, Ohio, resented the term and said so. The agent answered, "We have a special coach for your people." She registered a complaint with the Pennsylvania Railroad's passenger traffic manager, C. H. Mathews Jr. Mathews apologized to Mrs. Dalton in a letter saying the railroad maintains a nondiscrimination policy. He promised to discover the name of the ticket agent and take corrective, but unspecified, action.

A violent race-based hate crime had occurred in August 1939 in Cranbury, New Jersey, forty-three miles south of Newark. Ten white men dragged nine black potato pickers from their shacks at midnight, forced them to strip naked, lie on the ground with their hands taped behind them, and submit to beatings with rubber hoses while the white men threatened the black men with raping the lone woman of the group. They covered the pickers with white paint, kept their clothes, and forced them to walk three miles back to their shacks from the field where they had been driven. A local hospital refused to treat their injuries. An all-white District Court jury of nine men and three women in Newark deliberated nine minutes on May 10, 1940, before awarding $9,000 in damages to the pickers. Nine of the ten men, who ranged in ages from eighteen to twenty-four, threw themselves on the mercy of the court. They walked away with suspended sentences of two or three years each. The tenth member of the mob, a minor, escaped prosecution.[25]

O

Looking for better results on the diamond in the second half, Lundy revised the lineup in mid-July 1940 by moving Irvin from third to the outfield, Pearson from centerfield to the hot corner, and starting rookie Clarence Israel at second. Lundy's moves paid off initially. The Eagles took three straight from the Black Yankees. Manning won two games and Hill one. The team kept the streak going until it reached nine in a row by the first week in August, but lackluster effort characterized their play for the rest of the month. The Eagles again finished in third place while the Grays clinched the second-half flag.[26] The Manleys waited until mid-August to fine Lundy $25 for his altercation with Turner. Lundy resented the fine and quit the team instead of paying it. Effa asked Biz Mackey to take over the manager's job after Oscar Charleston refused it.[27]

Shortly after Mackey took the Eagles' reins, Josh Gibson returned to the Grays after three and a half months in Venezuela, where he earned $800 a month plus expenses for playing only on weekends. Posey, in a blatant and unapologetic violation of the three-year ban he had voted to support in February, wrote Effa a letter. "[S]o there won't be any controversies at the games," he told Effa. He explained that Gibson would be in the lineup against the Eagles in Griffith Stadium on August 18. Effa, taking it on her own to uphold the ban, told the Eagles' bus driver, Edison Thomas, to ask Clark Griffith, owner of the Washington Senators, not to open the park because the Eagles would not play the Grays with Gibson in the lineup. Effa chose to go to Chicago rather than Washington in an effort to bring the owners, who were attending the East-West game, to her point of view. Griffith told Thomas that he, not Effa, would decide when to open the park and who would play in it. Griffith arranged for the Stars to face the Grays. Gibson went one for six with a home run. An aide to Griffith, Edward B. Eynon, subsequently asked Effa to write a letter explaining why she made the request and why she should be "reinstated in the good graces of Mr. Griffith and the stadium." Effa gave Eynon the background on the ban. She explained that she had flown to Chicago to meet with the owners and that in a rare instance of getting the owners to agree with her, had convinced them to ban Gibson from all remaining games that season. She acknowledged to Enyon that "the most unfortunate part of whole affair, was putting the Eagles and their management in a bad light with you people and the fans." She pointed out, "Our organization is very carelessly run, and in many cases, rules and regulations are not observed." She offered to meet with Griffith or Enyon to "clear things up so that you know that our reputation for honesty and integrity continues." Things evidently were cleared up as the Eagles continued to play in Griffith Stadium.[28]

Gibson knew his comings and goings upset the owners. "They get angry with us when we go away," he said. But, echoing Paige's comments on the matter, Gibson asked a reporter what he'd do if a newspaper in Mexico offered to double his salary.[29]

Players other than Gibson cited money as one justification for their trips to Latin America. They also found the freedom attractive. Irvin found Mexicans to be more accepting of blacks than Americans were and, in one instance, more accepting than Puerto Ricans were. He, Day, Raymond Brown, Roy Partlow, and Clarkson lived on the second floor of the Hotel Bonair in the old part of San Juan. Momma Seta ran a brothel on the first floor. Irvin recalled, "We'd say 'Momma Seta, why can't we go downstairs? We got money. Pourque, Momma Seta?' She'd say with a smile and rubbing my hand, 'Wrong color.' So we'd go down to the waterfront where there's a lot of soldiers and sailors and where it was only a dollar a time or two dollars for all night. 'Course in Mexico they had wonderful night-clubs. You could dance all night; proposition a woman, and there's no problem. They'd accommodate everybody—first time I really felt free. People sent drinks to you. It took two or three weeks to get used to the regime back in the States."[30]

While players found money and freedom in Latin American, the owners of the teams they left in the United States found themselves over a barrel and em-barrassed, as their bans on players could never be fully enforced. No one in the business of Negro league baseball would keep Paige and Gibson out of action for a year or two because of a ban passed at a meeting. Besides, the owners had no legal recourse. Nothing in a player's contract spoke of penalties for "jumping." Effa knew if the situation continued, the Negro leagues would suffer, and as was her style, she proposed some alternatives. In a November 25 letter to J. B. Martin she said, "I feel I am being taken such undue advantage of . . . we have a vested right in these men and should be paid for them." She suggested that each team contribute $100 to a fund to pay a lawyer to negotiate a farm club arrangement with Pasquel, in which the Mexican league would buy players from the Negro leagues. "If these men," she wrote hopefully, "were informed of the true state of affairs, they would be glad to cooperate on a sensible, practical program." Three weeks later in a letter to Cum Posey, Effa reported she had spoken with a lawyer (Robert Hartgrove) who recommended she "sign ballplayers to a contract like fighters sign. When you have a vested right in a man he cannot leave you at will." She suggested "Tom" invite Hartgrove to an owners meeting. Neither the proposal to approach Pasquel, hire Hartgrove, or invite him to a meeting came to fruition then. It would take some years for the owners to see the value in Hart-grove's suggestion.[31]

Player problems of another sort had beset Effa in August when thirty-eight-year-old Darltie Cooper sued the Eagles for workman's compensation payments. Cooper, an itinerate pitcher and outfielder, was in his last year of an eighteen-year career during which he had played for nine teams. He fractured his foot running to first base on May 19. As was the usual custom in the case of injured players, Abe let him go without pay when his foot did not heal. Effa expressed regrets at the injury but thought Cooper should have healed faster than he did. The referee for the Workman's Compensation Bureau in the New Jersey Department of Labor disagreed and awarded Cooper twenty-one weeks worth of payments. In the course of the hearing in which Jerry Kessler represented Effa, she admitted the Eagles did not carry insurance and learned that the law required the team to do so. When Effa asked, "What if I don't have the money for insurance?" the referee told her, "You go to jail." Effa turned on her heel and left the room. She bought insurance from the Employers' Group of Boston, Massachusetts.[32]

Player problems continued. Pearson, whom Effa had talked out of jumping the Eagles for the 1940 season, disappointed her when he chose to play winter ball in Caguas, Puerto Rico, rather than stay in Newark to try out for Bob Douglass's New York Rens basketball team as Effa had arranged. Known as the Renaissance Five, after the Renaissance Ballroom in Harlem—the team's titular home —the squad was the country's first professional black basketball team. Its success earned Douglass a plaque in the Naismith Memorial Basketball Hall of Fame in Springfield, Massachusetts. Learning that Effa had made disparaging remarks about his decision, Pearson told her in a four-page handwritten letter that he thought her remarks "quite unfair," and he reminded her that he would have stayed if she had made him the loan she agreed to but subsequently reneged on. He said at the end of his letter, "I hope I have explained myself clearly, and if you feel I let you down, I am sorry, but you must remember you also let me down."[33]

On a more upbeat note, Newark's YMCA honored Effa at their First Annual Recognition Reception for her volunteer activities in 1939 and 1940. A notice in Ruth Shipley's column, Socially Speaking! in the *Afro-American* informed its readers of the award and went on to say that "the attractive Effa Manley was in town. She owns and manages the Newark Eagles." Shipley may not have known that Effa was neither owner or manager of the team, but she did know the extent of Effa's influence on the Eagles' affairs.[34]

# CHAPTER SEVEN

## *Cobbling Together a Lineup*

Wilson, Posey, and Bolden lay in wait for Effa and Abe at the start of the NNL owners meeting at the York Hotel in Baltimore on January 3, 1941. The first motion presented to the group by the trio proposed consolidating the office of secretary-treasurer into the secretary's office "for reasons of effectiveness." The group elected Posey to the office, thereby squeezing Abe out of the treasurer's office and bringing Effa's financial activities on behalf of the league to an end for the time being. The Manleys, strangely enough, made no protest. The meeting concluded on a peaceful note as the owners established the season's schedule and planned for a joint league meeting in March. The *Afro-American* hosted the group to a banquet with Art Carter as toastmaster.[1]

Once the Manleys returned to Newark, Effa began rounding up players for the campaign. She asked Mackey to manage the team. He agreed but Mackey, who lived in Los Angeles, wanted to meet the team in come to Newark before the team left for Florida, to give him collect unemployment insurance and pay off a debt. Effa agreed and it to coincide with the start of spring training.[2]

presented more of challenge. Hill had received a $50 fine in lieu of a for throwing a pool ball at a man and striking him on the arm. Hill paid part of it and wrote Effa asking for a loan for thirty-five, saying, "You know, Mrs. Manley, I don't want to go to jail." He also told her that he and Mary had married but that "she is younger [she was sixteen] and we wouldn't want that to go into no kind of papers." He asked Effa "not to expose us." Effa agreed not to expose them and to give the loan once she received Hill's contract, which he promptly returned, saying he "was very satisfied with the salary." A month later he requested money to cover doctor bills for an unspecified reason. Effa again agreed. But by April 12 Hill had not reported to spring training. Effa laid into him with a letter expressing her disappointment and dismay in his absence, saying in part, "I wonder if you have real good sence [sic]. . . . I have been more of an employer to you as you well know. . . . You should be a real star but that cannot happen until you make up your mind to act like a man, and not a child." She enclosed $5 with her letter.[3]

Effa had been trying to sign John Howard Davis, a big, power-hitting outfielder since July 1940, but Davis had been incarcerated in the New Jersey State Penitentiary. Having had no luck with the Parole Department in June 1940, Effa enlisted the help of Reverend Johnson, whose efforts failed to produce Davis, even though, as Johnson told Effa in May 1941, "Danny Burrows [sic] interceded for me." Dan Burroughs was a New York City assemblyman. Burroughs's efforts, nevertheless, pleased Effa to the extent that she offered him all the tickets he wanted for a Sunday game and asked him to bring a bill of his expenses with him.

Effa turned to another friend, Dr. Leroy Morris of Trenton, to ask the governor's office to make an appointment for Abe with New Jersey's director of the Division of Parole, Sgt. Alban Kite. Kite met with Abe and pledged his full cooperation. Davis joined the team in late June.[4]

Lenial Hooker returned his contract unsigned with the curt comment "terms not acceptable." Effa told him she "was quite surprised." She went on to say, "I cannot believe it was your idea. I cannot even understand you permitting it to be done." Effa told Hooker that anyone familiar with his record last year would feel "you had been treated more than fairly." She devoted the rest of her letter to detailing what a poor year he had had. She closed with, "I expect you to sign the enclosed contract, return it, and be ready to meet the bus in Raleigh about midnight April 3." Hooker met the bus.

Max Manning took a straightforward approach to asking Effa for a raise in early March. "A Negro baseball player's life is a hard one," Manning wrote. "He has to make money while he is still young. He must obtain his salary however and whenever he can." Manning asked for a $25-per-month raise. Effa granted it saying that to do so immediately was unusual but that Manning had finished the year "in grand condition." She said she hoped he would have a good season "and be worth even more next year."

Satchel Paige reappeared. He dropped Effa a line from Puerto Rico in early March saying he wanted to meet with her in any city of her choosing before he returned to Kansas City. "I don't belong to no one," he wrote, "and haven't signed a thing. . . . Bring your contract with you and if we can get together I will sign up . . . listen Mrs. Manley don't Beat around the Bush. I am a man. Tell me just what you want me to know." He signed the letter "Mr. Satchel Paige (Smile)." A reply could not be found, but Paige stayed with the Monarchs.

A week earlier Effa had written to McDuffie at his home in Jacksonville asking him for a favor, "which I know you'll do if you can." She wanted Willie Wells's address. She confided in McDuffie, "I can't understand the ballplayers. They don't seem to have any idea how much destruction they can cause, they seem to feel that just a word that they are sorry is all that's needed."[5]

Effa had written McDuffie just days after the joint league meeting held at Chicago's Grand Hotel. Led by Ed Bolden and opposed by the Manleys, the majority of owners had passed a resolution that allowed "a jumper" to pay a $100 fine to his team by May 1 or continue to be subject to the ban. In yet another attempt to reduce jumping by passing resolutions, the majority of owners then agreed to a five-year ban on players who jumped their team after May 1. The ban caused Dan Burley, *New York Amsterdam News* sportswriter, to wonder why—in much the same way Hazel Wigden had earlier—owners did not spend more time on developing American talent by supporting church, college, and other amateur baseball leagues, holding baseball schools, or stepping up scouting activities, while reducing their myopic focus on Latin America.[6]

O

In the midst of negotiating with her players, Effa found herself in negotiations over two real estate properties. Ruth Marie Brown, branch general secretary for Camden's YWCA, recalled Abe's foot dragging on repairing door hinges a year earlier and wrote Effa "a one woman to another" letter in April. The building at 822 Kaighn Avenue, the same building that had housed the Rest-A-While Club, had not been painted since the Y rented it in 1935. Noting that "only women can appreciate the importance of a clean house" and "that Negro women are especially aware of these things . . . we hope that you will see fit to influence the 'head of the house' to grant it." Brown's pitch registered with Effa, if only partially.

She agreed the house needed painting but said "the income is very, very little" and "the insurance is much higher, and taxes are steeper" than other properties because "this one is a public building." She offered to buy the paint and suggested Brown find someone to apply it, perhaps from the National Youth Administration, a New Deal agency that paid boys and girls from families on relief $10 to $25 a month for part-time work.

She asked the property manager for their apartment building at 1334 N. 15th Street in Philadelphia whether she could postpone the current insurance premium for a month as "I am under very heavy pressure this current month," and she promised to make sure the janitor for the building was covered by Social Security.[7]

At about this time Abe bought another piece of real estate, this one a large, three-story house at 71 Crawford Street in the Hill District of Newark's Third Ward, where he and Effa would live and work for the rest of their time in the city. They lived on the second floor and rented out the other two floors. One of their tenants, Estey Jones, seemed well satisfied with the Manleys as landlords, as he rented from them from 1943 to 1951. Other tenants stayed little more than a year before moving on.[8]

○

As Effa negotiated with players, tenants, and property managers, the *New Jersey Afro-American* shone its investigative light on prostitution in the Third Ward. In an attempt to develop public support to curb prostitution "from flaunting itself before hundreds of respectable women," the paper, in a front-page article, described how the world's oldest profession operated in the Third Ward and parts of the Seventh. While residents were now more knowledgeable about the business side of prostitution in their neighborhoods, the profession continued to flourish.

During their free time, some prostitutes attended Eagles games. First baseman Fran Mathews recalled being cheered on by one, a Mrs. Smith, whose services he did not use. "I had enough problems," he said. Mathews remembered the time he ran to the dugout to a chorus of boos for a throwing error he'd made earlier in the inning. "Mrs. Smith stood up," Mathews said. "A great big lady with beautiful silks and watches, she said: Don't worry, honey, we are all with you.'"

○

With her negotiations complete, at least for the time being, Effa set about preparing for another opening day. She invited black America's number one celebrity, heavyweight boxing champion Joe Louis, to throw out the first ball. In a February

10, 1941, letter to Louis's agent, Julian Black (who would make the decision), Effa cast her invitation in terms of racial pride. "I really feel that our Negro Athletes are one of the few things we have to work with, and can be really proud of," she wrote. "This is the thing that has kept me fighting this uphill battle of trying to organize Negro Baseball. . . . I want Joe to through [*sic*] out the ball." She approached the New York City office of the NAACP with a plan to sell buttons at the opener for the association's benefit but was told by Roy Wilkins, assistant secretary, that her request for a decision the next day by telephone was unrealistic. "Such matters . . . require the action of our Committee on Administration and our Board of Directors. No one executive can give his request on such a proposition." She invited all 2,500 colored soldiers of the 372nd Army Infantry—the only black federalized National Guard Regiment stationed at Fort Dix, New Jersey—to join Louis. She predicted the trucks driving them to Ruppert Stadium along with the police escort would stretch for more than a half-mile. With Effa and J. Mercer Burrell standing beside him in his office, Mayor Meyer Ellenstein, in one of his last acts as mayor, signed a proclamation that declared May 11, opening day, to be "372nd Infantry Day." The proclamation noted that the New Jersey State Legislature had cited the 372nd for its rescue work during the *Morro Castle* disaster in 1934. A fire had engulfed the ship during a nighttime nor'easter, causing many deaths and numerous injuries. The 372nd led the rescue effort.[9]

While Effa worked on the ceremonial side of opening day, Abe and Biz Mackey had the players hard at work in Daytona Beach, Florida, preparing for the game against the New York Cubans. The team's biggest improvement lay in its pitching staff. Leon Day, dissatisfied with life in Venezuela, agreed to pay the $100 fine and re-signed with Newark. James Brown, whom the press referred to as "the second Satchel Paige," returned. After a promising start, he had left the Eagles two years ago to be with his new wife in her hometown of Sharpsburg, North Carolina. Hill, Hooker, and Manning rounded out the staff. The other positions, except catcher, which Mackey covered, presented challenges. Wells and Dandridge both opted to ignore the owners' new ban and play in Mexico, as did outfielder Ed Stone, leaving Irvin as the only returning star. Abe, continuing his youth program, took Suttles's bat out of the lineup by trading him to the Black Yankees. The reconstructed infield featured Mathews at first, Clarence "Pint" Israel at second, Pearson at third, and rookie Leaman Johnson at shortstop. Irvin, Thadist Christopher (who had played part of the 1936 season with the Eagles and once shredded Ray Dandrige's new suit with a knife when Dandridge tried to break up a fight), Charles Thomason, and Leon Day (when he wasn't pitching), held down the outfield.[10]

A week before the opener, Julian Black declined Effa's invitation. The honor went to ex-Mayor Meyer Ellenstein. Lt. Col. Earl Davis, officer in charge of the twelve hundred soldiers of the 372nd, handed the ball to Ellenstein, who opened the season with his toss. Irvin's three hits, including one homer, went for naught, as the Cubans triumphed 3–2. Fran Mathews also hit a round-tripper and, because he did it first, received $100 for hitting the first home run of the season in front of the hometown fans. Mule Suttles, now a Black Yankee but still connected to Newark as a bartender at the city's Afro Club, watched the game unannounced from the Eagles' dugout. Police broke up six fights, prompting the concessionaires to shut off the tap in the eighth inning. Though she lost the game, Effa's take from the twelve thousand paid admissions pleased her, as did her retinue of celebrity guests. Carl Lawrence, who covered the game for the *New York Amsterdam Star-News*, noted that many "sepia" newsmen were "peeved" at Effa for giving the Eagles' publicity business to "a personable ofay [a contemptuous term for a white person] lad," Jerry Kessler.[11]

In a stroke of good financial fortune, Effa managed to secure two Sunday dates in Yankee Stadium through Gottlieb's booking office. Memorial Day saw the Eagles suffer a loss before $25,000 fans to the Black Yankees, who scored three runs in the ninth to win the game, 6–5. The game was so well played that one sportswriter said Negro league ball in New York would outdraw the major league games if teams kept up that level of play. Fans found entertainment in drinking and gambling as well as in watching the scene on the field. Ample whiskey and wine consumption led to a number of fistfights that police had trouble containing. A Newark woman successfully bet $50 on the outcome of one of Manning's pitches. Another woman's husband was not as lucky, losing $75 he had bet on the Eagles to win. Ignoring the custom that it was not a good idea to attend a Negro athletic event alone, unescorted women, many draped in fine furs, attended in larger numbers than in past years.

A week after opening day the Eagles lost the first game of a Yankee Stadium twin bill 6–3 to the Stars. Prior to the game both teams lined up along the baselines to listen to Rev. Adam Clayton Powell Sr. lead the crowd in prayer in memory of Lou Gehrig. The "Iron Man" first baseman of the New York Yankees had died on June 2. The two clubs were the first to honor Gehrig since the white Yankees were on the road.[12]

In spite of losing their first two Yankee Stadium games, the Eagles played well enough elsewhere to lead the league as Independence Day approached. The team's fortunes, however, took a turn for the worse, and the Grays nosed them out to claim the first half pennant.[13]

O

In between games Effa attended to a variety of other tasks. She thanked *Chicago Defender* sportswriter Frank A. Young for asking her for a picture of herself to run in the paper, which she agreed to with a pass at modesty. "I always argue," she replied, "that people do not care who owns the ball club, but all you newspapermen insist there is a human interest angle where a woman is concerned. I will have the picture for you at the meeting in New York."

She also sought permission from New York City's Transit Commission to register the team bus in the name of the Newark Eagles. Until now it had remained registered in the name of the Brooklyn Eagles Baseball Club. Her request triggered an inspection of the bus that identified needed repairs to the upholstery, brakes, gas tank, headlamps, fire extinguisher (not full), and windshield (needed to be made of plate glass). She made the repairs but Irvin found the bus, which the Manleys bought new in 1935, wanting. "I asked Abe, why don't you get us a decent bus to ride in. Here we are riding in this rickety bus." Abe declined.

Effa filed a claim on her recently purchased unemployment insurance for an injury that Pearson sustained on June 22. In her letter she went to great lengths to explain why she had the team doctor treat Pearson without first notifying the insurance company. The company had no problems with the treatment but did inform Effa that she needed to pay the premiums for the first and second quarter or face delinquency penalties.

She also made the public address system at Ruppert Stadium available to the New Jersey branch of the NAACP, which evidently had found the needed time to process her offer to aid them in selling buttons during the same game in which Pearson suffered his injury. The proceeds were to help support people from Newark who planned to participate in a July march on Washington, D.C., to protest discrimination in defense industries. Organizers of the march, A. Philip Randolph and Walter White of the NAACP and T. Hill Arnold of the National Urban League, called off the march following a meeting between Randolph, White, and

President Roosevelt on June 18. To avoid the embarrassment of 100,000 people marching in the streets of the nation's capital in protest of the federal government, FDR issued Executive Order 8802. The order prohibited discrimination in hiring workers for defense industries or government agencies and created the Fair Employment Practices Committee (FEPC) to serve as a watchdog over the defense industries. The order had an immediate impact in Newark when the Western Electric Company, which held several federal government defense contracts, ended a ban of many years and hired African Americans as clerks and typists. Blacks also found employment in large numbers for the first time at the U.S. arsenals located in nearby Picatinny and Metuchen, where men received upwards of seventy cents an hour.

O

Effa found an unexpected ally in her efforts to wrest control of Yankee Stadium from booking agents, Seward "See" Posey, the Grays business manager and Cum's brother. See wrote Effa suggesting the Grays and Eagles work more closely together to schedule games and rely less on booking agents. Effa quickly agreed. "The Eagles and the Grays," she said with feeling and by return mail, "can stop Gottlieb, Wilkinson, [Bill] Leuschne [who had succeeded Nat Strong as a booking agent for the New York area upon Strong's death], [Abe] Saperstein [a Chicago-based booking agent and better known as the owner of the Harlem Globetrotters basketball team], and all the other Jews who want to join them where Negro baseball is concerned." Their booking fees, Effa argued, would be better-spent if put in the league's treasury. This idea, like the reserve clause idea, would take time to come to life. She also asked See for help in replacing Wilson as NNL president. "Please get Tom out of there," she wrote. "He is really Gottlieb's stooge."[14]

On another matter concerning Wilson, Effa chose to work with Cum Posey. Effa, upset with Wilson's lack of accounting of the $1,400 he had received from the proceeds of the East-West game, wrote to Cum saying, "We should speak directly," and stressed the importance for "us Negroes to work together. While we are busy hurting each other, the O-Fays are all pulling together, and are even unlucky enough to have a few of the Negroes pulling with them." Referring to the upcoming league meeting in January, she informed Posey "I have a better man than yours [Wilson] for chairman." She wrote in closing, "You fellows are going to be sorry someday you didn't let me have a little more voice."[15]

In an effort to boost the image of the league with the public, she wrote a one-page article for the *Chicago Defender* in response to sportswriters who criticized unruly behavior in the stands, squabbles among the owners, and uneven quality of play. In it she described Negro league baseball's contributions as she saw them. Each team, she said, spent about $40,000 a year for salaries, park rent, government taxes, equipment, transportation, balls, bats, and uniforms, making the twelve-team enterprise a $480,000-a-year business. She predicted this amount would increase each year, so that "it will supply many jobs [and be] something my race can be proud of." She called for more exhibition games against white semipro teams as one way to increase growth. She pointed out that in such games arguments between players, a reason given by many for opposing integrated baseball, were practically unheard of, and that if the day ever came when black players had lives as luxurious as whites', "You would see balls hit further, men run faster, and, in general, see baseball that has never been played."[16]

That day would not come for some time. Meanwhile, four-team Sunday doubleheaders continued to be the staple of the league's scheduled games. In one of the only four games that Gottlieb allowed the Eagles to play in Yankee Stadium that year, the team met the Kansas City Monarchs, NAL champs in four of the last seven seasons, in the feature game of the August 24 twin bill. In addition to Paige, the Monarchs brought pitcher Hilton Smith, Johnny "Buck" O'Neil at first, and outfielders Ted Strong and Willard Brown. The latter two led the NAL in extra base hits. Paige and Smith bested Eagles pitchers Hill, Hooker, and Manning before 25,000 spectators by limiting the Eagles to six hits and three runs, while Strong and Brown rapped six hits between the two of them. Paige contributed two singles, a run batted in, and scored a run en route to a 6–1 Monarch victory. A special guest, Police Lt. Samuel J. Battle, who filled Gehrig's position on the New York City parole board, threw out the first ball from first base, where the Iron Man once ruled.

The final four-team affair for the season at Ruppert Stadium took place on August 31. Billed as Johnnie Borican Day, in honor of the sprinter, the games featured the Eagles against the Baltimore Elite Giants and the Stars against the Black Yankees. In pregame contests Leon Day won the hundred-yard dash in 11.1 seconds, Monte Irvin took top honors in the outfielders' throwing contest, and Eagle backup catcher Charlie Parks made the most accurate throw to second base. The Eagles didn't fare as well in the game, losing 7–2, largely owing to errors made and walks issued by Eagle players and pitchers. Mayor Bertram R. Aitken of Borican's hometown, Bridgeton, New Jersey, made a presentation to Borican. In November 1941 *Life* magazine would devote a four-page photo spread to him, with pictures by the world famous photographer Gjon Mili. Borican expressed his appreciation and said the day's events would enable him to hold an exhibition of his artwork in the fall. The Eagles played well enough through September to come up winners of the second half, but on the basis of a better season-long record, the owners awarded the pennant to the Grays. The two teams would meet once more before the year was out.[17]

Even though the United States had not yet entered World War II, Hitler's terrorizing of Europe alarmed Americans, many of whom thought he needed to be stopped, and soon. In support of that sentiment, the Grays and the Eagles played a benefit doubleheader at the Polo Grounds on September 14. All proceeds from the game went to the Fight for Freedom Committee, a group supporting America's entry into the European war led by Herbert Agar, editor of the *Louisville Courier-Journal*. Pregame publicity promised that Joe Louis and Fiorello LaGuardia would attend. They did not, but seven thousand others did to watch the Eagles fall to the Grays by the score of 6–4 in both games. Former Eagle McDuffie held the Eagles to seven hits in the second game.[18]

Three months after the Eagles dropped their last doubleheader of the season, the United States declared war on Japan and Germany. Many of the Eagles were in Latin America at the time. Lennie Pearson told Effa in a three-page handwritten letter that he had been meaning to write her, but the war declaration convinced him "it's time everyone got in touch with their friends because you never know when you may have the chance again." War with Germany heightened Pearson's sense of danger. War in the Pacific "didn't mean as much but this is a small island [Puerto Rico], and it wouldn't take too much to sink the whole island"—a reference to reports of German submarines patrolling coastal waters. He said he thought most of the men would soon be returning home. Wells, Dandridge, Pearson, and others did choose to play in the United States for the 1942 season, a decision for which Effa would be grateful. He signed his letter "Lennie."[19]

One of Effa's last letters of 1941 went to Joseph Rainey, a Philadelphia magistrate and former member of the Pennsylvania Athletic Commission. Effa told Rainey she believed him to be "a Negro . . . interested in the future of his race." She acknowledged that she "was putting a big load on your shoulders [by asking him to stand for the NNL presidency] but I honestly feel whether Negro Baseball goes forward or backward, depends on what happens now."[20] Wilson had notified all NNL owners that the annual meeting would take place at the York Hotel in Baltimore.

The year 1941 had treated the Eagles well financially. With a surge in attendance and an increase in ticket prices (Abe had raised the price of a bleacher seat from forty cents to sixty cents), the team took in $60,000, which allowed Effa to meet expenses without dipping into Abe's bank account as she had become used to doing. The next year would see Effa and Abe confronted with the usual round of league issues, player negotiations, and the unusual challenges of a world war—notably gasoline restrictions and the draft.

# CHAPTER EIGHT

## *War Comes to Newark*

As the country mobilized for war in the Pacific and in Europe, many people, including Major League Baseball commissioner Kennesaw Mountain Landis, wondered if baseball should continue. Landis wrote FDR to ask his opinion. Roosevelt replied in the affirmative on January 15, 1942, with the "green light letter." In it Roosevelt noted that the war effort would demand long hours of hard work and baseball would offer workers a morale boost. Congress agreed. By implication, Negro league baseball also had the green light.[1]

Assured of a season, Effa and Abe turned to the upcoming owners meeting. Abe's nomination of Judge Rainey to be NNL president went down to defeat with little discussion. Wilson won reelection by a vote of 5–0 with Abe abstaining. Once again frustrated in their efforts to bring in leadership from the outside, the Newark duo promptly walked out over the entreaties of Bolden, Wilson, Semler, Posey, and Pompez to stay. On their way out the doors of the York Hotel they once more threatened to quit the league and sell the team. Little else of importance happened, forcing the owners to call for another meeting in Philadelphia on February 28.[2]

The Manleys' actions provided good copy for the sportswriters. Dan Burley observed that Effa has long been a "sore spot" with the other owners, "who have complained often and loudly that 'baseball ain't no place for no woman. We can't cuss her out.'" At the same time Burley said she could not be faulted for sticking to her principles and protecting her franchise. Al Moses, feature writer for the Associated Negro Press, threw a bouquet her way in his April 4 letter to her saying,

"Effa. All I can say, privately or editorially of you is . . . more power to your type of aggressive womanhood."[3]

Greenlee told Abe that sponsoring Rainey "was a bad move" and suggested that Abe run for president to "put every member who opposed you on the spot. There are too many alibis against an outsider." Abe decided against Gus's proposal but offered to sell the Eagles to him. Gus declined, saying, "I appreciate the offer . . . but I would rather not be a member if you are going to withdraw."[4]

In a surprising move, the Manleys, still seriously thinking about getting out of the NNL if not quitting baseball altogether, considered joining forces with Syd Pollock, owner of the independent Indianapolis Clowns. The Clowns had been blacklisted by both leagues for their antics on the field and their booking agent, Abe Saperstein, whose booking practices Effa had previously denounced. Pollock argued that Saperstein's unmatched promotional skills would give Abe a chance to recoup much of his losses. In the end Abe and Effa decided that leaving the NNL would be too great a risk without league opponents to play at Ruppert Stadium. Abe thought 1942, with the expected increase in defense jobs, would be a good year at the turnstiles, and he wanted to give it a try within the league. "If it had been up to me," Effa told Art Carter, "we would be through."[5]

Effa's pique kept her in Newark for the owners meeting on February 28 in Philadelphia, where Abe retracted his threat to leave the league. Greenlee decided to form a new team but play in the NNL. The owners denied his application, as seventeen of the proposed players were under contract to other NNL teams.[6]

While Abe met with the other moguls, Effa turned her attention to the players. She thanked Pearson for his Christmas card announcing his marriage and sent him a newspaper clipping saying Congress was all for baseball in 1942. She then admonished him for asking if rumors of his being traded were true: "I cannot understand why you or anyone else who had been connected with this club would feel that you're not going to be treated fairly." Following a phone conversation to talk contracts, Pearson returned the four-and-a-half-month contract she offered him, saying he expected a five-month contract. He considered going to Mexico to play in Tampico, but Effa's letter to Pearson's draft board, pointing out that she had advanced him $75 on his salary and that he had signed a contract, evidently dissuaded him. He played for the Eagles in 1942.[7]

Irvin, who led all NNL batters with a .426 average in 1941, wrote Effa on January 22 telling her he was having a great season in Puerto Rico and expected a raise from the Eagles. She replied with a newsy letter about her plans for the team and concerns about the draft's potential impact on the team. When talking about his contract, she told him, "We will come to terms, I am sure."[8]

She became crosswise with Mackey, whom she replaced as manager with Wells. Mackey had left Newark at the end of the 1941 season without speaking to her. "I am sure you agree," she said in her February 19 letter to him, "a manager should have been interested in discussing plans for the next season, at the close of the last." She wanted him to return as a catcher and take charge of driving the bus for an additional $75 a month. He agreed and asked her for an advance to take the train from Los Angeles "because I do not want to ride the buss [*sic*] . . . so you had better send me $125 an[d] I will leave at once." Effa sent him a money order for $100 saying, "I am unable to send any more. Please do not ask me too [*sic*]."

Mackey did not, but kept the $100 and applied for a job at North American Aviation in Los Angeles instead of coming East. Without alerting Effa, he gave her name as a reference to his new employer, who wrote Effa asking for a recommendation. Effa agreed to supply one, telling Mackey, "If I could be assured you would return my money. It was bad enough not to not show up for work . . . but to have taken my $100 the way you did certainly makes me feel very badly." Mackey answered that he would have come back if she had sent the full amount, "but since I couldn't walk back there I had to get a job." Mackey assured her she'd be repaid in $25 installments. "I have played ball twenty two years an[d] I haven't taken a nickle [*sic*] from no one but they have taken plenty from me," Mackey told her. Effa now needed a catcher.[9]

In between letters to Mackey, Effa discussed by mail plans for the upcoming season with Wells, who was playing winter ball in Aguadilla, Cuba. Effa, adopting a collegial tone, wrote Wells that she had gone to Philadelphia to see Ed Gottlieb about Stars' pitcher Barney Brown, whom Wells had suggested she trade for. Gottlieb suggested a number of possible trades, including Barney Brown for three Eagles players—Hill, Leaman Johnson, and Christopher—and added that Gottlieb wanted Clarkson badly and would like to trade Gene "Spider" Benson to the Eagles for Clarkson. Gottlieb's ideas did not excite Effa. She wrote Wells, "I think we have a pretty fine club with Pearson, Dandridge, Wells, and Clarkson in the infield, and Stone, Davis, and Irvin in the outfield. "Our pitching staff," she said, "is really pretty good," but she did ask Wells what he'd think about giving Hill and someone else for Barney Brown and trading Clarkson for the Stars' Pat

Patterson. Effa also suggested Wells rethink his proposal to trade pitcher James Brown because "he is married and has a child, which might keep him out of the draft and he can play outfield better than most of the regulars." Effa brought Israel to Wells's attention, saying, "[T]here is another boy we have not spoken of. He looks like a really grand prospect. He was beaned and has been a good deal slower since but I still think he might come around." She closed with a thought about salaries: "Of course we would like to keep the payroll down as far as possible, but on the other hand we must be practical." The two finalized the Eagles' lineup, much along the lines described by Effa above, before Wells arrived back in the States in late March.[10]

Hill, unaware that he was the subject of trade talks, returned his contract unsigned along with a letter in which he asked for a raise, because "I think I pitched as good as them" (several pitchers making more money than he was) and "food and every expense you can think of is higher." She told Effa that his and Mary's baby had died at three weeks old. If Effa did not agree to a raise, he'd stay home and take a job as director of a recreation center. If she did, he'd like to borrow $40, because "I had a job selling whiskey and the law got me. I'm supposed to have the money Saturday. If I don't get it, I'll have to stay down here and work it out." Effa wrote him a letter, reminding him of the extra money she'd given him, the doctor bills she'd paid, and the full salary he received for that season in which "you were no good." "I can't believe you could be as unappreciative as your letter sounds." She ended by saying she was "very sorry to hear about the baby. You are both young and will still have time to raise a big family." Perhaps the baby's death softened her anger about Hill's request for a raise. She sent him a contract calling for a raise and offered to pay his debt directly to the person who held it. Three weeks later Hill had not reported to camp prompting Effa to write him telling him to go to camp "at once . . . so the Eagles can start off this year looking good and I can make money in order to give you more."[11]

Fran Mathews notified Effa that he would not sign his contract because "I believe we could come to better terms." Effa told him that her first reaction was "to accept your refusal to play, and forget about it." But she reconsidered and, as she had told Hill, told Mathews that his performance did not merit a raise. Their negotiations stayed alive until Effa ended them by wiring him transportation money and told him to meet the team in Baltimore on May 28, which he did. The terms of Mathews's contract could not be determined.[12]

The other Eagles had signed or arrived at understandings sufficient to get them to spring training in Richmond, Virginia, which opened the last week of March. Those who came to the United States by boat from Puerto Rico and Cuba—Wells, Irvin, Day, Pearson, Clarkson, Stone, and Dandridge—faced potential danger from German submarines thought to be patrolling the water between the islands and the United States. Flying from Puerto Rico was out of the question, as officials there would not issue plane tickets to civilians. Fortunately, everyone made it safely to Richmond, where Wells had the makings of a championship team. Stone, Davis, and Irvin made up the league's premier outfield. The first-rate infield consisted of Dandridge, Wells, Israel, and either Pearson or Mathews at first. Hill, Day, Brown, and Manning could be counted on for strong performances on the mound. Only the catcher's position presented a question mark. Abe promoted Mackey's former backup, Charlie Parks, to starting catcher and acquired Leon Ruffin in trade from the Stars for Clarkson and Carter, the players that the NAL had awarded to the Eagles to settle the Paige affair. The Stars included in the trade Eugene "Spider" Benson, an accomplished outfielder who used the basket catch before Willie Mays popularized it, but Benson refused to report and remained with the Stars.[13]

The Eagles broke camp to start a series of exhibition games with the ever-powerful Homestead Grays, featuring Josh Gibson, Buck Leonard, Vic Harris, and Ray Brown, considered by many observers the league's best right-handed pitcher. After several single games both teams met for a final preseason show-down, a doubleheader at Griffith Stadium, on April 19. The Eagles humbled the Grays 13–8 and 9–3 before eight thousand spectators, with Hill and Day holding the Grays to six hits in the opener, while Lenial Hooker, the Eagles' knuckleball-ing right-hander, bested Ray Brown in the second game. Irvin led the way at the plate with six hits, three walks, four runs batted in, and one run scored.[14]

While the exhibition games were being played, Effa divided her time between preparing for the season opener and lobbying Wilson and Martin to donate the proceeds of the East-West game in Chicago and a later all-star game she proposed to be played at Griffith Stadium to benefit war charities. She used Joe Louis's ex-ample of twice donating his fight winnings to war relief efforts as an example that should "inspire us to play such a game." They promised to consider her proposal at a later date.

Not surprisingly, they had not considered it by mid-June when the *New York Amsterdam Star-News*, noting that Effa's suggestion remained buried, criticized the NNL for not helping more servicemen see the games and creating more interest in purchasing war bonds and savings stamps. Shortly thereafter, the owners of both leagues agreed to send both teams from the upcoming East-West Classic on August 18 "in-tact" to Cleveland for a night game on August 20, with all proceeds to go to the Army-Navy Relief Fund. Effa said she'd preferred the second game be played in Washington so that eastern fans could see the teams, but "where it is played is not so important and having it played." Effa also agreed to captain a team of volunteers that raised $19,150 for Newark's Boys Clubs. In exchange for a season's pass, she took Jocko Maxwell up on his offer, as a member of the New York Sportscasters Association, to recruit white sportswriters, such as Bob Considine, Tom Meany, Jimmy Powers, Dan Daniel, and Tim Cohane to publicize Eagles games.

Gibson and the Grays spoiled the Eagles' May 3 opening day game and Wells's managerial debut at Ruppert Stadium by edging the Eagles 3–2 on a Gibson clout. Wells hit two home runs to give the Newark nine a 2–0 lead going into the ninth inning. Jimmy Hill started the top of the ninth by walking Sammy Bankhead and Buck Leonard. Leon Day, known for his sizzling fastball, relieved Hill. Day pitched two quick strikes on Gibson and tried to slip a third fastball by him. Gibson cancelled Wells's home runs by launching Day's next offering over the centerfield fence. As both teams were getting on their bus after the game outside of Ruppert Stadium for the ride back to the Grand Hotel, Effa sought out Gibson, telling him, "Josh, you should be ashamed of yourself ruining our opener the way that you did. You broke everybody's heart." To which Gibson replied, "Mrs. Manley, let me tell you this. I've been known to break a lot of hearts. I hate to have to do it to you, but that's my job."[15]

A few days after the game Irvin received a telegram from Jorge Pasquel offering him $500-a-month salary and $200-a-month toward an apartment to play in Mexico. Irvin told Effa about the offer and said he'd stay if she'd give him a $25 raise. Effa countered, "Monte you're young. You got plenty of time to make your fortune." Irvin replied, "Mrs. Manley, I don't want to hear that. I want to get married. [He was dating his high school sweetheart and future wife, Dee Otey.] I'll need at least twenty-five dollars a month more to make it. Jorge wants to give me five hundred a month plus two hundred for an apartment plus a maid but I want to play on this team. It's the best team I've ever been on. We'll fill the park, make a great reputation for ourselves." She did not budge. Dandridge received a similar offer two months later, and after Effa said no to him too, Dandridge joined Irvin in Mexico. "How bright could she have been?" Irvin wondered.

Later Irvin said he had had "a great year in Mexico. I was having fun. It was really terrific down there. I could have run for mayor. I told my draft board in 1943 that I wanted to go back. I got a baby. They said 'we can't let you go.' They would have tripled my salary."

In an interview years later, Effa remembered events differently. Effa told William Marshall that she had told Irvin and Dandridge what she remembered she had told Dandridge two years earlier, that she did not want to enter a bidding war with Pasquel and his brothers. So, she told Marshall, she advised both players to go to Mexico.[16] Irvin remembered no mention of the Pasquels.[17] Regardless of why she denied Irvin's and Dandridge's requests, Effa's tight hold on the purse strings cost the Eagles the services of three eventual Hall of Famers—Mackey, Irvin, and Dandridge—for the 1942 season.

In hopes that a lawyer might succeed in stopping the flow of players to Latin America, Effa again hired Robert S. Hartgrove, this time to plead her case with the Mexican consulate, Juan E. Richer. Hartgrove pointed out to Richer that players obtained passports under false pretenses (tourism or seeking work not available in the States), and that Mexico extended their visas illegally to cover the length of the Mexican baseball season. Before taking the case to the U.S. State Department, Hartgrove told Richer, "I want to . . . procure the cooperation of the Consul General." Such cooperation failed to materialize, so Hartgrove had what he called "a very encouraging conversation with Mr. Haig of the State Department." Hartgrove also spoke with New Jersey Senator William H. Smathers, who said, "You know that I will do everything I possibly can to assist you in this matter." Nothing came of Hartgrove's efforts, however, and the Manleys remained powerless—except in Pearson's case—to block players from enjoying the fruits of baseball in Latin America. Hartgrove's attempts did signal a new chapter in owner cooperation, as Effa coaxed agreement from each owner to pay an equal share of Hartgrove's $360 retainer fee.[18]

The team that Effa did field won three and lost two games following their opening day loss, to put them in fourth place by mid-May 1942. They ran into the Baltimore Elite Giants for a Sunday doubleheader on May 24, and Hill, who may not have been in shape given his late arrival at camp, took both losses, 3–0 and 5–3. Manning relieved him in the third inning of game one with the Eagles behind. Hill relieved Hooker in the seventh frame of game two and gave up four runs. By mid-June Wells had shifted the lineup for the upcoming barnstorming tour with the Grays. Day, who had been holding down centerfield in Irvin's absence, went back to his role as starting pitcher. Pearson went from third to center field; Wells stayed at short, Israel took over second base, and recently reported Fran Mathews covered first. James Brown and Stone completed the outfield. Mule Suttles had returned from the Black Yankees as a player-coach. For the June 29 game scheduled for Builder's Park in Norfolk, Virginia, Effa sent a notice to Percy Simon, whose address this time appeared as 401 Chappel Street in Norfolk, asking him to prepare placards and passes for the game. In recognition of Norfolk's segregation mores, she asked Simon to reserve part of the grandstand for whites.

With Day back on the mound and the team returned from its two-week tour of the South, the Eagles took care of the Cubans 9–2 on June 19, behind Day's six-hitter in front of the home crowd. Two days later, however, the Black Yankees clipped them 2–1 and 1–0, bringing the Eagles' record to 7 and 8, good for third place behind the Grays and Elite Giants. Hill pitched brilliantly in game two but failed to get any run support from his mates. Day had enough run support a week later at Forbes Field in Pittsburgh to beat the Grays 6–2, as did Hooker, who went the distance in game two, winning it 11–1 behind thirteen base knocks.

The Eagles' up-and-down season continued to July 4, when they not only lost 8–4 to the Elite Giants before twelve thousand people at Yankee Stadium, but almost lost Wells. A fastball from Giants pitcher Bill Byrd caught Wells on the temple and dropped him to the ground, unconscious. He was rushed to the hospital, where he came to, but he would not play again for a week and a half.

Some observers point to Wells's beaning that day as the event that prompted him to invent the first modern-day batting helmet by cutting down a construction worker's hard hat. Wells did invent the modern-day batting helmet but not because of this incident. He had worn a helmet as early as 1937, and the event that prompted him to do so is not known.[19]

July held good news for the Eagles in the person of rookie "Larry Walker," who joined the team in early July, and whom the press reported Abe had discovered in Los Angeles. The seventeen-year-old rookie gave the team a boost with a hot bat at the plate and with a sure glove at third. One reporter said, "He looks as good as most veterans on any ball club." He should have. Walker's real name was Larry Doby. (He played under an alias to protect his amateur status in basketball.) Doby had graduated from Paterson, New Jersey's Eastside High School in June and had a basketball scholarship to Long Island University. Unlike Irvin, who played only in away games during his stint as Jimmy Nelson, Larry Walker played in both home and away games in 1942. Doby picked his alias because Walker was his mother Etta's maiden name.[20]

Doby had moved to Paterson from Camden, South Carolina, after graduating from grammar school. He remembered his early years as being comfortable. "I've lived comfortable all my life. When I came up in the South, I may have eaten the same thing every day but I wasn't hungry. In other words, if my mother had rice and black-eyed peas Monday, Tuesday and Wednesday, I was full. Or if she had greens, I was full. I'd wear sneakers to school. The overalls . . . the things that they got now, I wore those a long time ago. I had a sweater. I had one suit for church. As far as luxuries went, I didn't know what luxuries were all about. The home was comfortable. Wasn't elaborate or anything. Sheets were clean. My mother probably made fifteen hundred dollars a year doing domestic work, but it went a long ways. . . . I'd pick up money for movies by scrubbing floors."[21]

At Eastside he lettered in baseball, basketball, football, and track, becoming the school's first student to win twelve letters. He remembered Paterson fondly and said he did not take much notice of segregation except in one area, dating. He said about his wife-to-be, Helyn Curvy, who was a year younger than he, "She was a very pretty girl and we didn't have too many pretty girls in my high school . . . particularly black girls. There were a lot of pretty white girls but that was like forbidden fruit at that time."[22]

In the same way that Irvin had, Doby came to Abe's attention playing semi-pro ball. An umpire from his hometown of Paterson suggested him to Abe. Abe liked what he saw and asked Doby's mother if Doby could play for the Eagles after graduation. Doby's mother told him, "Yeah, if you bring him home after the game's over with," and that's what Abe did. If Doby had to stay overnight, he stayed with Abe.[23]

O

Without Irvin, Mackey, and Dandridge, the Eagles struggled to a third place finish, but the record number of blacks finding employment in Newark validated Abe's decision to stay in the league. Weekly paychecks of $150 were not uncommon for those who worked as radio assemblers, solderers, chemical workers, clerks, testers, powder and detonator carriers, and who worked in other jobs formerly held only by whites. "Just venture," said Floyd Snelson, a writer for the *New York Amsterdam Star-News*, "into Newark on a Saturday and Sunday. Taverns, bars, grills, and vice resorts are doing a flourishing business." The largesse spilled over to Ruppert Stadium, where more fans than ever came to the games.[24]

O

While more blacks held jobs than ever before in Newark, discrimination in employment still held sway in the city. African Americans, while now making up 10 percent of Newark's 500,000 residents, held only 3 percent of the jobs. The president's FEPC summoned representatives from twelve industrial plants in New York and New Jersey, including Newark's Tite Flex Metal Hose Company, to answer charges of discrimination, against both blacks and Jews. The FEPC found eight of the twelve companies, including Tite Flex, guilty and ordered them to "cease and desist" discriminatory hiring practices.[25]

At the same time, integration moved forward within the city's administrative offices. In late June Mayor Vincent J. Murphy appointed William R. Jackson, executive secretary of Newark's Court Street YMCA, to become the first black to serve on the city's school board. Jackson pledged to increase the number of black teachers at all levels. Only eight blacks taught in Newark's public schools, which were not segregated but did discriminate against blacks during hiring.[26]

Enterprising moviegoers at the Savoy Theater on Springfield Avenue developed a system for foiling the Jim Crow requirement that blacks sit in the balcony or in a designated orchestra row. Patrons endured the ticket seller's explanation about the balcony, knowing the seller would soon call for the manager. Persistence with the manager paid off in the form of an orchestra ticket. While the purchaser walked quickly inside, the seller pressed a buzzer that alerted all orchestra ushers to intercept the ticket holder and direct him or her to the orchestra's segregated row on the left. Knowing about the buzzer, the moviegoer darted for the center of the orchestra, arriving there before the ushers did and daring them to do anything about it. The manager's only recourse was to call the police, which rarely happened unless a fracas broke out.[27]

O

Prospects for integrating Major League Baseball seemed brighter when Pittsburgh Pirates president William Benswanger said he would hold tryouts for four Negro leaguers selected by Wendell Smith. Smith picked Josh Gibson and Grays out-fielder Sammy Bankhead along with Willie Wells and Leon Day. "Plans for the tryout are almost complete," Benswanger was quoted in the *Courier*'s front-page article. The Pirates head scout, Bob Rice, would select the date and conduct the tryouts because, Benswanger said, "he is especially interested in this tryout and asked me to permit him to conduct it." Neither Benswanger nor Rice came up with a date, and by the end of August Benswanger had quietly backed away from any tryout.[28]

O

The Eagles first felt the effect of the draft in late August, when Uncle Sam reached out for Clarence "Pint" Israel. The Army assigned him to the 54th Aviation Squadron at Mather Field, ten miles outside of Sacramento, California. He wrote Effa a four-page letter, addressed to "Mrs. Manley and Members of the Base Ball Club," the day after he arrived, September 9, 1942, telling them, "I know you are quite surprised to learn that I am so far away from home." His only regret, he said, "was not playing ball with the fellows," and he said he hoped to play with the team on the base. He assured her that "there is no way for you to get lonesome, because there is to many soldiers around here." Saying he hoped to hear from her soon, he signed his letter "Pvt. Clarence C. Israel."[29]

The Eagles would lose more players to the draft but not until the 1943 season. The team entered September three games behind the Grays, even though Wells had recovered from his beaning and the Eagles had won nine straight games during July and August. They could cinch the pennant by winning the upcoming two doubleheaders between the two teams. Posey's nine, however, prevailed, winning the first doubleheader in Newark and the second in Ebbets Field, the first time the Eagles had played in the Dodgers' confines since leaving them in 1935. Only two members of Abe's Brooklyn Eagles, Leon Day and Ed Stone, were still with the Newark Eagles, who finished the second half in fourth place.[30]

Even though the Eagles fell short of the pennant, four of their number ended up in a postseason championship game. Pearson, Day, Stone, and Buzz Clarkson, an Eagle for part of the season before going to the Stars, signed on with the Grays for the fourth World Series game against the Kansas City Monarchs after the Grays had lost three straight to bring them within a game of losing the series. Posey claimed he had Kansas City General Manager Thomas Baird's permission to use the four because the Grays had lost the services of four of their starters to the draft. Day outpitched Satchel Paige, who gave up nine hits, five of them to the Eagles players, to lead the Grays to a 4–1 win. Monarchs owner J. L. Wilkinson disputed Posey's claim. League officials upheld Wilkinson's protest and nullified the results of the game. The Monarchs won the rescheduled fourth game to sweep the Grays.[31]

O

Pearson and Day opted to forgo Latin America this winter and applied for jobs with the Thomas Edison Company in West Orange, New Jersey. Both asked Effa for letters of recommendation. She overlooked their contract disputes when she of Pearson wrote, "[H]e has always been most cooperative and helpful. . . . He is also a real team man. I am sure he will show the same spirit in any field of employment he finds himself in." She had similar words of commendation for Day.[32]

Effa continued her war effort work by coleading the Volunteer War Service Committee of Newark, which brought entertainers to Fort Dix to entertain the soldiers. She paid $42 a week for the bus that transported the entertainers from their gathering spot, the 1229 Reception Center in Newark, to Fort Dix. The project gave her great satisfaction. "I really don't know anything in my life that I've enjoyed much more," she said. "I went down with them almost every week, and we carried it on for the entire duration of the war. Several of those entertainers married soldiers." Entertainers included Al Cooper and His Savoy Sultans from Harlem's Savoy Ballroom; dancer Bobbie Green; and blues singer Maude Mills, sister of the much beloved Florence, who died of appendicitis in 1927 at age thirty-one, in the midst of a star-studded career. Effa had been a fan of Florence and said of her, "There's been no other entertainer like her, black or white. She was really in a class all by herself." In August Effa had joined with Burrell and his American Legion Post to stage an official "send-off" in Newark's Frederick Douglass Park for the black draftees from Local Board #22. The Post had raised money to supply the men with cigarettes and small gifts.[33]

O

In between her volunteer activities she kept up the heat on Tom Wilson, and now seemingly had garnered the support of both Posey and Pompez. Posey told her in December 1942 that he thought the first order of business at the upcoming owners meeting should be to elect "a president who knows the problems of Negro baseball . . . knows some of the heads of the various agencies in Washington, D.C. . . . and lives in Washington, D.C." He proposed Judge William Hueston, who had been NNL commissioner from 1926 to 1931. "He is," said Posey, "a disciplinarian and a personal friend of Mr. [Paul V.] McNutt [head of FDR's newly created Federal Security Agency and a former ambassador to the Philippines] and Mr. [Harold] Ickes. . . . Alex [Pompez] was enthusiastic."[34]

While the annual battle over Wilson loomed, the Manleys were pleased that they again did well at the gate. The team, however, would have put on a better showing had Effa been a bit more generous with Mackey, Irvin, and Dandridge, whose departures caused the team, in Irvin's words, to go from "great to shinola."[35] This is one instance where Effa's judgment, usually on target, failed her. For an additional $25 to Mackey for transportation and $50 a month in payroll, for the raises requested by Irvin and Dandridge over the course of the six-month season—a total of $325 dollars (a sum Abe could afford)—the Eagles would have attracted more fans to the games, enriched their bottom line, and likely captured the pennant and the series.

# CHAPTER NINE

## *The Eagles Adapt to the War*

By 1943 the war effort commanded the nation's attention and resources. During that year, Soviet troops entrapped the Germans in Stalingrad, the Allies deposed Mussolini, the all-black 99th Fighter Squadron fought in Sicilian and Italian airspace, and the pogrom in the Warsaw ghetto began. At home, as defense employment in Newark and other cities continued to boom, more blacks migrated to cities along the eastern seaboard where many of the jobs could be found, millions of young men answered the draft call, and the Office of Defense Transportation (ODT) banned the use of gasoline for pleasure driving.

Joseph P. Eastman of the ODT interpreted the ban to preclude the use of team buses for baseball games. His ruling meant that Negro league teams would have to travel by rail, regular service buses, or private cars—each a more expensive option than the team bus. Art Carter described Eastman's ruling as a "death blow." Owners in both leagues considered halting play for the season. But encouraged by the ODT's subsequent decision to allow teams to use 40 percent of the gasoline they used in 1942, NNL team owners, whose cities were closer together than were those of NAL teams, decided at their April meeting at the Columbia Lodge Elks Home in Washington, D.C., to carry on, albeit with a reduced schedule. NAL owners later also decided to play a reduced schedule of games.[1]

Another threat to bus transportation in New Jersey, according to New Jersey Public Utilities Commissioner Joseph E. Conlon, was brought on by a lack of replacement and repair parts and a shortage of labor. "Nonsense," said Leonard H. Goldsmith, Congress of Industrial Organizations representative. "The shortage is caused by bus companies refusing to hire Negroes." Goldsmith offered to provide Conlon with "proof and testimony that blacks were turned down for no reason." Conlon never asked for the testimony.[2]

Even with the gas dilemma resolved, the teams still faced the draft and the lure of defense jobs that some players found more remunerative than playing ball. In addition to Israel, the draft had claimed Manning, outfielder Charlie Thompson, and catcher Charlie Parks by the end of January 1943. Wells and Dandridge received draft deferments because each was the father of two children, a point Abe stressed to Posey in Abe's offer to sell Dandridge to the Grays for $1,000. Knowing Dandridge's fondness for Mexico, Posey declined. As expected, Wells and Dandridge took off for Mexico, where the minimum salary came to $400 a month, plus travel and living expenses, leaving a decimated Eagles team in their wake. (Minimum salary in the NNL was about $175 a month.) Fortunately, with the exception of Mackey, who stayed in Los Angeles, and Leon Ruffin, who took a defense job in Portsmouth, Virginia, and played in weekend and night games, the Eagles did not have to compete with defense jobs for players.[3]

In spite of the challenges they knew the war would pose, the NNL owners expressed optimism over the upcoming season at their January 23 meeting at Philadelphia's Quaker City Elks Home. Those looking forward to the usual first-of-the-year fireworks were disappointed. Wilson was reelected president after "a short but heated discussion," led no doubt by Effa. Posey said he now agreed with her that "league officers" should not have a financial interest in any of the clubs, but subsequent events put a cloud over his statement. Ed Bolden was reelected as vice president, and Abe got his treasurer's job back from Posey, who was again elected league secretary. The owners appointed Effa to the position of promotional director for war relief activities, making her responsible for arranging for each team to participate in a war relief game and for a league all-star game to benefit the war effort. Wendell Smith, not always a fan of Effa's, took the occasion of her appointment to laud her "manipulations" over the past four years. He said, "She has made the owners sit up and take notice. Although they have always resented her presence at the pow-wow tables, they've had to admit she's helped her husband build up a good berth in Newark." Effa liked the column and let Smith know, telling him, "[Y]ou really flattered and complimented me. . . . You stuck your chin out, because there are still a lot of folks resisting a lady in baseball. I sincerely hope I won't let you down."[4]

A "manipulation" that Smith did not know about was a letter from Effa to Posey's partner, Rufus Jackson. She had written "private" on the envelope. She wanted to arrange a meeting between several owners with the Washington, D.C., law firm of Houstin, Houstin, and Hastie (the same Hastie she had unsuccessfully proposed to be commissioner) "to get some of our problems straightened out and maybe get some little idea of what to expect about the gas situation, etc." Remembering the fate of her previous proposals to the moguls, she wanted Jackson to present the idea. She told him, "Please don't tell anyone it is my suggestion. It would have two strikes on it before it started." No record could be found of Jackson's reaction to her letter, nor of any meeting with the law firm.[5]

Effa did not share the owners' optimism but foresaw a bleak season in which teams would be "lucky to play weekends [when players, many of whom on other teams had taken defense jobs, could play] and get in a game or two a week." Following the meeting, Effa went to work on another hindrance, namely, the annual trek of players to Mexico. She asked both Gottlieb and J. B. Martin to provide her with the names, addresses, and draft numbers of players headed south, saying, "As you may know by now I never give up until the last horn blows." She wanted the names for a meeting with "someone really important in Washington who might help us." Whether she had the law firm in mind or whether she went to Washington with the names that year is not known, but she did receive an unfavorable ruling from the New Jersey Selective Service in the case of Wells and Dandridge. Maj. P. E. Schwehm reminded her that both had family-based deferments and added that barring them from play in Mexico "might be definitely misconstrued, particularly because of their color."[6]

Having heard the sound of the last horn, at least for now, Effa turned to the affairs of the team in her usual fashion of signing players and planning an elaborate opening day, while Abe, in a move to conserve gasoline, took the team to Trenton's Dunn Field for spring training with Mule Suttles as the new manager. Player negotiations went more smoothly than usual for Effa, save those with Jimmy Hill. After several letters and two telegrams, to which she received no response, Effa wrote to his mother in Lakeland, Florida, asking what had become of him, the $30 railroad ticket to Trenton, and a $20 cash advance. She reminded his mother, "The law does not allow anyone to accept money under false pretenses." Hill eventually made his way to Trenton.

In her correspondence with Larry Doby, who had transferred from Long Island University to Virginia Union College in Richmond, Virginia, Effa asked him to check his leaving with his basketball coach, Henry Hucles, saying, "It would be better if he was satisfied to have you leave." Hucles, who had a distinguished coaching career at Virginia Union from 1926 to 1950, winning 247 games and losing 110, gave Doby his permission. Doby would play under his real name this year.[7]

Effa kept up with those Eagles who had been drafted and, in one instance, interceded for Max Manning, stationed in Richmond, Virginia, with the Army. Manning wanted to help his friends find work after they left the Army. She asked Harold Lett of New Jersey's Urban League how Manning's friends might find qualifying jobs. Lett directed Effa to Robert Monroe at the Plate Shop Federal Shipyard in Kearney, New Jersey. Lett said the men should contact Monroe for interviews, which they presumably did.[8]

Effa's opening day invitation list included the usual New Jersey politicians, headed this year by Democratic Governor Thomas Edison, son of Thomas Alva, and both Republican U.S. senators from New Jersey, W. Warren Barbour and Albert W. Hawkes. None of the three attended. Andy Razaf, a baseball fan as well as a musician and admirer of Effa's, did accept her invitation, saying he and his wife and two friends would be pleased to attend. He added in his acceptance letter, "Would like to see you sometime as I might have some ideas for the good of your team." Since the major league Dodgers, Giants, and Yankees were also training near New York, Razaf wanted the Eagles to challenge one or more of them to a game on their turf, Ebbets Field, the Polo Grounds, or Yankee Stadium. He proposed to send the proceeds to the Red Cross or the Army or Navy relief funds. Razaf's idea went nowhere.

Effa, remembering that on opening day a year ago the ballpark special police, feeling overwhelmed by a crush of fans arriving at the last minute, closed the entrances before many could enter, wrote Newark public safety director, John B. Keenan, asking for reinforcements from Newark's finest. Keenan agreed. In the tradition of black athletes throwing out the first ball, Effa contracted with Beau Jack, thirty-one, to make the toss this year. Jack held the world lightweight title twice.[9]

Jack did not arrive at Ruppert Stadium until the fourth inning of the May 16 Sunday opener against the Stars under cloudy skies, but Effa, nevertheless, stopped the game to allow the prizefighter to make his ceremonial pitch for the twelve thousand in attendance. The Eagles had scored six runs in the previous inning on their way to a 9–1 victory behind Leon Day's strong right arm and his bat; he contributed a double and two singles.

Effa had again invited soldiers from Fort Dix, the black members of the unit of Free French Forces, and in a postscript on her invitation to Lieutenant Colonel Beauregard, she invited the white members of the unit as well "if there was room." The presence of thousands of defense workers and women clerks from the Office of Dependency Benefits, an army agency located in Newark's Prudential office building charged with cutting checks to Army dependents, underscored the military tenor of the times.[10]

The Eagles did not fare as well in their next league game, played the following Thursday under the lights against the Grays at Griffith Stadium. Grays pitcher John Wright, age twenty-six, who had been an Eagle in 1937 and would be the second black player to be signed by Branch Rickey, pitched a 6–0 shutout. A week and a half later, as part of a four-team Sunday doubleheader at the Polo Grounds, the Cubans paid the Eagles back for their opening day loss with an 11–1 thrashing. Day and Hill gave up six runs between them in three innings to put the game out of reach.[11]

One bright spot for the Eagles during the first half was the no-hit, no-run game that Hill threw as the Eagles beat the New York Black Yankees 4–0 at Ruppert Stadium on a Sunday afternoon, June 6. Had it not been for two walks, Hill would have had a perfect game. In the fifth inning, Yankees outfielder Bill Bradford disagreed with umpire Henry Moore's third strike call, knocked Moore down, jumped on him, and beat on him until other players pulled him off. Moore required two stitches to his face. Effa, upset by the incident, called on Wilson to make an example of Bradford and to advise how she should respond to several white sportswriters who had carried the story and wanted to know what punishment Bradford would receive. She told the papers she was writing to the league president for an answer.[12] A response from Wilson could not be found. The Eagles had few other bright spots during the first half. Their 9–10 record put them in fourth place.[13]

The start of the second half was a different story. Buoyed by pitcher Lenial Hooker's failure to pass his Army physical, Effa's successful "snatching" of Ed Stone away from the Black Yankees, and the play of Suttles, Day, Doby, and Pearson (Irvin had been drafted in March), the Eagles had won six straight by the end of July to take a commanding lead. The team, unfortunately, slumped during late August, losing three of four league games, while the Grays went 5–2 to nose out the Eagles by two games for the NNL flag. The Grays helped their cause by beating the Black Yankees in an unscheduled game and declaring it a league game. Effa protested to Wilson to no avail. In the absence of a response from Wilson, Effa had no qualms about allowing three of her charges, Pearson, Day, and Hooker, to don the uniform of the Philadelphia Stars for their final two games of the season, which just happened to be against the Grays. The Grays, however, won both games.[14]

During the season Effa busied herself in her role as director of relief games by planning an NNL all-star game on the night of September 9 at Griffith Stadium. The North team consisted of players from the Eagles, Cubans, and Yankees, while players from the Elite Giants, Grays, and Stars played for the South. The proceeds did not go to the armed services but went instead to a cause that Effa believed was advancing the well-being of African Americans, the Lend-a-Hand Club in Washington, D.C., which needed funds to renovate its home for black unwed mothers. The South won 6–4 before six thousand fans who braved chilly, cloudy weather.[15]

O

Racial tensions persisted during the late summer and fall in Newark. Six women walked off their jobs at the American Transformer Company when supervisors ignored their complaints that white women with less experience were hired into more skilled, higher paying jobs. The women filed a complaint with the FEPC. Officials at the National Housing Agency announced on November 6 "the definite possibility" of new housing for those black defense workers already residing in Newark, although they said a final decision would not be forthcoming for several weeks. The announcement offered little relief to the 86 percent of blacks the agency's survey found to be living in "overcrowded or poor housing." Plans by the Church of Illumination to build the new Sojourner Truth YWCA sparked debate over its membership. Some argued that a branch was needed in "the Negro section" while others argued that it should be integrated. The latter argument won out. The New Jersey Congress of Industrial Organizations Council continued its campaign for integration, calling on President Roosevelt to end segregation in the armed forces by executive order, which he did not do, and pledging to maintain its opposition to all forms of racial or religious discrimination.

Effa as a young woman. (National Baseball Hall of Fame and Museum, Cooperstown, NY)

# An Asset to Baseball

## THOMAS T. WILSON

PRESIDENT
NEGRO NATIONAL BASEBALL LEAGUE

OWNER
BALTIMORE ELITE GIANTS

Thomas T. Wilson (1888–1947), owner of the Baltimore Elite Giants
and president of the Negro National League.
(National Baseball Hall of Fame and Museum, Cooperstown, NY)

Alejandro "Alex" Pompez (1890–1974), owner of the New York Cubans. (National Baseball Hall of Fame and Museum, Cooperstown, NY)

Willis "Cum" Cumberland Posey (1880–1946), owner of the Homestead Grays. (National Baseball Hall of Fame and Museum, Cooperstown, NY)

Edward "Chief" Bolden, owner of the Philadelphia Stars. (National Baseball Hall of Fame and Museum, Cooperstown, NY)

Left to right: Charles Ebbets; Wilbert Robinson, Brooklyn Dodgers manager; Stephen McKeever; and brother Edward McKeever in 1916. Ebbets and the McKeever brothers built Ebbets Field. Robinson managed the Dodgers from 1914 to 1931. (Huggins and Scott Auction House, Silver Spring, MD)

Ruppert Stadium circa 1942. (Author's collection)

Left to right: Kennesaw Mountain Landis and Jacob Ruppert. (National Baseball Hall of Fame and Museum, Cooperstown, NY)

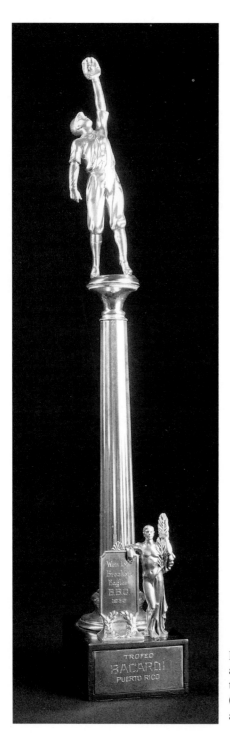

Bacardi Rum Company Trophy
awarded to the Eagles for winning
the Puerto Rican championship.
(National Baseball Hall of Fame
and Museum, Cooperstown, NY)

The 1935 Crawford's Championship dinner. Top row from left to right: John Clark, Romeo Dougherty, Abe Manley, Candy Jim Taylor, Oscar Charleston, Roy Sparrow. Bottom row, left to right: Ferdinand Morton, Alex Pompez, Gus Greenlee, Effa Manley, Josh Gibson. (Noirtech Research, Inc.)

Monte Irvin as a rookie.
(Author's collection)

Newark Mayor Vincent J. Murphy throwing out the first ball for the 1942 opener. (National Baseball Hall of Fame and Museum, Cooperstown, NY)

Raleigh "Biz" Mackey. (National Baseball Hall of Fame and Museum, Cooperstown, NY)

Cramped quarters on the bus. Front to back left row: Len Hooker, Len Pearson, Bob Harvey, Johnny Davis. Monte Irvin on right. Note the players are dressed in suits and ties. (National Baseball Hall of Fame and Museum, Cooperstown, NY)

Eagles pitching staff. Left to right: Jimmy Hill, Russell DeDeaux, Leon Day, James Obgood, James Brown, Len Hooker, and Max Manning. (National Baseball Hall of Fame and Museum, Cooperstown, NY)

Abe's new bus. (National Baseball Hall of Fame and Museum, Cooperstown, NY)

Larry Doby as a Newark Eagle.
(Author's collection)

# NEGRO AMERICAN LEAGUE PRESIDENT

## *A Real Baseball Fan*

WHEN Doctor J. B. Martin, one of the famous "Martin Brothers of Memphis, Tennessee," became president of the Negro American League in 1939, baseball fans saw one of their own take the helm. His interest in the game runs back prior to 1925, the year he and his brothers, Doctors W. S., A. T., and B. B. Martin, purchased a baseball park now rated one of the finest used in the League as well as the only Negro owned park.

The affable president of the western circuit knows baseball from the ground up, and his remarkable experience with the Memphis Red Sox Baseball Club owned by the Martin Brothers, as president of the Southern Baseball League in 1934, and currently owner of the Chicago American Giants, stamp him as an executive of proven ability. During his administration of League affairs, attendance has gained in all parks, cash receipts mounted to unprecedented heights, new talent developed and the annual East-West Game reached its peak.

In 1940 Dr. Martin took up residence in Chicago, the home of his lovely wife, the former Lula McGuire. He has two sons, Doctor J. B. Martin, Jr., of Detroit, and William Martin who operates the South Memphis Drug Company. In Chicago President Martin opened League offices at 412 E. Forty-seventh Street from which he conducts the business of giving the fans genuine entertainment in the great American sport.

☆

### DR. J. B. MARTIN
*Host to the*
*East-West Baseball Classic*

J. B. Martin, president of the Negro American League.
(National Baseball Hall of Fame and Museum, Cooperstown, NY)

Another gala opening day crowd, this one for the start of the 1946 season.
Ben Holmes, member of the 1888 Cuban Giants, is sitting at far left.
(National Baseball Hall of Fame and Museum, Cooperstown, NY)

Bill "Ready" Cash tags Larry Doby. This photograph of the disputed play on
opening day 1946 shows Doby was out even though the umpire called him safe.
(National Baseball Hall of Fame and Museum, Cooperstown, NY)

Program for the 1946 World Series with the lineups for the Eagles and the Monarchs. (National Baseball Hall of Fame and Museum, Cooperstown, NY)

1946 World Champion Eagles. Back row left to right: Monte Irvin, LF; Johnny
Davis, LF, P; Lennie Pearson, 1stB; Len Hooker, P; Max Manning, P; Cecil Cole, P;
Rufus Lewis, P; Larry Doby, 2ndB. Middle row left to right: Leon Ruffin, C; Warren
Peace, P; Jim Wilkes, CF; Bobby "Cotton" Williams, P; Bat Boy. Front row left to
right: Selton, SS; Charles Parks, C; Clarence Israel, 3rdB; Raleigh "Biz" Mackey, C
and manager; Bob Harvey, RF; Leon Day, P. (National Baseball Hall of Fame and
Museum, Cooperstown, NY)

Eagles new Stratoliner bus.
(National Baseball Hall of Fame and Museum, Cooperstown, NY)

The Almendares team that Irvin played for during the 1948–49 winter. Irvin is at the far left in the back row. Others in the back row from Irvin's left are Rene Gonzalez, Santos Amaro, Michale Sandlock, Ken Conners (better known later as TV actor Chuck Connors), Wesley Hamner, Morris Martin, Sam Jethroe, Ed Wright, Octavio Rubert, and Vincent Lopez. Second row, left to right: Domingo Carrillo (trainer), Agapito Mayor, Hector Rodriguez, Rodolfo Fernandez (coach), Fermin Guerra, (manager), Sungo Carreras (coach), Al Gionfrido, Andres Fleitas-Utility, Jorge Comellas, Manolo Fernandez Masajista. Bottom row, left to right, Rene Solis, Ramiro Ramirez, Sojito Gallardo, Humberto Jordan Cargabates, Sandlock, Jr. (mascot), Avelino Canizares, Conrado Marrero, Gilberto Valdivia, Wally Miranda. (Author's collection)

Effa Manley (far right) with the Heritage Group.
(National Baseball Hall of Fame and Museum, Cooperstown, NY)

Monte Irvin and Effa Manley admiring a glove awarded to Effa by the Negro League
Baseball Old Timers Association at the 1978 Ashland meeting, during which she was
voted Woman of the Year by the returning players. Effa is wearing the stole
she bought with part of the proceeds from the Giants for Irvin's contract.
(Courtesy of Monte Irvin)

Governor Edison expressed his views on how blacks could best make progress to a reporter for Baltimore's *Afro-American*. The governor counseled blacks to go slowly, exercise caution, and learn not to antagonize whites. He told the reporter, "[M]ost of your problems come from people who are in a hurry." To make his point he recounted a personal story. A "colored" chauffer, "a very fine boy," had driven the governor's aunt to a "nice Christian resort," where Edison was staying. The resort did not allow the chauffer to sleep in one of its rooms. "The boy," who was actually a grown man, Edison said, "did not raise hell but I was indignant." The resort administrators, upon learning of the governor's feelings, promised "to make provisions for such emergencies." Edison viewed their promise as "a victory" and added, "if the boy had insisted on his rights, he would have only antagonized people."[16]

O

The Eagles were coping with tension of another nature, the draft. As the end of the year approached, more Eagles had heard from Uncle Sam, and by November, Thompson, Parks, Ruffin, Day, Davis, and Doby were also gone. The Manleys' only solace was that the other teams had also lost players to the war effort.

Even though many star players were overseas, the Eagles and other Negro league teams had their best year to date financially thanks to the increase in employment generated by the war. Effa's volunteer service resulted in her name being added to the New Jersey Afro Honor Roll, which honored distinguished New Jerseyans, for her work with the Volunteer War Service Committee. She saved the newspaper article in her scrapbook and wrote "More Bouquets" at the top of the page. She included a rhyme she wrote about the effort. Some of the words did not survive the page being copied:

**Chant of the V.W.S.C.**
Come join with us in helping
To spread a little cheer
Among our soldiers
Each Tuesday in the year.
The performers gladly volunteer
And do a show that's . . . .
Won't you help us to . . .
To get them to the . . . .[17]

Owners looked forward to more of the same in 1944. Wilson and Martin called for a meeting of NNL and NAL owners at New York's Hotel Theresa on January 5, 1944. Effa gave her effort to unseat Wilson a rest, and Wilson, Bolden, Posey, and Abe won reelection to their respective offices by acclamation. Keeping the tradition of controversy at the meetings alive, however, Gottlieb asked Martin if any of his league's clubs had played the St. Louis Stars. Martin had earlier assured NNL owners that no NAL teams would play the Stars after Wilson revoked the Stars' NNL membership for failure to pay their 1943 dues. Gottlieb, of course, knew that the Memphis Red Sox and the Stars had divided a doubleheader on September 12. Sox owner B. B. Martin said that neither league president had notified him of the ban. B. B. and J. B. Martin were brothers. Gottlieb let the matter drop after a "heated exchange" took place between several NNL owners and the Martins.[18]

A month after the meetings Effa and Abe and all of Newark learned the tragic news that Charles Tyler, from whom Abe had purchased the Newark Dodgers, had been felled "gang-fashion like" at 1:15 a.m. on Sunday morning, February 6 by a "pellet about the size of a marble fired from an old-fashioned type shotgun." The pellet struck Tyler as he stood at the cash register counting money in his popular tavern and restaurant, the Chicken Shack, located on St. George Avenue in Avenel, New Jersey. Tyler had operated his tavern with his wife, Carrie, for fifteen years. The pellet split his head into several pieces. The shooter, Clarence Martin's, thirty-two, opened the door, fired, and took off. Carrie told police she believed the shooting stemmed from a confrontation between Tyler and a relative of Martin who had refused to pay for a drink the evening before. The FBI arrested Martin a month later in a New York apartment, where he had hidden to avoid a dragnet that stretched from New York to Florida. Martin received a life sentence.[19]

Abe and Effa returned to Newark from the January meetings and set about filling out their roster. Effa asked Mackey whether he would be interested in returning at a salary of $250 a month and did he know of any players with the potential to make the Eagles. He was not, and he did not. His legs bothered him, he told Effa. "I would very much like to play ball again but I'm afraid my legs won't stand it." Mackey did tell Effa that he had married a woman named Lucille since last playing for the Eagles. "You should see Lucille," he wrote. "She is too fat for words."[20]

Undaunted by Mackey's refusal, Effa thought she had a good nucleus of a club with Wells, who had promised to return; Dandridge, whose draft board kept him home; and returning veterans classified 4-F, Pearson, Hill, Hooker, Davis, outfielder Bob Harvey, and utility infielder Murray Watkins. Suttles, with his explosive bat, returned to manage the team. Abe cast his recruiting net to the Canal Zone, where he found, thanks to the recommendation of Bill Yancey, who played ten seasons in the Negro leagues and was directing the YMCA in Colon, Panama, heavy-hitting outfielders Archie Braithwaite and Victor Burnett. Both made the team.

Little did Effa know that a future major leaguer would soon appear on her doorstep. Don Newcombe, who would play ten seasons in the majors, joined the Eagles that spring as a result of being chided for losing at checkers at Pryor's Barbershop on Magnolia Avenue in Elizabeth, New Jersey, on a December afternoon in 1943. After he lost seven straight games to a man named Buddy Holler, an onlooker said to the seventeen-year-old, two-hundred-pound, six-foot-plus Newcombe, "If I was your size I'd give up checkers and try football or maybe baseball." At the time Newcombe was pitching for a sandlot team in Roselle, New Jersey. The checkers loser made this known to Holler, a department store clerk and acquaintance of Abe's, who two months later, drove Newcombe to the Manley's apartment to introduce him to Abe. Abe was out, so Effa answered Holler's knock on her door. Effa asked Newcombe, "[H]ow is it a big fine-looking boy like you isn't in the service?" Newcombe replied, she said, "I've been in and out. I knew what to do." Newcombe met Abe the next morning at the Grand Hotel just before the bus left for Richmond. Abe liked what he saw and took the youngster with him. Hill had yet to be heard from.[21]

The roster suffered a blow when Wells, even though he had promised to return, flew to Mexico instead to manage the Vera Cruz Blues in the Mexican league, where he would appreciate the $10,000 salary and the freedom. His decision sparked criticism in the press. Sam Lacy said he could understand a man's desire to seek employment at the best possible salary, but thought it "neither understandable or excusable for a ball player to agree to join a team and then willfully and deliberately run out on that agreement." Wells responded by saying, "I understand that there is a lot of adverse talk about me in the States because I quit the Newark Eagles and returned here to play ball. I hate that, but there's always two sides to every story."

Wells told his side while getting a haircut. "Not only do I get more money playing here but I've found freedom and democracy," Wells said, "something I've never found in the United States. I was branded a Negro in the States and had to act accordingly. They wouldn't even give me a chance in the big leagues because I was a Negro, yet they accepted every other nationality under the sun. Well, in Mexico I am a man. I will encounter no restrictions of any kind because of my race. Not only do I get more money here but I live like a king." As a measure of the respect Wells had earned in Mexico, the barber, after releasing Wells from the chair, turned to grin at Smith and say while pointing to Wells, "El Diablo, El Diablo." Wells, translating for Smith, said, "That means 'The Devil' in Spanish. It's what they call me here." Smith replied, "Yeah, that's what they're calling you in Newark but they don't mean it the same way."[22]

O

While Smith was interviewing Wells, signs of progress, resistance, and protest could be seen in New Jersey and Newark. The New Jersey State Senate and Assembly put teeth in New Jersey's civil rights laws by ordering the attorney general's office to enforce them. New Jersey was one of the first states to enact such laws, and by taking this step in late March became the first state to offer protection against discrimination through the attorney general's office.[23] The taxpayer-supported City Hospital's continued refusal to integrate its staff inspired playwright Hughes Allison, whose play *The Trial of Dr. Beck* had been performed on Broadway, to pen *It's Midnight over Newark*. The play depicted not only the hospital's ban against black medical professionals, but other race-related issues, including prostitution and housing problems. In a manner that Governor Edison would not have approved, the idea, said Dr. Charles M. Harris, president of the Newark chapter of the Alpha Phi Alpha fraternity, which presented the play, "was to put race discrimination right on the stage where the general public can see it gnawing at the very foundations of democracy." The play was well received but despite requests by both whites and blacks, including one by Lucy K. Milburn, the white president of the city's Interracial Council, the hospital's practices went unchanged. The medical board of the hospital said the ban against Negro physicians "will remain unchanged."[24]

O

The Eagles opened the 1944 season at Ruppert Stadium on Sunday, May 14, with a twin bill against the Stars. They overcame poor pitching by Hill, who had finally joined the team but had not rounded into shape. Hill gave up three runs to the Stars including two round-trippers in the first inning. Hooker relieved Hill and held the Stars to one run while getting five runs from his teammates for the win, 5–4. Eagles pitchers struggled in game two as well. Percy Forrest walked six Stars in the first inning and had to be relieved by Newcombe, who was in turn relieved by Eddie Jacobs, but the Eagles' bats again came to the rescue for an 11–6 win. Forrest's lackluster performance prompted Abe to trade him a month later to the Black Yankees for, of all people, the temperamental but effective McDuffie.

The Eagles and the Grays met a week later in a doubleheader on neutral turf at Ebbets Field on a sunny afternoon on Sunday, May 21. Posey and Effa chose Ebbets Field because they could book the park without having to pay Gottleib his 10 percent booking fee. An hour before the game started, Maj. Miles A. Paige, commander of the Third Separate Battalion, New York National Guard, led the battalion and its band on a march from its armory at 801 Dean Street, down a mile-long stretch of Washington Avenue into Ebbets Field and on to the center-field flagpole, where Paige raised the flag to the sounds of the National Anthem. He led the band back to the mound, where he threw out the first ball in front of 6,732 fans. The Grays, who had not been weakened as much as the Eagles had been by the draft and the flight to Latin America, still had their core players, Buck Leonard, Josh Gibson, Ray Brown, and Sam Bankhead. They beat Effa's charges 5–1 in game one behind the five-hit pitching of Brown and drubbed the Eagles in game two, 12–2.

Several weeks after the Eagles' doubleheader loss, one of the Eagles who had been drafted, Leon Day, joined other black soldiers during and following the D-day invasion of France in June 1944, to drive army DUKWs, six-wheel amphibious vehicles built by General Motors, between the beaches at Normandy and supply ships stationed offshore to keep soldiers on the beaches supplied with food and ammunition.[25]

From their .500 start, the Eagles righted themselves so that by the last week in June they were contesting the Grays for first place. By July 4 only one game separated the two teams. They had split a doubleheader at Ruppert Stadium on Sunday, July 2. Hill and Davis combined to shut down Gibson during his five trips to the plate and hold the Grays to seven hits, while McDuffie cracked a pinch hit, grand slam homer in the bottom of the tenth inning to lead the Eagles to an 11–7 win. Roy Partlow allowed the Eagles nine hits and five runs in the nightcap but won the game 14–5 behind the heavy hitting of Gibson, Leonard, and company.

The Eagles faced the Cubans two days later for an Independence Day doubleheader, again at Ebbets Field. The games featured a war bond rally, arranged by Effa and directed by Mrs. Mary McCloud Bethune, the first African American and the first woman to be honored with a statue in a public park in Washington, D.C., for her many civil rights achievements. The rally helped raise funds to build a Liberty ship to be named after Harriet Tubman, a runaway slave from Maryland who risked her life guiding other slaves to freedom along the Underground Railroad. The rally raised $80,000, one-third of the entire quota assigned to the New York area.[26]

The first-half championship was usually decided by July 4, but this one went undecided until August 18. The Grays and Eagles ended the first half tied, but the Manleys protested Partlow's appearance in the July 2 games, claiming that Partlow belonged to the Stars and not the Grays. It took Wilson over a month to decide that Abe and Effa had a point and to call for a playoff game. The teams met for a night contest at Ruppert Stadium that drew ten thousand "free-spending, hell-bent for victory" fans who forked out over $5,000 for rye, rum, and scotch at the stadium's bar. Effa was too nervous to talk to a reporter during the game. "Oh Carl," she said to Carl Lawrence, "please go away and don't bother me now. This thing is too serious." Gibson decided the game in the Grays' favor, 8–4, with a towering blow over the left-field fence in the ninth inning.[27]

With the first half flag in doubt, the second half began with the Eagles meeting the Stars at their home park, Parkside Field, on Saturday night, July 8. Newcombe, still struggling, accounted for one of Stars' runs in the first inning by walking the bases full and hitting the Stars' first baseman, Jim West, in the ribs. Three batters later, Newcombe's errant ball found the thigh of Stars catcher Bill "Ready" Cash. Hill, on in relief in the third inning, issued two walks and a wild pitch that helped the Stars score eight runs in the third to increase their lead to 12–0. The Stars took the game 13–2. The next day Ruppert Stadium's nine dropped a doubleheader to the Baltimore Elite Giants 4–1 and 3–1 at the Giants' home park, Bugle Field. The Eagles fared no better for the rest of the second half. Johnny Davis, in a bright spot, pitched a five-hitter a week later against the Elite Giants for one of the Eagles' rare wins. More typical was the doubleheader loss administered by the Grays on August 17 in Pittsburgh at Forbes Field, the home of the Grays before they moved to Washington, D.C., in 1940. The first game pleased those fans who liked offense with twenty-three hits and seventeen runs, but the Grays got more of each, winning 9–8. Newcombe, after setting down the side in order in the first inning of the second game, gave up two walks and, after hitting a batter, walked the fourth batter to bring home a run. Then he gave up a bases-clearing single to spot the Grays four runs on their way to a 6–2 win. By season's end, the Eagles had floundered their way to a next to last place finish.[28]

As 1944 drew to a close the owners in both leagues met again at the Theresa Hotel in Harlem on December 16 and 17. Once again they discussed the issue of a commissioner for one or both leagues. The press, and particularly Wendell Smith, had become increasing critical of the leagues' "slipshod operation." Smith estimated that Negro league baseball was by now a $2 to 3 million business and a source of livelihood for two thousand people. To insist as Martin and Wilson continued to do, that no qualified person could be found to take a commissioner's post was, in Smith's opinion, "tommyrot." A more likely possibility, Smith maintained, was that such people were available but would require a decent salary, on the order of $10,000 per year, and complete autonomy, neither of which the owners were likely to grant. The owners, in the words of Sam Lacy, "shriveled" at the thought.

To no one's surprise, the NNL officers all won reelection without opposition. J. B. Martin was reelected as president of the NAL but encountered opposition for the first time. Two owners, Thomas Hayes of the Birmingham Black Barons and Syd Pollock of the Cincinnati Clowns, voted for Cleveland attorney John G. Shackelford. The owners, perhaps becoming increasingly uncomfortable with the press's criticism of them, appointed a four-man committee to search for a potential commissioner and report on their findings at the May meeting. Abe and Pompez represented the NNL. The NAL selected Ernest Wright of the Cleveland Buckeyes and Thomas Baird of the Monarchs. The committee evidently satisfied Effa, as she did not make her annual appeal about the matter.[29]

She did begin the business of negotiating players' contracts as the war entered its fifth and final year. The Allies were putting the finishing touches on Germany and had entered the Nazi death camps, in which six million people died. President Roosevelt died in Warm Springs, Georgia, elevating Harry Truman to the presidency. Germany surrendered in May and Japan in August.[30]

Those Eagles who had been drafted started returning home, but their full presence would not be felt for another year. One of the last to return, Monte Irvin, who would not set foot on American soil until August, had kept up a correspondence with Effa from his unit in France and, in a January 12, 1945, letter, thanked her for the Christmas package she had sent to him. He told her that he'd run into Max Manning, who "was fine but homesick like the rest of us."

Effa turned first to Mackey. Displaying none of the reticence she had displayed toward Mackey's salary and expenses request in 1942, Effa now agreed to his requests for a $400-a-month salary, an assurance that he would not have to catch all the games, full round-trip train transportation from Los Angeles, and payment of his rent for five months. She sweetened the deal with a $20-a-week stipend while he was in training camp (salary payments did not start until opening day) to help make up for the loss of income from his defense job.

She extended the stipend offer to every player who reported to camp, held again this year in Richmond at Virginia Union College. She wanted Mackey to use his coaching talents with Newcombe and Hill, who again asked for a loan to help him get to camp. Effa obliged. Hill reported late to Richmond after a short, to-the-point scribbled note to him from Abe. Effa, in a turn about from her earlier refusal to compete with offers received by players from Latin America, satisfied McDuffie's salary demands, which amounted to $4,000 for the season, because that's what he said he'd been offered to play in Cuba. Mackey, Irvin, and Dandridge would no doubt have been outraged if they had known Effa so quickly agreed to pay McDuffie the equivalent of $800 a month based on McDuffie's claim of what he could earn in Cuba, since Effa had denied their similar requests for far smaller sums.

Newcombe held out for more money and threatened to go to Mexico with Hooker, which angered Effa. Newcombe's rookie year had not impressed Effa. He had been, in her estimation, "absolutely next door to nothing." Newcombe was 0–4 in league games for which he got the decision and had to be relieved in many others. In a one-page, single-spaced letter to his parents, Effa explained that he had the makings to "become one of the outstanding pitchers" but "he is showing a big head. This is bad." She explained that she was paying "a big salary" to Mackey partially so he could help Newcombe, and that, in spite of his record, she had offered him a raise from $170 to $200 a month. She wrote, "I wish Donald the best of luck, but I do hate to see him getting off so completely on the wrong foot." Her letter had the intended effect.

In a letter to utility infielder Murray Watkins, who had been filling in for Wells and Dandridge the past three years, she agreed to most of the raise he had asked for and again voiced her frustration with such requests, saying, "They seem to have forgotten the years we had to go to the bank to pay salaries." With these players on board; a commitment, which this year would be honored, by Wells; and the return of Pearson, Mathews, and Davis, the Eagles' prospects for 1945 looked promising.[31]

While Mackey no doubt helped Newcombe with his pitching as Effa had expected, the big rookie also benefited from Wells's coaching. Again the Eagles' manager, after Abe had fired Suttles from the post for undisclosed reasons, Wells told Newk just to run the first week of camp. When Wells finally let the fire-balling nineteen-year-old throw, he asked him to "just lob the ball to me." This did not sit well with the young Newcombe, who said to Wells, "You're pretty rough, aren't you?" "No," replied his manager, "I just want you to be in good shape." Over repeated protests from Newcombe, Wells limited his pitching to three to four innings in spring exhibition games. Newcombe would win fourteen games in 1945.[32]

As Abe supervised training camp, Effa set about her managerial duties. She had a misunderstanding with H. B. Webber, a reporter for the *New York Amsterdam News*, whom she had hired to score the games, take publicity photos, and send publicity notices to the press. Having not heard from her shortly before the season started, he assumed she did not want him to continue with press notices for opening day. Effa did want Webber to continue, but hearing nothing from him, she fired him much as she had fired Mackey after he left Newark without speaking with her at the end of the 1941 season. Effa did not inquire into the gray areas of misunderstanding between herself and her employees. Webber, upon hearing the news, told her, "I am not offended when you push me around, as I expect it." Effa justified her action believing, "It was just one of those things, and there is no reason for any hard feelings."[33]

She sent a long letter to Abe, addressed "Dear Baby," that showed her attention to detail. She asked Abe for names of promoters for exhibition games the team would play and gave him instructions for how he should pay bills for posters and placards and arrange for rain insurance. She apologized for the players' jackets not arriving on time and wanted to know the shoe preferences of those players still in need of them. She inquired about those rookies who might make the team, McDuffie's condition, Newcombe's progress, and other information she needed "as I must give the fans some information." She signed her letter "Love Effa."[34]

Several weeks later, after hearing of a small turnout for a preseason exhibition game between the Eagles and Cubans in Norfolk, she laid it on the line to the game's promoter, Brady Johnson. "I'm sure it was caused by the bum booking you are doing down that way." Among other complaints, she accused Brady of lying to the fans by promising them Negro league games and then delivering semipro teams. "You have good territory," she told him, "but you are ruining it. . . . I do hope you change your methods before it is too late."

When the Eagles arrived in Newark, McDuffie was struggling with stomach problems. Effa sent him to see Dr. Chainey at 1890 Seventh Avenue in New York. Chainey wanted reports from the doctor who had treated McDuffie earlier in Norfolk. Effa asked Percy Simon, now residing in Norfolk, to retrieve the report and send it to Dr. Chainey. McDuffies's large salary—and the fact that, as Effa put it, "he has looked like two cents"—and rained out games had put the Eagles $5,000 in debt by June 10. "If the baseball keeps on like this," she told Simon, "I will be asking you to take me in as a partner in the hotel business. Ha."[35]

While the press paid little attention, the Eagles' season opened at Ruppert Stadium on May 6, 1945, against the Cubans. The Eagles won 6–0. For the rest of the first half the Eagles struggled to play .500 ball and hang on to fourth place. McDuffie lifted the team's mood in a mid-May game when "The Great One," whose stomach problems had cleared up, beat the Cubans practically single-handedly, pitching shutout ball and tagging two homers.[36]

Soon thereafter Wells brought some excitement to the team by walking out on it. He had little patience with anyone who second-guessed his decisions, even if it was the club owner. Abe, who still bore hard feelings toward McDuffie, ordered Wells to start McDuffie, who Wells thought was not ready to go. Abe wanted to make the pitcher look bad in the eyes of Effa and her girlfriends. Wells called a clubhouse meeting after the game with Abe in attendance and said, "He doesn't have to pay me any more as manager of this team. I am finished." The feeling was mutual, as Abe had said earlier that he'd trade Wells for a broken bat. Instead Abe traded Wells for a pitcher, Spec Roberts from the Black Yankees. Abe installed Mackey as manager.

Effa was fed up with Wells as well. She was "so disappointed in Wells for letting me down" that she took $150 out of his final paycheck, which was the money she had sent to Wells to pay his fare from California, where he had been playing in the California Winter League.[37]

In mid-June the Eagles dropped two games to the Grays 7–2 and 3–2 before 8,367 fans in Griffith Stadium. Highlights for the Eagles included Hill retiring twelve Grays in a row in game one before Buck Leonard blasted a home run over the thirty-two-foot wall in right field, and forty-eight year old Biz Mackey reaching first safely on a drag bunt. Hooker, recently back from Mexico, lost the second game.

Two weeks later Hooker dropped another decision, this one by the score of 4–1 against the Stars on Sunday, July 1, before nine thousand spectators in one of the Eagles' few games at Yankee Stadium. The Eagles' lone run came on Mackey's 350-foot shot into the right-center field stands. The Eagles managed a fourth-place finish at 11–9, with most of their wins coming at the expense of the Cubans and Black Yankees, both of whom played a mere .200 ball for the first half.[38]

To add to the Eagles' problems, Pearson received a call from Uncle Sam that would make him the thirteenth Eagle to be drafted. Just before Independence Day, however, Effa wrote a letter to Pearson's Selective Service Board asking that they delay his induction until the end of the season. She couched her request in terms of Pearson's value to the team, the "big part that baseball plays in the lives of Negroes in New Jersey," and the fact that he had previously been declared 4-F owing to a bad knee. Asking the board to "understand my motive for writing this letter," she gave them the names of three women who would testify to her war-related volunteer work. Pearson finished the season with the Eagles.[39]

Before the first half ended, the NNL and NAL owners met in Chicago on June 12 to again take up the issue of a commissioner. The four-man committee had nominated two men. The NAL representatives nominated Robert Church, sixty, a millionaire, close friend of the Martins', and an influential Republican in Memphis politics. The NNL representatives nominated William Hueston. Neither received the required three-fourths votes. All NAL owners voted for Church, as did Abe because Effa said she'd heard many good things about him. The other NNL owners voted for Hueston. Again, the owners had failed to shore up their organization and remained a target of criticism from sportswriters and the public.

A month later at a meeting in New York, the NNL owners showed a bit of mettle. They fined the Black Yankees $500 for twice forfeiting a game by walking off the field to protest an umpire's decision and again imposed a ban on players who jumped to Mexico. They set this ban, initiated when they learned that Marvin Williams and Barney Brown of the Stars had joined McDuffie on a flight to Mexico, at five years.[40]

The Eagles' fortunes picked up in the second half following a slow start, when they dropped a Sunday doubleheader on July 8 to the Elite Giants at Bugle Field, 3–2 and 3–1. Hooker was again tagged for a loss in game one. As Hooker was struggling, Newcombe was showing the benefits of Wells's and Mackey's coaching. Referred to in the press "as one of the rising young stars of the NNL," he turned in a "brilliant performance" on July 22 at the Polo Grounds by beating the Black Yankees 6–1. On August 5, he threw a one-hitter against the Elite Giants to lead the Eagles to an 8–1 win at Bugle Field. Mackey, manager and part-time catcher at age forty-eight, was batting .300. Irvin rejoined the team in late August to help the Eagles lead the NNL in batting. Oscar Charleston, a scout with Branch Rickey's ill-fated Brooklyn Brown Dodgers, brought newcomer Jimmy Wilkes to Effa's attention. Wilkes performed well at bat, in the outfield, and on the bases. His speed earned him the nickname "Sea Biscuit" after the famous racehorse.

The Eagles played better than any NNL team throughout most of August to earn the top spot in the standings. On August 26, before five thousand fans at Griffith Stadium, however, the Grays nicked the Eagles in both games of a doubleheader by the identical scores of 3–2 to cut the Eagles' lead to one game. A week later the Grays again took two Sunday games from the Eagles, 5–2 and 4–3, to knock the Eagles out of first place. Had they won the nightcap, the Eagles would have held on to first place, but Mackey, who had played a pivotal role all year, committed a throwing error that allowed the tying and winning runs to score. The Eagles finished in second place.[41]

Effa kept the players busy with exhibition games after the season ended, and the result of one prompted a letter from her to "The Newspapers of Newark N.J. Sports Editors." Umpires had refused to halt play when a rainstorm occurred during a game between the Eagles and the semipro East Orange Base Ball Club. Mackey disagreed with the umpires and took the Eagles off the field in protest, an event widely reported by the Jersey papers. Effa wanted it known, "because we value the reputation of the ball club very highly," that the rain was "heavy and not light" and that "just a little rain makes [a field] impossible to play on." By justifying Mackey's actions in her letter to the state's sports editors, she publicly took a stance at odds with her earlier vote to fine teams for leaving the field on their own.[42]

While Effa did not feel the owners' fine against the Black Yankees should apply to the Eagles, she fully supported their ban on players jumping to Mexico. In October Effa hired Newark attorney James A. Curtis to take the matter up with U.S. Senator Howard Alexander Smith of New Jersey. Though reportedly sympathetic, he noted, as others before him had, that urging the State Department to deny players visitor visas would be discriminatory. Smith did, however, promise he would consult with "Senator Chandler when he returns from the World Series." A. B. "Happy" Chandler, a U.S. Senator from Kentucky, had been elected by major league owners to succeed Landis, who had died in 1944, to the post of major league baseball commissioner in April.[43] Chandler resigned his Senate seat in October before having a chance to confer with Smith, whose efforts on Effa's behalf came to naught. Effa would have dealings with Chandler in the years ahead.

O

As Chandler assumed his new duties, black and white soldiers were returning home from a long and costly war that successfully thwarted the Japanese and Axis threats at home and around the world. They returned to a society in which segregation still reigned, as it had in their units overseas. Employment statistics for blacks during the defense industry boom showed more blacks employed but few in prominent positions. Only 10 percent of blacks employed in Newark held foremen positions.

In spite of those dismal figures, some progress could be seen. Assemblyman James O. Hill of Newark, the lone black representative in the state body, shepherded an act through the legislature that made discrimination illegal in public organizations employing six or more persons. The directors of City Hospital approved the applications of five black physicians but placed them on a waiting list rather than hiring them. Newark physician Dr. Thomas Bell integrated the State Department of Education with his appointment by Governor Walter E. Edge as a member of the department's Division of Discrimination.

In the world of baseball, Branch Rickey loosened Jim Crow's hold on the game when he signed Kansas City Monarch's infielder Jackie Robinson to a contract with the Montreal Royals, a Dodgers farm club, on August 28, 1945. Rickey swore Robinson to secrecy that day, saying he could tell only his family and his fiancée, Rachel Imus, until Rickey decided when he wanted to make the signing public. That day came on October 23 at a press conference in Montreal.[44] While moguls, players, black sportswriters, African American citizens, and many whites applauded the move, the way forward would be anything but smooth.

# CHAPTER TEN

## *Branch Rickey Drops the Color Bar*

Several months prior to Robinson's signing, two black sportswriters tried to get Negro league players in the majors. Joe Bostic of the Communist-affiliated *People's Voice*, took McDuffie and Dave Thomas of the New York, Cubans to the Brooklyn Dodgers' training camp at Bear Mountain, New York on Saturday, April 7, 1945. Although they had not been invited, several Dodgers, including manager Leo Durocher, watched as McDuffie pitched to Clyde Sukeforth, a coach and confidant of Rickey, while Thomas batted against Frank Wurm, a southpaw whose major league career consisted of throwing one-third of an inning for the Dodgers the year before, and right-handed Claude Crocker, who appeared in a total of three games for the Dodgers. Nothing came of the tryouts. Wendell Smith of the *Pittsburgh Courier* arranged for Robinson, Sam Jethroe of the Cleveland Buckeyes, and Marvin Williams of the Philadelphia Stars to travel to Boston on Monday, April 16, for a tryout with the Boston Red Sox. The Sox received them cordially and held the tryout in front of manager Joe Cronin and business manager Eddie Collins, but made no further contact with the players or their teams.

Potential competition for the Negro leagues came in May when Rickey called a press conference to say he had formed a new team, the Brooklyn Brown Dodgers, to play in a new Negro league, the U.S. League, to be headed by Gus Greenlee. The Brown Dodgers actually served as cover for Rickey while he scouted black players for the Brooklyn Dodgers. Only two representatives of the Negro leagues, Effa and Curtis Leak, secretary to the New York Black Yankees, attended the press conference. Rickey had invited both. He also invited the presidents of both the NAL and NNL—Tom Wilson, who did not reply, and J. B. Martin, who said he was not interested in attending. The conference soon became a verbal battle between Effa, "who fired questions at Rickey with machine-gun rapidity," and Rickey. The unflappable Rickey said the existing Negro league teams or leagues could apply to the U.S.League but if they chose not to could expect stiff competition. In response to Effa's question about why he chose to support the new league instead of the existing ones, Rickey said it was because Greenlee, and the proposed league president, Cleveland attorney John G. Shackelford, had approached him.

The two may have approached Rickey, but in truth, he held the existing leagues in contempt. "They are not leagues and have no right to expect organized baseball to respect them," Rickey said. "They have the semblance of a racket. I felt," he said some years later, "both the American and Negro National League clubs were in the control of racketeers—men exploiting the colored players for their own purposes. They had no contracts, no league schedules and no constitution, and almost without exception, no written contracts with players." Rickey said he had talked with people in both leagues to suggest they remedy what Rickey felt the leagues were lacking but found that "my proposal was not at all acceptable."[1]

Rickey continued talking publicly about the U.S. League and the Brown Dodgers as he scouted black players for the Dodgers. By August 1945, the same month he signed Robinson, Rickey had Sukeforth contact Monte Irvin, who had recently been discharged from the service. Sukeforth told Irvin he was contacting several Negro leaguers about trying out for the majors. Was Irvin interested? Irvin said he was not in the shape he wanted to be in but would let Rickey know when he was ready, which he thought would be in about a year.[2] Irvin was considered the best player in the Negro leagues at the time, at least by Effa, who said Irvin "would have been our first choice if we'd been asked." In addition to his skills on the field, Irvin had two years of college and the temperament to handle the stress of being the first black in the majors. Rickey said he understood and, in the meantime, kept up the ruse of the Brown Dodgers. We'll never know whether Rickey would have signed Irvin before Robinson, had Irvin said yes to Sukeforth.

When asked by the *Pittsburgh Courier* whether he had spoken to Jackie Robinson in late August, as had been rumored, Rickey said he had. Asked if the meeting had been about Robinson playing for the Brooklyn Dodgers, Rickey said it had not. "That was never discussed," Rickey said. "I am interested in investing in a Negro team and would like to use Jackie Robinson on that team." The Brown Dodgers and the U.S. League would fold before the end of the 1946 season, but by then Rickey no longer needed to be secretive about scouting black players.[3]

Rickey did not pay J. L. Wilkinson, Kansas City Monarchs owner, for Robinson's services, nor did Rickey even talk to anyone besides Robinson in the Monarch's organization. Rickey had stolen Robinson, and no one could do anything about it. This did not sit well with Effa. Putting it politely, she said, after complimenting Rickey for democratizing baseball, "I didn't know it was good business for an owner of one team to negotiate solely with a player of another."[4]

J. B. Martin, owner of the Chicago American Giants and still president of the NAL, the league the Monarchs played in, also felt owners were entitled to payment for their players. At the same time, Martin did not want payment concerns to jeopardize Robinson's chance to make the majors. Martin told Effa, "I have Tom Baird's [co-owner of the Monarchs] assurance that whatever they [the Dodgers] offer for Robinson he will accept it. What we are trying to do is set up a principle for the others to follow. There will be no price named, for we are not going to jeopardize Robinson's chance. If they say $500 or five thousand, all well and good. . . . But when they get other players, if they get them, we will place a reasonable price on them and demand it."[5] Rickey, of course, said nothing. Effa wanted several owners to meet with Ford Frick, president of the National League, to assure him of the owners' interest in Negro leaguers making the majors, while at the same time letting him know she and the others expected to be compensated. Effa arranged for Rev. Johnson, now a member of Mayor LaGuardia's interracial Committee on Unity and chairman of a subcommittee charged with making recommendations on integrating baseball, to set up such a meeting. Martin agreed, but Wilson and Posey wanted to go straight to the top man and meet with Chandler. Wilson and Posey won out. Posey and Effa wrote a joint letter to Chandler on November 1, 1945, expressing their belief that "the clubs of Organized Negro Baseball who have gone to so much expense to develop players . . . should be approached and deals made." Posey and Effa invited Chandler to attend a meeting in New York to discuss the matter.[6]

Demonstrating that the quality of play in the Negro leagues compared favorably with that in the majors would improve the leagues' respectability in the eyes of people like Rickey and Chandler. The chance came when Rickey invited

Effa's Eagles to play a doubleheader against his Brooklyn Dodgers the first Sunday in October, just weeks before he would announce Robinson's signing. Wanting to enlarge the invitation, Effa successfully negotiated for a five-game series that would include a core of players from each team supplemented with several all-stars. Dodgers coach Chuck Dressen would manage the major leaguers while Biz Mackey would pilot the Negro leaguers. Effa invited Satchel Paige to pitch in the games for a fee of $1,000, and asked Robinson if he would also play for an undisclosed sum. The other players would receive $260. Effa contacted Paige and Robinson directly, committing the same error that she had criticized Rickey for when he signed Robinson. She later apologized to Baird, saying she should have contacted him first. Her lapse of protocol made little difference as both Paige and Robinson were already committed to play in a North-South all-star game.[7]

She delegated player selection to Mackey, who chose eight Eagles—Irvin, Davis, and Harvey in the outfield; Pearson, Wells (now with the Black Yankees), and Watkins in the infield; and pitchers Newcombe and Hooker. Mackey rounded out the team with Showboat Thomas of the Cubans at first; pitcher Bill Byrd and catcher Roy Campanella, both of the Elite Giants; and Frank Austin and Roy Partlow of the Stars at short and pitcher, respectively. Day was still in military service, as was Doby. Posey refused to make Gibson, Bankhead, and Leonard available from the Grays, as they also had been committed to play in a North-South game in New Orleans, but Posey did allow Johnny Wright to pitch.

Dressen chose Dodgers Goody Rosen and Frency Bordagaray in the outfield, Eddie Stanky at second, and pitchers Ralph Branca and Hal Gregg. Tommy Holmes of the Boston Braves, who led the National League in homers, batting average, and hits that year (with 224), completed the outfield. Whitey Kurowski of the St. Louis Cardinals was at third, Buddy Kerr of the New York Giants played shortstop, and Frank McCormick of the Cincinnati Reds completed the infield at first. Others included catcher Clyde Klutz of the Giants, and pitchers Van Mungo of the Giants and Virgil Trucks from the newly minted World Champion Detroit Tigers. If Mackey's team was missing some NNL heavyweights, so Dressen's was missing the likes of Ted Williams, Joe DiMaggio, Bob Feller, and Stan Musial.[8]

Anticipation ran high as the teams took a rain-soaked Ebbets Field on October 5 for the first Sunday doubleheader. Mackey's charges narrowly lost both games, 5–4 and 2–1. Friday night at Ruppert Stadium the major leaguers shellacked Mackey's team 10–0. Back at Ebbets Field for another Sunday doubleheader, Trucks won the first game 4–1. Umpires called the second game, a scoreless tie, in the fifth inning because of rain.

Effa's disappointment in the games' outcomes showed in her letter to Elite Giants general manager Vernon Green. Citing "awful weather both Sundays," three errors by Watkins, instances of players being caught off base, and two men covering the same base, Effa concluded, "One thing the series showed me was how dumb our ball players are. The white boys looked so smart . . . and our men constantly showed how dumb they were. . . . They just did not know what to do half of the time." The series gave her no ammunition to use against those who considered play in the Negro leagues to be second-rate.[9]

The series did, however, provide a chance for Rickey to offer Roy Campanella a contract. After one of the games at Ebbets Field, and after he had signed Jackie Robinson (but before he had announced the signing), Rickey told Campanella during a meeting in his office that he had investigated dozens of Negro leaguers. Oscar Charleston had, Rickey said, investigated Campanella's background and found it to be "good." When asked by Rickey, "Would you like to play for me?" Campanella said, "I'm doing all right where I am." Rickey said he understood and would be back in touch, and asked Campanella not to sign with another major league club without talking to him. Campanella agreed.

Campanella thought Rickey was asking him to play with the Brooklyn Brown Dodgers. It was not until Campanella returned from his meeting with Rickey to the Woodside Hotel in Harlem, where Robinson and other players were gathering prior to a barnstorming tour of Venezuela, that Campanella learned from Robinson, in a breach of Robinson's promise to Rickey to stay mum about his signing, that Robinson had signed with the Brooklyn Dodgers. Campanella and Rickey met again on April 4, 1946, and cleared up the misunderstanding when Rickey signed Campanella to a contract with the Nashua Dodgers, a New Hampshire farm club of the Brooklyn Dodgers.[10]

Rickey also signed Don Newcombe to a contract with the same club on April 11 without talking to Abe or Effa. Newcombe's signing prompted calls from the papers asking Effa for a comment. Rickey's actions infuriated Effa. "Rickey took Robinson, Newcombe, and Campanella from our Negro baseball and didn't even say thank you," she said. "He took Newcombe from me, so I know what I'm talking about."[11] She told Abe, "I am going to have to make a statement. I am going to . . . seek some advice from Council, but it is really quite a question. We have so many boys who are major league material we may wake up any morning and not have a ball club, if this keeps on."[12]

Effa decided against legal action but made her feelings about Newcombe clear in a letter to Mackey, at which time she thought Newcombe would sign with the Brown Dodgers. She said that would not surprise her, "as he is quite a problem child anyway." Mackey replied, "That is bad about Newcome. Something is wrong with his head. Is his wife with him?"[13] Effa wanted to be compensated by the Dodgers for the same reason she had expressed to Chandler. She wrote several letters to Rickey protesting the lack of payment for Newcombe but received no answer.[14]

Mad though she was, she had the upcoming 1946 season to deal with. She looked forward to it with enthusiasm. In a letter to Pat Patterson, an infielder with the Philadelphia Stars who recently returned from the war, and for whom Effa wanted to trade, she wrote, "[W]e have a chance to win the pennant this year, in fact run away with it."[15] Such upbeat forecasts were rare for Effa. Unlike the prewar years when profits were nil, necessitating repeated trips to the bank on the first and fifteenth of each month to meet payroll, attendance during the war years had enabled Effa and Abe to turn a profit even though a dozen of their best players had been lost to the draft. Prospects of even greater profits danced in her head because Effa knew every one of those players would be back in uniform in 1946.

# CHAPTER ELEVEN

## *A Reunited Team*

The meeting that Effa and Posey wanted with Chandler occurred, but not in New York. They met in Cincinnati in Chandler's office at the Carew Tower on January 27, 1946. Wilson attended, as did Martin. Also present were the National and American League presidents, Ford Frick and Will Harridge, respectively, and attorney, Herold "Muddy" Ruel, better known as a catcher for eighteen seasons with six American League teams.

Chandler did not address the payment issues but suggested ways the Negro leagues could improve their reputation as a legitimate business in the eyes of the majors, holding out the possibility of affiliating with the majors if they did so. He suggested Negro league team owners build their own stadiums to reduce the fees paid to booking agents and, as the owners had already done, adopt a constitution similar to that of the major leagues, and pattern their player contracts after those in the majors to prevent jumping and raiding. The owners demurred on building stadiums, but within a month they had printed the contracts and constitution the owners had agreed to at their December 1945 meeting.[1]

The owners were starting to organize their operations along lines that Effa had long proposed. Still lacking, of course, was a commissioner or president without ties to a team. Effa again ramped up the pressure on the NNL owners to oust Wilson and elect an independent president. Now she championed Samuel Battle, age sixty-two, the same Battle who had replaced Gehrig as a member of the New York City Parole Board and who was now its commissioner. She had hoped to nominate him at the December meeting but decided not to because Posey, who also supported Battle, could not attend because he was ill.[2]

Posey did attend the 1946 owners meeting in New York at the Hotel Theresa on February 21, but his illness (he had lung cancer) kept him in his room. Rufus Jackson joined Effa "in a heated session," to take up the cause of nominating Battle and demanding Wilson's ouster, but the others were not yet willing to turn over power to an outsider. Wilson had offered to resign in 1945, but several of the owners insisted that he stay on. Those owners' insistence surprised and irritated Effa, who thought she had their support for a change in leadership. "Several of the members got hold of Tom," she wrote to Posey after the meeting, "and asked him not to resign. . . . I can't understand how people can be so deceitful." Little other business took place because, Effa said, "Cum is so sick everyone hated to do anything without him being present. One of the faults of our organization is there has always been more sentiment than business."[3]

On April 4 Posey died at Pittsburgh's Mercy Hospital. Baseball officials and politicians offered testimonials to a man who had made his mark in sports, politics, and education as a member of the Homestead School Board since 1931. He left his one-half interest in the Grays to his widow Ethel. His brother Seward continued to serve as the team's business manager, as he had since 1936.[4]

In between attending to league affairs, Effa got down to business with the players. In an exchange of letters with Mackey, whom she asked to manage the team again, Effa refused his request for a raise, saying they had a verbal agreement he'd play for the same salary as last year. She had advanced him $150 on the basis of that agreement and told him, "[I]t certainly shows a very bad spirit to accept money and not keep your word." In lieu of a raise, they settled on a two-year contract, at a rate of $350 per month, and an understanding that Mackey again would not have to catch full-time. At age forty-nine, his legs were still giving him problems.

The army gave Manning, Doby, and Day their releases during the spring. Manning and Day agreed to terms, but Doby held out for more money. This did not please Effa. After not receiving an answer to her letter to Doby inviting him to talk, she wrote a second in which she scolded him "for not giving me the courtesy of a reply," and told him, "[H]aving met your mother, I know you were not raised this badly. There is only one conclusion to reach, that is you are being very poorly advised by someone both stupid and ignorant of baseball conditions." Doby took the hint and signed.

Concerned that Irvin might be tempted by the Pasquel brothers, she wrote a lengthy letter to him in Puerto Rico, where he was playing winter ball, explaining why it would work to his advantage to play for the Eagles. Namely, the long Mexican season would interfere with his returning to school, should he choose to use the GI Bill of Rights, and he had a better shot at the majors if he were around to be seen by the scouts. Irvin agreed to return to Newark to talk with Effa before deciding where he'd play.

By way of further enticement, she met him in her negligee when he appeared at her door. Explaining "Abe won't be back until tomorrow," she invited him into the living room and sat across from him. She kept hiking her negligee up as they talked until it got to her navel. "This," Irvin said, "made me uncomfortable because I had a lot of respect for both Abe and her." She told Irvin not to be uncomfortable because it was warm and she just wanted "to air things out a bit." Irvin decided his better course would be to leave and continue the talks later. He did and signed with the Eagles for $400 a month.[5]

The team was now nearly complete. Abe decided to drop Jimmy Hill owing to his lackluster performance the last two seasons and his continual requests for special treatment. Abe wanted to add the Stars' Pat Patterson to the infield in a trade for Watkins. Usually, Effa left those decisions entirely to Abe, but not this time. Word had spread that Abe wanted the trade, and some women in the stands asked Effa about it during a game. She replied, "[L]isten darling that's not my department." The fans would have none of it saying, "[W]e know you run this team, girl." Effa said nothing more, "knowing they couldn't understand me saying I didn't know anything." That night she asked Abe if maybe he was not making a mistake; "the fans are very upset about Watkins being traded." "Effa," he said, "there's no comparison between two. The only reason I can get him [Patterson] is he's not getting along with the manager." Effa never questioned Abe's trade ideas after that. She did, however, take up the negotiations with Patterson, after getting clearance from Bolden and Gottlieb, and eventually coaxed him to sign with the Eagles, promising to pay him $350 a month and delay his reporting date to accommodate his attendance at Wiley College in Marshall, Texas, where he was pursuing an education degree.[6]

By mid-April the *Newark Herald* touted the Eagles "as the team to beat." Even allowing for the paper's hometown bias, the prediction looked solid. The outfield consisted of Irvin, Johnny Davis, and Bob Harvey, who had been a reliable

.300 hitter since joining the team in 1943. Pearson, Doby, Israel, and Patterson were to man the infield. The pitching staff, now led by Day, Manning, and Hooker, had power even without Newcombe, Hill, and McDuffie (who flew to Mexico along with Dandridge). Parks would catch when Mackey did not. Three rookies, Rufus Lewis, Cecil Cole, and Bob Cheeks, rounded out the roster.[7]

Leon Day, in his first NNL outing since he had returned from three years in the Army, boosted the *Herald*'s predictive reputation when he pitched a no hit, no run opening day game against Barney Brown and the Philadelphia Stars before 8,514 spectators at Ruppert Stadium on Sunday, May 5 to claim a 2–0 win. Stars manager Homer Curry and catcher Bill Cash enlivened the festivities by attacking umpire Peter Strauch after he called Doby safe at home when he tried to score on an infield out. Cash punched Strauch in the left eye. Curry ran from the dugout and got in several swings before the police ejected both from the game during the thirty-minute delay. A photographer's picture showed Cash had tagged Doby before Doby's outstretched hand reached the plate.[8]

The incident upset Effa, who, having received no response from Wilson about the Bradford umpire bashing episode the year before, wrote directly to Gottlieb. Gottlieb assigned umpires to Eagles home games, and Effa asked him whether Strauch, who was white, should continue to work "games for the colored teams." "I really think," she continued, "the Negro men are as prejudiced against the white umpires as the white people are against the colored." She noted that Strauch worked a game with the Black Yankees last year that was forfeited and that "[w]e have the Yankees here Sunday." Strauch did not work that game.[9]

Despite the fisticuffs, Day's performance excited Effa. "I'm sorry you did not see that no-hitter Sunday," she wrote to Art Carter. "It really was a beauty. He gave up one walk and our rookie shortstop made two errors that caused men to reach first. The last man up . . . was a pinch hitter, McHenry [Henry], and Day blazed three fastballs right over the heart of the plate, and he swung at each one of them. Went down swinging. Can you imagine what a thrill that was."[10]

Two weeks later at a meeting of NNL owners in Philadelphia, the moguls got serious about protecting umpires. They fined Cash $50, suspended him for three days, and agreed that future incidents would bring a $100 fine and a ten-game suspension. While they were at it, they banned eight players, including Dandridge and McDuffie, from the NNL for five years for jumping to Mexico.[11]

By late May the Eagles and Cubans each owned a share of the lead, but Patterson had still not arrived after promising Effa he would leave Houston by May 17. She let him know how she felt about his delay, telling him, "I was quite shocked and annoyed when I received your letter this morning telling me you had not yet left Houston. . . . Your absence is causing us a lot of inconvenience and set back." The setback consisted of losing a doubleheader to the Elite Giants 4–3 and 5–3 at home before an expectant crowd of six thousand. Those losses, plus recent games lost to the Stars, dropped the Eagles into fourth place.[12]

A letter of rebuke appeared on letterhead of the Third Ward Republican Club from one Reginald Simpson. Simpson, speaking on behalf of "the 3rd Ward Boosters Club," said Mackey was falling short in his duties as manager because "he has permitted Irvin, Harvey, Israel, and [William] Felder [a rookie shortstop], to remain in the lineup and none of them are hitting the ball a lick." He suggested it might be time to hire another manager. Effa thanked Simpson for his letter and interest in the club. She acknowledged that only two players, Pearson and Davis, were "hitting well," but that it was "a little unfair to pass final judgment so soon. . . . They will all come around. In the meantime we must all be a little patient." Mackey was reported to be upset over the team's slump and to have plans to correct it.[13]

Whatever he did worked. Mackey's men overwhelmed the Cubans in a doubleheader at the Polo Grounds before twelve thousand on Sunday, June 9, 7–1 and 6–2. Patterson, who had finally made his way to Newark, contributed a 450-foot triple to deepest centerfield to drive in two runs in game one. Day not only held the Cubans to four hits in the first game but had a perfect day at the plate with three singles and a walk. Rookie pitcher Rufus Lewis won the second game behind the now strong-hitting Eagles. The wins continued with eight straight victories that started with a 16–2 trouncing of the Grays behind Day and ended with 6–1 and 3–1 wins over the now third place Cubans on June 23 at Ruppert Stadium. A 13–11 loss to the Grays the following week interrupted the string, but the Eagles took the remaining three games of the series. Both teams hammered the ball throughout the series, scoring a total of seventy-seven runs. A double shutout of the Stars, 3–0 and 5–0, on June 30 at Ruppert Stadium, behind the strong arms of Day and Lewis and the by now wide-awake bats of Irvin, Pearson, Doby, Davis, and Patterson, each hitting over .330, assured the Eagles of the first place flag in what was described as "the most sensational drive in the history of the Negro National League."[14]

Effa's call for patience and Mackey's managing had paid off. "Mackey is a story all by himself," Effa wrote to Art Carter. "It is really remarkable the ball he is playing, and the response he is getting from the team." Mackey, described in the press as "pauncy" at age forty-nine and old enough to be many of the players' father, caught an occasional game. His ability to work with pitchers when he did play often meant a win for Effa's team. In a game against the Baltimore Elite Giants, Eagles pitcher Max Manning kept shaking off Mackey's signs for a curveball to Felton Snow, the Giants' third baseman, in the first inning. Mackey called time, walked to the mound, and told Manning, "Don't shake me off, I know these guys." (Mackey had played with the Elites from 1936 to 1939.) Manning agreed and fed a steady stream of curveballs to Snow, who struck out four times that day. After the fourth time, Snow slumped on the bench and shook his head. Mackey yelled over to him, "[I]t's a good thing you're not coming up again 'cause we'd do it again for a fifth time."[15]

While Effa appreciated the wins and the record proceeds from the turnstiles, the contribution that the team made to entertainment for blacks in Newark pleased her the most. She told Wendell Smith, "[T]he important thing is large crowds of Negroes have somewhere to go for healthy entertainment. Up to the baseball start, you must admit there was not a lot of entertainment for the average working man."[16]

The Eagles started the second half slowly, dropping a doubleheader to the Stars on July 14, 7–5 and 3–0. Uncharacteristic wildness on Day's part allowed the Stars eleven hits in the opener, while three errors undermined Lewis in the nightcap. Following the double loss, the team departed Newark on a rented bus for a series of exhibition games against the Cleveland Buckeyes in Cleveland, Dayton, Toledo, and Erie, Pennsylvania. The ten-year-old team bus had broken down in Elizabeth, New Jersey, on June 24, forcing Effa to charter a bus for the western trip and use players' cars for subsequent games in the East.

In one game against the Buckeyes, Mackey again pulled the team off the field in protest of an umpire's decision. Wendell Smith criticized the move in his column, saying the fans saw less baseball than they paid for, there are other ways to solve such disputes, and Mackey's decision "simply substantiates Branch Rickey's charge that 'Negro leagues do not actually exist.'" Effa did not like this column. In a "Dear Friend" letter to Smith she said, "I don't know when I have ever felt much worse than I did when I read your column this week." She justified Mackey's reasoning to Smith in detail, adding, "I will never condone any unsportsmanlike conduct from the Eagles, but on the other hand I do not expect them to accept stupid decisions like this one without protesting." She asked Smith to be fair and give her point of view as much credence as he had given his own. He did by reprinting her letter in full in his next column. It was not a proud day for Effa, the Eagles, or Negro league baseball.[17]

Back in Newark, the team regained its first-half form and by late July had attained the top spot by taking three out of four from the Grays, including a 17–3 thumping in Wilmington, Delaware, on Friday night, July 26. Four Eagles—Irvin, Doby, Davis, and Day—were hitting over .340. Lewis, Manning, and Day had won twenty-three games while losing only six between them. As expected, they rolled on to clinch the second-half pennant and the win NNL championship behind Irvin's league-leading .389 average.[18]

They would face the Kansas City Monarchs in the World Series. Paced by Hall of Fame pitchers Hilton Smith, who had swung the bat at a .449 clip; Satchel Paige; first baseman John (later to be better known as Buck) O'Neil, hitting .353; and Willard Brown, who led the NAL in homers, the Monarchs promised to make the series competitive.

Rules for the best four-out-of-seven series had to be worked out. Tom Baird suggested that Effa start in the Newark area with three games "anywhere you want to where we can get the most money" and then move the series to Kansas City for the fourth game (plans for additional games were not made at this time). The teams could perhaps play an exhibition game or two while en route from Newark to Kansas City, and a three-man commission (one man appointed by each league and one jointly appointed) should be formed to settle any disputes that might arise.

In the same letter, Baird said he was meeting with Cleveland Indians pitcher Bob Feller who was planning a coast-to-coast barnstorming tour between a team of major leaguers, the Bob Feller All-Stars, and a like group of Negro leaguers, the Satchel Paige All-Stars. Baird said he would soon let Effa know which of the Eagles he'd like for the Paige All-Stars. J. B. Martin weighed in with a statement that he opposed playing the World Series games anywhere but in Newark and Kansas City. Wilson did not comment.[19]

Effa agreed to Baird's proposals, save for the en route exhibition games, lest they cheapen the series. The two, for unknown reasons, scheduled a fifth game if needed for Chicago's Comiskey Park. Dates were set, hotel arrangements made, and publicity distributed throughout Newark and Kansas City. Effa chose Sam Lacy and Baird chose Fay Young as two of the commissioners. Martin said if any disputes arose, he, and not any commissioners, would resolve them. Martin claimed to have Wilson's support. Fortunately, no disputes arose. Baird agreed with Effa's suggestion that box seats be made available to the wives and girl-friends of the players. Effa visited Joe Louis in Pompton Lakes, New Jersey, where he was training for his title defense against Tami Mauriello, to ask Louis to throw out the first ball at the second game, scheduled for September 19 at Ruppert Stadium, the night after the Louis-Mauriello bout in Yankee Stadium.[20]

The series opened Tuesday night, September 17, at 8:30 p.m. before 19,423 fans at the Polo Grounds (the Newark Bears had Ruppert Stadium occupied). The Eagles took the field in their new white home team uniforms, which Effa had provided at a cost of $700. Hilton Smith held the Eagles scoreless for six innings while the Monarchs managed one run in the first inning. Defensive gems by Irvin, Doby, and Pearson kept Day, whose wildness resulted in several walks and hits, from yielding more runs. Paige relieved Smith in the bottom of the sixth and promptly struck out Irvin and Pearson, but Doby singled, stole second, and scored on Davis's single to right. Lewis had replaced Day in the fifth inning and gave up a single to Paige in the seventh. Paige took second when Doby threw wide of first and scored on Herb Souell's single to left field. There the game ended; Monarchs 2, Eagles 1.

The series moved to Ruppert Stadium on Thursday night. This time, Joe Louis, as advertised, threw out the first ball. He had had an easy bout the night before, knocking out Mauriello in the first round. Ben Holmes of Orange, New Jersey, an Eagles fan and a member of the 1888 Cuban Giants who had won a tournament that at the time represented the championship of black baseball, presented the ball to Louis—a silver baseball won by the Cubans for their championship. Ten thousand fans saw Louis mark the beginning of game two with a toss of the ball. Trailing 4–1 in the bottom of the seventh inning, the Eagles unloaded for six runs against Monarchs starter Ford Smith and Paige, who relieved Smith following Doby's four-hundred-foot, two-run shot over the fence in right. Four singles off Paige and two Monarch errors accounted for the remaining runs. Doby came away from the game $50 richer. Mayor Murphy had offered $25 dollars to the first Eagle to score a run, which Doby did in the third on Irvin's double, and a like amount for the first Eagle to homer.

Tied at a game apiece, the series moved to the Monarchs' home field, Blues Stadium at 22nd Street and Brooklyn Avenue in Kansas City, for game three on September 23. There the Kansas City nine feasted on Newark pitchers Hooker and Bill "Cotton" Williams for fifteen runs and twenty-one hits. The Eagles managed five runs. They rebounded the next evening before a smallish crowd of 3,836 paid fans. This time the Eagles dominated the offense with fourteen hits and eight runs, while Lewis went the distance and held the Monarchs to four hits and one run. Irvin's 350-foot homer over the right-field fence off Paige in the seventh completed the Eagles' scoring.

Now it came down to a two games out of three series. Chicago's Comiskey Park hosted game five the following evening, September 25. Both Manning and Hilton Smith pitched complete games, but Smith emerged the victor, 5–1. The Eagles' only run came in the eighth when Irvin singled and scored on Pearson's double to center. With the Monarchs now up three games to two, the series came back to Ruppert Stadium, where the Eagles would have to win both games to claim a world championship. Both offenses opened up during game six on Friday night, September 27, as soon as each team came to bat. Willard Brown drove in three runs for the Monarchs on his homer in the top of the first inning. The Eagles answered with four in the bottom half of the first on singles by Pearson and Ruffin, several walks, and Irvin's first of two round-trippers. Day again had trouble with his control and had to be relieved by Hooker, who, fortunately for the Eagles, did better than he had in Kansas City. He held the Monarchs to only four more runs while five more Eagles crossed the plate for a 9–7 win.

Now it was winner take all. Mackey gave the ball to Rufus Lewis for Sunday's final game before a slim crowd of 7,200. The twenty-eight-year-old rookie held the Monarchs scoreless until the sixth inning, when Buck O'Neil slammed a 350-foot homer over the left-field wall to tie the game at one all. Irvin had singled Patterson home for the Eagles' first tally in the first inning. Two more Eagles scored in the sixth inning when Johnny Davis doubled home Doby and Irvin, both of whom had reached base on walks from Ford Smith. The Monarchs managed one more run in the seventh. The Eagles held on to win the game and the series 3–2. Fans showed their excitement by throwing seat cushions in every direction leading the Newark Bears' management to remove the cushions at all future Eagle games in Ruppert Stadium. The only thing that marred the festivities was a fight in the stands that resulted in a fan receiving three stab wounds to the neck. Effa distributed the winners' shares to the Eagles players. In Patterson's case she fattened his check by $25 "because," she told him, "I want the twins' mother to get them a little gift from the Eagles. I do hope they are both well. Ask their mother to send me a card and tell me how they are doing."[21]

The series could have turned out differently had Paige and Hilton Smith been available to the Monarchs for game seven, but both had left the Monarchs to join the Paige-Feller barnstorming tour as members of the Paige All-Stars. The tour opened in Pittsburgh, and by October 4 Feller's team had won three and Paige's one. The tour continued west and eventually ended in Los Angeles. Whites and blacks turned out in large numbers to "see the games between the races." The games demonstrated that spectators of both races would turn out to watch whites and blacks play on the same field and do so without any incidents on the field or in the stands, as evidenced by a peaceful crowd of 27,463 turning out for a game at Yankee Stadium on October 6, 1946, to see Paige's All-Stars beat Feller's 4–0.

Both teams had players of exceptional talent. Feller's team had four future Hall of Fame players—himself, Bob Lemon, Stan Musial, and Phil Rizzuto—as well as Mickey Vernon (that year's American League batting champion with a .353 average), Johnny Sain (of "Spahn and Sain, then pray for rain" fame), Rollie Hemsley, Frank Hayes, Charlie Keller, Sam Chapman, Spud Chandler, Jeff Heath, Jim Hegan, Johnny Berardino, Ken Keltner, and Dutch Leonard, among others. Satchel Paige's team had two future Hall of Famers—himself and Hilton Smith—plus Buck O'Neil, who signed on after game seven of the Eagles-Monarchs series; Quincy Trouppe; Howard Easterling; Gene Benson; Chico Renfro; Sam Hairston; Max Manning, also a post–game seven addition; and Neck Stanley, among others.[22]

Jackie Robinson played in the first three games but wanted more money and left to form his own team. Monte Irvin, Roy Campanella, and Larry Doby joined Robinson's team. One can only imagine how Paige's team would have been improved had the four future Hall of Famers played for him.[23]

The tour did make clear, however, what the Dodgers-Eagles games at the end of 1945 had failed to: that whites had no monopoly on baseball talent. Feller said about the tour, "We played on equal terms. They didn't train like we did, but they were no better and no worse than the best major leaguers."[24]

With the championship had also come another year of profits for Abe and Effa, allowing them to be more generous with their players. They gave each player a ring with an intricately designed Eagle on the top and an inset solitary diamond of about .45 carats. "Negro World Champs 1946" was printed in raised letters on one panel, and the player's position and number on the other panel. For $15,000 they replaced the bus that Irvin had complained about and that had recently broken down with a new, air-conditioned Stratoliner that sported "Newark Eagles Baseball Club" in large letters along each side and "Negro World Champions" along the top of each side, and that had room for twenty-three passengers.[25]

The bus took the Eagles on a post-series barnstorming tour through the Jim Crow South. A truck with several farmers passed the bus on a Mississippi highway. "Golly, look at the jigaboos," yelled one farmer. "Your mother didn't think so last night," Pearson fired back through an open window. "We almost killed him," said Irvin. Mackey told Pearson to let the whites say anything they wanted. To make amends, Mackey shouted to the farmers, as the bus passed their truck, "Okay, anything you say." Mackey, Irvin, and others wanted to keep the farmers from calling ahead to alert the state troopers or the Klu Klux Klan to Pearson's remark.[26]

O

Jim Crow still resided in New Jersey as well as in Mississippi. The Palisades Amusement Park, eighteen miles north of Newark, banned Negroes in defiance of the state's civil rights statute, which, as noted earlier, had few teeth but was in the process of getting more. Whites could buy tickets to the park's swimming pool. Ticket sellers told blacks they had to buy a membership card, before purchasing swimming tickets, at the administration building. There officials told several black women who sought to buy a card that they were not aware of the need to purchase one.

Signs of progress, however, could be seen elsewhere. The City Hospital hired its first black doctor in mid-January, Dr. E. Mae McCarroll, a graduate of Fisk University, the Woman's Medical College in Philadelphia, and Columbia University. Newark's African American boys in search of a summer camping experience could now attend the YMCA's Camp Wawayanda, an integrated camp located forty miles west of Newark in Andover, New Jersey. They had previously been limited to the all-black Camp Osceola outside of Trenton.[27]

Cracks of light kept appearing in the veil of segregation both on and off the field as 1946 drew to a close. The brightest burst of light in baseball had occurred in the International League on April 18 when the Montreal Royals with Jackie Robinson on board took the field against the Jersey City Giants at the Giants' Roosevelt Stadium. Robinson's appearance was the first for a black player in organized baseball since the color bar had been established. Typical of the accolades Robinson received was a telegram sent two days after the game from James Malloy, director of the National Maritime Union. The telegram read, "Every time you sock the old apple it is a blow against Jim Crow and all its Fascist manifestations. Remember, we seamen are behind you."[28]

The cracks would become larger and more numerous in 1947 and would bring with them far-reaching changes for baseball, both black and white, and for the wider community in New Jersey and in Newark.

# CHAPTER TWELVE

## *Striving for Respectability*

"Negro league baseballdom was rocked on its heels this week," sportswriter Dan Burley said, referring to the NNL owners' ouster of Wilson as president on January 5, 1947, at their winter meeting at Harlem's Theresa Hotel. Four of the six NNL ownership groups—Abe and Effa, Grays' owners Rufus Jackson and Mrs. Ethel Posey, the Cubans' Alex Pompez, and the Black Yankees' James Semler— voted for Effa's handpicked candidate, Rev. John H. Johnson, with whom she had worked in Harlem during the Citizens' League for Fair Play boycotts of white merchants along 125th Street. Only the Stars' Ed Bolden and Eddie Gottlieb voted with Wilson. Effa had finally gotten her way, but without A. B. Chandler's suggestion that the Negro leagues would appear more respectable if a team owner was not also league president, Wilson may well have remained in office.

Forty-year-old Johnson had no previous experience with professional baseball other than his two-year chairmanship of New York Mayor Fiorello LaGuardia's Mayor's Committee on Baseball and periodic visits to Ruppert Stadium as Effa's guest. Johnson acknowledged as much. He said he "did not feel the need for counsel from the club owners," and his objectives included drawing up a new constitution and getting recognition from Major League Baseball.[1]

He wasted little time. Six weeks later, at a meeting at the Appomattox Club in Chicago's Grand Hotel, the NNL owners adopted a Johnson-drawn constitution, patterned after that of the International League. Johnson's document included more protective measures for players, umpires, and owners than did the league's existing constitution; it also restricted World Series play to the cities of the competing teams and reaffirmed the five-year ban on players who jumped to Mexico. This time it looked as if the owners would enforce one of their bans. They denied "Double Duty" Radcliffe the right to play for any Negro league team as punishment for his having left the Grays for Mexico five days before the 1946 season ended.

In another move toward respectability, New York Yankees president Larry MacPhail agreed to Effa and Semler's request that Semler, and not Gottlieb, book Negro league games at Yankee Stadium. Understandably, Effa left the meeting with MacPhail smiling. Conceivably, she made a convincing pitch to MacPhail about the benefits to Negro pride of a Negro taking charge of arranging the games. Black fans, she may have also argued, would now be sure that more of their money was going to other blacks, which would entice more to attend, thereby enlarging MacPhail's take from each game.

The agreement ended years of contention over Gottlieb's practice of booking the games. His refusal to hire blacks for his professional basketball team, the Philadelphia SPHAs (South Philadelphia Hebrew Association), because "it wouldn't work out," while he participated in NNL deliberations as part owner of the Stars, irritated Effa and others. Wendell Smith, commenting on Gottlieb casting his one-half vote to retain Wilson, said, "I ask in all sincerity, is there not a stranger among us."[2]

In the midst of these changes Branch Rickey reportedly struck again. Wendell Smith, citing "reliable sources," reported on February 1 that the "Mahatma" (Rickey) had promised Monte Irvin, Larry Doby, and Stars shortstop Buzz Clarkson a thorough tryout during the Dodgers' spring training. The *Chicago Defender* reported the three had inked their names to contracts. Biz Mackey said the loss of Doby and Irvin would be a blow to the Eagles, but he wished them well. He need not have worried. The reports were false. Mel Jones, business manager of the Montreal Royals, issued a statement saying that Irvin and Doby "are in no way associated with this club."[3] The same held true for Clarkson.

Two other Eagles, however, were truly not with the club as Effa and Abe made their plans for spring training, held again in Jacksonville. The team's ace battery—Day and Ruffin—jumped to the Mexican league. Where such defections in the past had caused Effa considerable angst and stirred her to appeal to various agencies of government for return of the players or compensation, she said simply of Day's and Ruffin's departures, "[I]f Mexico took Mickey Owens from the Dodgers, [Harry] Feldman from the Giants, and Max Lanier from St. Louis, how do you expect me to keep them from taking Day and Ruffin from me?" Apparently she had resigned herself to the fact that if the majors could not stop such departures, she would not be able to either.[4]

The rest of the championship squad reported to Jacksonville. Sportswriters picked the team to again garner the top spot. Their first test in the New York area came against the Cubans on a Sunday afternoon at the Polo Grounds on April 27. The Cubans overwhelmed them 10–2, before six thousand fans, who witnessed a bench-clearing brawl as well as the game. Doby, late to second base for a tag attempt on Cubans runner Silvio Garcia, nevertheless slammed his mitt into Silvio's midsection. Silvio and Doby flailed away at each other as their teammates rushed to join in. The umpires finally separated everyone and play resumed. NNL President Johnson, wanting to signal that he would not tolerate such fights, called a hearing the next morning in which he fined both players a modest $10 each, gave them a tongue-lashing, and promised that he would deal more severely with future incidents. Fortunately for the Eagles' won-lost ledger, the game was an exhibition game.[5]

Opening day, May 11, was another story. President Johnson presented watches at home plate to Monte Irvin, for winning the batting title the previous year, and to Max Manning, for being the league's best pitcher with an 11–1 record. The Eagles treated the crowd of twelve thousand to a doubleheader win over the Stars 10–2 and 4–0. Manning limited the Stars to five hits in game one, while Pearson and Doby contributed a homer each. Lewis gave up but three hits in game two while assisting his own cause with a 425-foot, two-run homer.[6]

A week after the season started, the NNL lost another of its moguls. On May 15, Tom Wilson died of a heart attack at age sixty-one on his farm, twelve miles outside of Nashville, just four months after being voted out of office. Vernon Green, the Elite Giant's longtime business manager, became the team's new owner.[7]

As the season progressed, the Eagles lived up to their press notices by beating the Black Yankees in Hartford, Connecticut, besting the Elite Giants three in a row, and subduing the Cubans in a single game. The Grays, however, managed to clip their wings by taking both ends of a doubleheader, but the Eagles were atop the NNL at the end of May after taking a Memorial Day doubleheader from the Grays at Ebbets Field. A crop of young pitchers—Cotton Williams, Warren Peace, and Nelson Thomas—and Irvin's and Doby's sizzling bats contributed to the Eagles' successes. Irvin led the league with forty-five runs batted in. Doby hit for the circuit three times in the Eagles' win against the Black Yankees and went into Memorial Day with seven homers to his credit. By early June he led the league in hitting with a .508 average: thirty-two hits in sixty-three at bats, including twelve doubles, three triples, and ten homers. He became the consensus choice to be the next Negro leaguer to attract Rickey's attention.[8]

Doby, in fact, was no stranger to Rickey—he'd had his eye on Doby as early as 1946. Dodger scout Clyde Sukeforth, who had given Rickey the final OK on Robinson, sat in the stands for every game Doby played in the New York area that year. A Dodger scout had seen all of Doby's games in the previous three weeks. In the spring of 1947 Roy Campanella, former catcher for the Elite Giants and now with the Dodger organization, called Doby to tell him he'd soon be in Montreal, where the Dodgers' farm club, the Montreal Royals, played.

Bill Veeck, Cleveland Indians president, also knew of Doby and had by now compiled, in Doby's words, "a foot-high notebook that had everything I'd ever done in my life from the time I was born." Veeck explained the notebook, saying, "We had the transcript of his grades and we knew he had been to college for one semester. We knew what there was to know about him second or third hand. This played a part [in Veeck's upcoming decision to sign Doby]. This was going to be a rather ticklish situation." Rickey and Veeck decided that since Robinson had integrated the National League, Doby should do the same for the American League. Wendell Smith speculated that Rickey, a shrewd operator who had spent a lot of money scouting Doby, "let" Veeck have Doby so the critics of integration would have a second target. Veeck signed the twenty-three-year-old Doby to an Indians contract on July 5 at the Congress Hotel in Chicago.[9]

Doby played his last game with the Eagles, the first game of an Independence Day doubleheader against the Stars at Ruppert Stadium. At a ceremony at home plate between games his teammates gave him a toilet kit with shaving lotion, soap, a brush, and a comb. The Old Timers Athletic Association of Paterson, New Jersey (Doby's hometown), gave him $50. Accompanied by his mother, wife, and Louis Jones, Lena Horne's ex-husband, the first black major league front office employee when Veeck hired him into the Indians' organization, and the person who had done the background checks on Doby for Veeck, Doby left Ruppert Stadium for Newark's Pennsylvania Station. There the two men boarded the Admiral for the overnight trip west to join the Indians in Chicago. When the train came to a stop in Chicago at 10:45 a.m., Doby said he "felt a little funny because it was a little strange to me in terms of being alone."[10]

Veeck helped him overcome his funny feeling, at least momentarily. "I walked into his office," Doby told William Marshall, "and he got up from the desk and he walked over and he shaked my hand and he says, 'Lawrence,' he says, 'I'm Bill Veeck.' And I said, 'Nice to meet you Mr. Veeck.' So he says, 'You don't have to call me Mr. Veeck. Call me Bill.' And it stuck with me because it's an old Southern tradition, strictly from respect, that those who are your elders you say 'Mister' to. I had never said 'Mister' to anybody else and got that kind of response. I said 'Mr. Jones' and he'd say, 'Hello, son,' or 'Hello, Larry,' or whatever. And when he said that it was a strange thing. . . . But as I grew older and as I had contact with him, I recognized what he meant and what it was all about." Following the introduction, Veeck had a heart-to-heart with Doby to prepare him for slights and insults he could expect. "He told me the same thing that Mr. Rickey told Jackie," Doby said.[11]

It took only a couple of hours for the first indignities to surface, when he met his Cleveland teammates later that afternoon. Jones accompanied Doby to the Indians' locker room, where each player, in uniform, stood in front of his locker. Jones introduced Doby to Lou Boudreau, the Cleveland manager, who led Doby past the lockers while introducing him to each player. Some turned their back on him. Some responded to Doby's outstretched hand with a "limp-fish" handshake. Some made no response at all. A few, among them second baseman Joe Gordon, catcher Jim Hegan, and coach Bill McKechnie, gripped Doby's hand and welcomed him to the club.[12]

Following the introductions, Doby put on his uniform, left the locker room, and walked up the tunnel leading to the field, where he could hear the smacks of ball against leather as players were warming up. No one looked at him as he stood on the top step of the dugout. Doby later said about this moment, "I have never before or since been that lonely in my life." Then he felt a tug on his sleeve and heard a voice saying, "Hey rookie, you gonna pose in your new uniform or do you want to warm up?" It was Joe Gordon. Doby said, "he became immediately friendly with me. He talked to me about situations." Doby also cited Indian players Al Rosen and Bob Lemon as being supportive.[13]

There would be no minor league experience for Doby as there had been for Robinson. "I'm going to get one [a black player]," Veeck said, "that I think can play with Cleveland without having to go to the minors first." Veeck thought Rickey had put too much pressure on Robinson by starting him in the minors. "When I find a man I realize the spot he'll be in and will try to ease up on this sort of pressure. . . . I'll handle him just like any other rookie." Rickey did not seem displeased by the signing, saying, "[I]f Doby is a good player, and I understand that he is, the Cleveland club is showing signs that it wants to win."[14]

Nor did Veeck steal Doby. While the terms were not pleasing to Effa, they at least tempered her ire. When Veeck telephoned on July 1 to say he wanted to sign Doby, Effa asked him, "[W]ell, what do plan to give me for him, Mr. Veeck?" Veeck said $10,000. "Well, I'm not a millionaire," Effa replied, "but I am financially secure, I think, and ten thousand dollars looks like ten cents. I know very well that if he was a white boy and a free agent you'd give me a hundred thousand. But if you feel you're being fair offering me ten, I guess I'll have to take it." Veeck promised Effa an additional $5,000 if he kept Doby for thirty days.

Effa would not give her OK without clearing the deal with Abe, who thought the price was "ridiculously low." Effa told Abe, "We're in no position to bargain." She meant they had no leverage by which to force Veeck to up the ante, and, if they refused the offer, Effa knew they'd be accused by black fans and the press of depriving Doby of his shot at the majors. After some more pleading on her part, Abe consented. In talking with interviewer William Marshall about Doby's signing years later, Effa said, "So it's the whole story has been just one of those kind of things where the strong have taken advantage of the weak. And, of course, that's true of life. I learned that all through life."[15]

Veeck came through with the $15,000 even though he could have stolen Doby. Unlike Rickey, who considered the Negro leagues to be "a racket," Veeck's assessment of the leagues was less harsh: "They were at best marginal. They just scuffled." Veeck knew Rickey paid nothing for Robinson because Tom Baird could not stand in Robinson's way. Veeck also knew Effa could not stand in Doby's way, just as she could not have prevented Rickey from stealing Newcombe from her. "We could," Veeck said, "just have reached out and said 'Come on.' But we didn't want to do that and we did purchase his contract."[16]

As meager as Veeck's offer seemed to Effa, she knew Veeck was willing to pay for Negro league stars. With that in mind, she extended an offer to Veeck to "take a look at Irvin for a thousand dollars and then pay me what you think he's worth." Veeck declined the offer, saying, "Effa, I'm going to have enough trouble bringing in one black." He regretted not taking Irvin and later told Irvin, "That was the dumbest deal I never did." Irvin agreed, saying, "Well, Bill, you blew it."[17]

O

Doby's promotion and the Eagles' winning the first-half flag put the team and its business manager in a favorable light among writers and fans, many of whom gave much of the credit to Effa. She responded, as she always did, that Abe deserved more of the credit for the team's success than did she. "My husband is the real owner and boss of the Newark Eagles," she said during an interview with Wendell Smith. "He made the Newark club what it is today, not I. I work for him. . . . He knows ten times as much baseball as I do." She considered their division of labor "a magnificent partnership." This was not false modesty on her part. While she tended to day-to-day management issues, Abe made the decisions on new players, salaries, trades, and managers. He supported, and at times may have initiated, the reforms that Effa championed at the owners meetings. Her high-profile ways of doing business and her eagerness to talk candidly with the press, owners, and anyone who would listen, while Abe rarely talked for publication, made it appear to many as if she were the one calling all the shots.[18]

The Eagles missed Doby's bat throughout the rest of the season. They failed to repeat as champions in the wake of the Cubans' eleven straight wins in the last month of the second half. The Cubans got the World Series nod without having to play the Eagles in a playoff on the basis of winning the most NNL games throughout the entire season.[19]

By the end of the 1947 season every NNL team had experienced a drop-off in attendance, owing in part to the end of the war boom and in part to Robinson's appearance as a Brooklyn Dodger, and the anticipation that Newcombe, Campanella, and others would follow. Negro league teams playing in Yankee Stadium were hard-pressed to make a profit if Robinson and the Dodgers were playing across town in the Polo Grounds or in Ebbets Field. Robinson, a hero to millions, had confirmed Rickey's faith in him by earning the National League's Rookie of the Year award.

In light of these developments, Wendell Smith called on the league to develop more young players, conduct itself in a "dignified and business-like manner," cut player salaries, hire a real publicity director, and no longer "promote games in a haphazard, devil-may-care manner." "We know it is a big job," he said. "But it is a job that must be done and be done immediately." There were signs of progress in Smith's direction. Rev. Johnson's election as NNL president and his early actions signaled a new seriousness about the business of Negro league baseball. The 1947 East-West Classic in Chicago continued as a big draw by attracting 48,112 spectators, more than the forty thousand that had been predicted. The eastern version of the game a week later drew a record 38,402 fans to the Polo Grounds.[20]

O

Hopeful signs could also be seen for Newark's African American citizens. More than ever before, blacks found jobs with Newark's telephone company as switchboard operators, clerks, stenographers, installers, coin collectors, and technicians. Fourteen white girls at Upsala College, a private school in nearby East Orange, formed a new sorority, Delta Beta Delta, whose purpose became to abolish discrimination in college sororities. Voters approved the new state constitution, including the clause that banned discrimination in citizens' civil or military activities and in the public schools. The *Philadelphia Tribune* called the clause a "new emancipation clause" and applauded the work of its author, Attorney J. Oliver Randolph of Newark. Nevertheless, two days of "heated debate" on the floor of the convention were necessary before the delegates approved the clause by a fifty-one to eighteen vote.[21]

That much still needed to be done, however, was apparent as the Palisades Park Pool continued its discrimination against blacks prompting the Committee of Racial Equality (CORE—the group would later replace the term Committee with Congress) to file a $270,000 suit against the pool's owners, Rosecliff Realty Company. In another instance of discrimination, Quock Gee and Fong Min, the manager and a waiter at the Far Eastern Restaurant at 226–228 Mulberry Street, refused service to two African Americans, C. Ronald Hightower and Kenneth Worde in mid-August. J. Mercer Burrell represented the two in a suit against the café in Essex District Court.[22]

Effa, looking for civil rights volunteer activities now that the war had ended, became treasurer of Newark's NAACP chapter.[23]

O

It had been an uncertain year for the Manleys and the Eagles. The NNL, through the election of Johnson, was finally getting its house in order as Effa and sportswriters had long pleaded with it to do. On the other hand, the team had fallen short of a second championship. Falling attendance meant Abe again had to resort to his bank account to meet expenses. Veeck's purchase of Doby provided some financial relief, but it also marked the departure of another star Negro leaguer to the majors without another player of Doby's talents to replace him. Attendance at Ebbets Field, where the Eagles purposively played more games in the hope that Brooklyn's blacks would turn out, fell below expectations. Effa took the low turnouts personally. "The fans," Effa said, "deserted us to go see the boys on the white team. Deserted us like they say rats desert a sinking ship." She told Abe the time had come to get out of baseball, but Abe convinced her to try one more year.[24]

In their first move of the 1948 season, they gave Mackey his unconditional release in January. The team's failure to win the second-half flag coupled with Mackey's age (he was fifty-one) and his fondness for drinking late into the night at the Grand Hotel sealed his fate. Without mentioning Mackey by name, Effa said, "The game requires a real disciplinarian who is able to get the most out of his players. Their conduct on and off the field must be beyond reproach." The man deemed to possess those qualities, William Bell, joined the team as its manager just prior to departure to Jacksonville for spring training. Bell had managed and pitched for the Manleys in Brooklyn and Newark in 1935 and 1936, and came with a reputation for handling pitchers well and being a gentleman. The team that Bell inherited had, like most Eagles teams, a core of returning veterans, in this case Irvin, whose injuries kept him out of action for the first two months of the season; Davis; Harvey; Manning; Hooker; and Lewis. Others in camp included a few players returning for their second or third year and several promising rookies.[25]

The arrival of one rookie shortstop—Willie C. "Curly" Williams, an eighteen-year-old working as a soda jerk in his hometown of Orangeburg, South Carolina, and playing for the semipro Orangeburg Tigers when Abe signed him to a contract in the winter of 1947—illustrated Abe and Effa's division of labor. Acting on the recommendation of former Eagle Jimmy Hill, on whose Lakeland, Florida, semipro team Williams occasionally played, Abe pulled up front of the store where Williams worked. "Hey Curly," somebody in the store yelled, "there are some people out there looking for you." On seeing the long, black, chauffer-driven Lincoln Continental with three men inside, Williams said he was "scared. It could have been the FBI." Fear turned to joy when Abe offered him a contract for $250 a month—big money compared to the $10 to $15 a week plus tips Williams made at the soda fountain. When the team reached Newark, Effa found Williams a room at the corner of Market and Howard Streets and stopped by occasionally to see how he was faring. She wrote him a check at her apartment each month and took the occasion to advise him. "She gave advice all the time," Williams said. The advice included tips on how to manage his money, avoid the wrong crowd, travel in pairs when going out, and conduct himself as a gentleman. "Abe," Williams said, "didn't have that much to say about anything." Williams adored them both. "They were," he said, "just great people. Playing for the Eagles was the start of my life."[26]

As the season opened Day and Ruffin remained in Mexico. Patterson decided to stay in Texas. The *New York Amsterdam News* dubbed the Eagles the "dark horse" in the race for the pennant. They spoiled the Elite Giants' home opener, 2–1 at Bugle Field in Baltimore on May 2, defeating the Giants' ace pitcher, Joe Black. The Eagles again beat the Giants by the identical score two nights later under the lights at Bugle Field. Returning to Ruppert Stadium for opening day, they stumbled in a 5–4 loss to the Grays on Sunday afternoon, May 9. The combination of two Buck Leonard circuit clouts and brilliant pitching by Tom Parker, a twenty-year veteran, proved too much to overcome. Twelve thousand spectators, more than had attended any other NNL game, turned out for the festivities.

Rainstorms postponed a doubleheader against the Cubans at the Polo Grounds the following Sunday and a midweek game against the Elite Giants in Chester, Pennsylvania. After the rains let up the Eagles played themselves into first place by Memorial Day. By mid-June Manning led all league pitchers with a 4–0 record, and in a game against the Black Yankees he helped his own cause with a single, double, and two homers. Effa still organized an occasional benefit game, including one on July 1 against the Grays for the benefit of Community Hospital. The hospital did better than the Eagles, who dropped the game, 10–2. Bell welcomed Irvin back to the lineup but saw his team fade to a disappointing third-place finish for the first half.[27]

As the Eagles fell from first to third place, Jackie Robinson dropped a bomb on the Negro leagues with his article in the June 1948 issue of *Ebony* magazine, "What's Wrong with the Negro Leagues." Players were, he said, allowed to drink whenever they pleased, some stayed up all night, and many owners had questionable business connections. He also aired his hard feelings about low pay, long rides in uncomfortable buses, unprofessional umpiring, NAL president Martin also owning a team, and the lack of coaching from older players or management. All of what he said had been said before, even by Robinson, so his article did not come as news.

Robinson had derided the Negro leagues the previous October during an appearance at the Howard Theater in Washington, D.C. The Howard, located at 7th and T Streets NW, just a block from Griffith Stadium, was the center of D.C.'s jazz scene from 1910 to the late 1960s. Robinson had said then that the bus rides were too long, food and accommodations were poor, and he was "disgusted" during his one year in the Negro leagues. Had Rickey not signed him, he said he would have quit the Monarchs to work with underprivileged boys.[28]

If his *Ebony* article did not come as news, it did come as traitorous—a case of a man biting the hand that gave him his start. His motive for writing the article remains a mystery. Reactions came immediately from practically every black sportswriter and, of course, from Effa. "Frankly," she said, "no greater outrage could have been perpetrated. No greater invasion of the good sense of the American people could have been attempted. No greater ingratitude was ever displayed. I charge Jackie Robinson with being ungrateful and more likely stupid. How could a child nurtured by its mother turn on her within a year after he leaves her modest home for glamour, success, and good fortune."[29]

Robinson's article; declining attendance; the owners' decision to cap the amount a team could devote to player salaries at $6,000 a month, down $2,000 from a year before; sports editors who covered Robinson's spring training but not the Negro leagues' World Series (unless the teams paid their expenses); and other of what Effa called "unpleasant facts" were taking their toll on her. In her frustration she blamed blacks, saying, "Negroes have to develop some race consciousness and stop ramming themselves down white peoples' throats." She felt she alone was the only one speaking in support of the Negro leagues. "I am compelled to speak out," she said in an interview with the *Chicago Defender*'s Frank Young, while fighting to hold back tears. "Nobody in Negro baseball has the prudence or the courage to say these things. Not that they are cowards by any means but fate put me in this spot. Therefore I must speak the truth." She would continue to speak the truth as she saw it, including in a speech to the Optimist Club at Bambergers, Newark's largest department store, in which she flailed Rickey for his "unfair handling" of players and praised Veeck for his treatment of Doby.[30]

As the second half dragged on, Effa gave more thought to getting out of baseball. She invited local reporters to her home at 71 Crawford Street on Thursday, September 16 to air her views. "Yes," she told the assembled scribes, she was "seriously considering" disbanding the team. Attendance this year had been one-fourth of the attendance at Ruppert in 1946. Negro fans, whom she said were "acting like damn fools," deserted the team to follow the blacks now in the majors. She excoriated the black press for not "educating" the fans about the Negro leagues' contributions to advancing the fortunes of blacks. Both fans and the black press, she said, "express the inferiority complex of Negroes." She did not believe integration of the majors would continue, because "the Negro youngsters in the minors are most unhappy" and several big league owners, whom she did not name, do not want black players to "become the targets for adulation by white women."[31]

Later she said Larry MacPhail had been the one who said in essence, "[I]f we signed a Negro player and he began to hit home runs, white women would become attracted to him." MacPhail had long opposed blacks in the majors. Six years earlier, when he was president of the Brooklyn Dodgers, MacPhail had said there was no demand for Negro players, and even if there were a demand, few, if any, of the current players in the Negro leagues could stick with a major league team. MacPhail added there was no reason to raid the teams thereby ruining their games, and finally, "most leading Negroes," he said, "were opposed to breaking down the custom."

MacPhail's statements, all without merit save the consequences that would follow "raiding" Negro league clubs, were nonetheless representative of the rationalizations put forth by many whites in organized baseball that opposed integration.[32]

Caught between what she saw as the disloyalty of many African Americans and the unyielding resistance of the white power structure, Effa's frustration contributed to more barbs coming her way. Upon hearing her comments, the *Kansas City Call*, a black weekly, reprimanded her, saying, "The day of loyalty to Jim Crow anything is fast passing away. Sister, haven't you heard the news, democracy is coming fast." A. J. Jones, owner of an interracial barber college in Atlantic City and president of the Equal Rights League, a baseball league for boys both black and white, upon hearing that Effa had also said that blacks in majors have set the race back fifty years, said she should retract her words before it damages "the morale of your players." Her comments were also wearing thin on Wendell Smith. When he heard her chastise Rickey yet again for not respecting Robinson's contract with the Monarchs, he responded, "[S]he knows Kansas City never had Robinson signed to a legitimate contract. She knows that, boys and girls."[33]

Not all of the black press had negative things to say about Effa. In November 1948 the *New Jersey Herald Tribune* honored Effa and forty-one other New Jersey citizens with induction into its Hall of Fame on November 7 at its twenty-first anniversary jubilee. Others inducted included entertainers Count Basie, Sara Vaughan, and Paul Robeson; attorneys and civil rights activists J. Mercer Burrell and Oliver Randolph; Mrs. Charles Tyler, widow of the slain former owner of the Newark Dodgers; Larry Doby; and Mrs. Grace B. Fenderson, teacher and NAACP executive.[34]

Two months after her press conference, consideration turned to certitude. This time, Abe agreed. In early November the husband and wife duo announced they were disbanding the team. "We're not quitters," she explained. "It's just impossible for us to continue. Baseball has become a rich man's hobby, and we're not rich." Two other teams, the Homestead Grays and the New York Black Yankees, made similar announcements. The remaining NNL teams joined the NAL bringing to an end the Negro National League.[35]

Later in the month Abe and Effa sold the Eagles to Dr. W. H. Young, a Memphis dentist, and Hugh Cherry of Blytheville, Arkansas, for a reported $15,000. That was a fraction of the $100,000 often reported as the sum Abe had invested in the team. Young, a star third baseman on the diamond and left halfback on the gridiron at Bishop College in Marshall, Texas, opened a dental practice in Blytheville, Arkansas, after graduating from the dentistry program at the University of West Tennessee in 1921. In Blytheville he became a business partner of Hugh Cherry. In 1944 Young moved to Memphis, where he met fellow dentist and baseball enthusiast Dr. B. B. Martin, brother of longtime Memphis Red Sox official J. B. Martin. The two were often seen together at social events such as Memphis's Cotton Makers' Jubilee, touted by the *Chicago Defender* as "Dixie's greatest Negro celebration." Young often made announcements concerning Eagles personnel moves from B. B. Martin's office.[36]

With the team, which the new owners moved to Houston, Texas, went the new bus; all the equipment; players' contracts, which now included a reserve clause; and an agreement that if a major league team bought one of the Eagles' contracts, the Manleys and the new owners would share in the proceeds.[37]

Young and Cherry would soon have reason to be thankful the last provision was part of the sale. While Effa and Abe were in Chicago negotiating the sale, Rickey tried to steal another Eagle, Monte Irvin, who was playing winter ball with the Almendares club in Cuba, from them. Irvin agreed to a contract with a Dodger farm club, the St. Paul Saints in the American Association. After reading an account of Irvin's signing the day she returned to Newark in late November, Effa wrote Irvin asking if he had signed with Rickey. He wrote back saying he had and felt he was within his rights to do so. Effa decided to fight this time. While realizing that many would turn on her for blocking Irvin's chances to make the majors if she opposed Rickey, her business sense and her pride told her she could not let Irvin go for nothing, as she had done in Newcombe's case. She again hired Jerry Kessler, this time to represent her in a suit against Rickey. Upon hearing that Effa was suing him, Rickey investigated the matter and decided that Irvin held a valid contract with the Eagles, albeit now the NAL Houston Eagles, and said, "We don't want any player illegally." He withdrew his offer.[38]

The predictable press reaction followed. Wendell Smith charged Effa, whom he called "the publicity-mad 'Queen of Newark,'" with hypocrisy, fighting for human rights while at the same time denying Irvin his. Her position, Smith said, "provided us with the biggest laugh we've enjoyed since the funeral of the late Senator Bilbo of Mississippi." (Theodore Bilbo, a white supremacist, had died the previous August.) Smith ended his column, "Human rights? What about Monty Irvin's right to make a living as a ball player, Mrs. Manley?" A disappointed Irvin called Effa's decision "spiteful" and said she had acted "selfishly with only her own monetary interests at heart."[39]

Effa, however, did not want to keep Irvin out of the majors. She asked Kessler to contact the New York Yankees, who, as noted previously, were not ready for a black player, on Irvin's behalf and then Horace Stoneham, president of the New York Giants, who were ready. Stoneham had signed Ford Smith from the Monarchs. Stoneham paid the Manleys $5,000. Irvin suggested to Effa, "I've always been underpaid so instead of giving Kessler half the money, why don't we split it?" Effa said no. She gave Kessler half of the money, as had been their agreement, sent $1,250 to Young and Cherry and, with the remaining $1,250, she bought herself a mink stole.[40]

By signing Irvin and Smith, the Giants had lowered the major league color bar another notch. Other sports-related color bars had also fallen—one with the help of Larry Doby and one assisted by the Eagles. In January 1948 Doby did for the American Basketball League what Robinson had done for baseball when he signed a contract to play for the Paterson (New Jersey) Crescents, previously an all-white team in an all-white league. The Eagles and the Black Yankees stayed at a white-owned hotel in Rochester, New York, that previously barred blacks as guests, while the teams were in town for a series of games during the last week in May 1948.[41]

O

Integration continued apace in both baseball and in Newark and its surrounding areas. As more opportunities opened up for blacks in previously all-white institutions and organizations, the questions and concerns about the impact of integration on previously all-black enterprises, including baseball, continued.

# CHAPTER THIRTEEN

## *Effa's Life After the Eagles*

Relieved of running the Eagles, Effa nevertheless stayed mad, venting her anger toward those she held responsible for the Eagles' demise and the decline of the Negro leagues—the press, the black fans, and most of all, Branch Rickey, whom she demonized in a January 2, 1949, three-page, single-spaced, typed letter to one of the nation's foremost civil rights leaders, Mary McLeod Bethune, the founder and president of the National Council of Negro Women. In her letter, which began "Dear Lovely Lady," Effa impugned Rickey's motives in signing Negro league players. Rickey, Effa said, "was not sincere" and "wanted to wreck Negro Baseball and get rid of Negro's once and for all where White Baseball is concerned." To support her contention she told Bethune several falsehoods. Effa wrote that Rickey had purposefully selected Negro leaguers whom he felt would have a hard time making the majors—Jackie Robinson and Don Newcombe—and that Rickey had returned pitcher Johnny Wright to the Homestead Grays "because he looked too good." It was known at the time that Rickey carefully researched every black player he signed and that Wright could not cope with the pressure. Effa said Rickey signed Campanella only to develop Campanella so he could sell him to another team at a handsome profit. (This Rickey did not do. Campanella played with the Dodgers his entire ten-year major league career.) Remembering that Bethune had told Effa at a previous meeting that she knew Robert Hannegan, a St. Louis, Missouri politician, who, with corporate lawyer Fred Saigh, had purchased the St. Louis Cardinals in 1948, Effa asked Bethune to arrange a meeting with Hannegan and Saigh in the hopes that "a meeting of the minds could be arranged." She gave

Bethune her private phone number, Market 3-0555, and closed saying, "[I]f I do not hear from you, I will give up, and realize I am trying to fight a losing battle." A response from Bethune could not be found, but Effa was never one to give up.[1]

A chance encounter several months later with George Lyle, sportswriter for the *Norfolk Journal and Guide*, on the beaches of Atlantic City, where both were vacationing, gave her yet another chance to criticize the print media for articles that were critical of Negro league baseball. Lyle, writing about the encounter, said that while she made a few good points, only the incorporation of intact teams into organized baseball's minor leagues could salvage the black teams. The idea had surfaced before.

Effa herself had pursued it with George Trautman, president of the American Association, one of the better minor league systems, during a self-appointed trip to Washington, D.C., in August 1945. Trautman expressed no interest in the idea.

She continued to vent her feelings at formal occasions, such as in the speech she gave to the National Negro Publishers Association in Washington, D.C., in mid-June 1949—a speech that grated on Sam Lacy. He devoted his June 25 column to her, saying, "[T]he applause [for her departure from baseball] was premature, baseball still has Effa Manley. . . . The bleating from Crawford Street continues." Lacy took the occasion to take Effa and the other moguls to task for not acting on his and other writers' advice to develop younger players, scout college games, and seek ways to collaborate with organized baseball. He added, "[W]hat it [Negro league baseball] hasn't done in the past to commit suicide, it most certainly is doing now."[2]

Lacy had not always been so peeved at Effa. In an undated "Dear Friend" letter to Effa, probably written in the mid-1940s, when he had just joined the *Baltimore Afro-American*, he asked her for a loan of $150 to pay for two bad checks he'd written to cover his hotel expenses for a vacation at New York City's Hotel McAlpin. He explained he had spent more than he should have, and "I was silly enough to hope that a good day at the races would put me in the clear." He asked her to keep his request confidential because "[i]t may mean my job." He included a phone number where she could reach him at the *Afro*. It's not known how she responded, but the relationship between the two had cooled in the interim.[3]

Frank Young joined Lacy in defending the press against Effa's broadsides, saying, "Since some of our newspapers have been very fair to Negro baseball, we regret the blast at us as a unit. Those which haven't been fair should be named," something Effa never did in public.[4]

Wendell Smith treated her more kindly. He noted that the tears she used at meetings to try to get her way, hardly ever successfully, "brought an atmosphere of moisture, whereas before her arrival . . . it was always as dry as an African desert." He credited her with always making good copy, even though "she tried to tell us how and what to write." Smith recognized that Effa "was trying to fight off the inevitable and cling to the great days. But," he continued, "the old days have gone. So has gracious, charming, eccentric Effa Manley. The boys in the press box are gonna' miss her—tears and all."[5]

The players, at least as represented by Monte Irvin, had feelings about the Negro leagues' demise that differed from Effa's. When asked if he was ever concerned about the Negro leagues' decline, he said, "We [the players] weren't that much concerned. It was progress. It's gonna happen sooner or later anyhow. Now that we have the opportunity we might as well take it and make the most of it. We had no compunction about breaking up the league at all."[6]

Effa gradually resigned herself to the inevitable and discontinued her attacks but managed, nevertheless, to generate publicity for herself in areas other than baseball. She appeared as the subject of a feature article in *Ebony* on "How to Stay Young After 40," in which the author noted "she admits to being 50 but looks nowhere near that age."[7]

She also kept up her relationships with former players. George Crowe, a first baseman for the New York Black Yankees in 1948, credited Effa with recommending him to Harry Jenkins, head of the Boston Braves farm system, with launching his career in organized baseball. Crowe played in the minors for several years before beginning a nine-year stint in the National League. She and Abe agreed to be godparents to Larry and Helyn Doby's first child, Larry Doby Jr. In the same spirit in which she had helped Day, Pearson, and Manning during the war years to secure jobs, she helped Irvin with a loan so that he could put a down payment on a house. Pearson called Effa "a beautiful, beautiful person in all ways" after she paved his way with contacts and a loan to purchase a tavern in Newark.[8]

The next several years brought more signals that the heyday of the Negro leagues had vanished. Ed Bolden died on September 17, 1950, at Fitzgerald Mercy Hospital in Darby, Pennsylvania, where he'd been brought the day before after suffering a stroke. Bolden had been a force in Negro league baseball in the Darby-

Philadelphia area since 1913. The New York Yankees, after selling the Newark Bears to the Chicago Cubs (who moved the franchise to Springfield, Massachusetts), gave up hope of organized baseball returning to Newark and decided to demolish Ruppert Stadium in October 1952. The Associated Press account said the stadium's history is "a story of some of the biggest names ever to grace a scorecard—Red Rolfe, Tommy Henrich, Joe Gordon, and Ed Walsh"—all of whom played for the Newark Bears and went on to the majors. Not a word appeared about Monte Irvin, Larry Doby, Mule Suttles, Willie Wells, Don Newcombe, Ray Dandridge, Dick Seay, or Terris McDuffie. The article must have been difficult reading for Effa. It had taken only four years for the Eagles to fade into invisibility, at least in the white press.

Newark's Board of Education bought Ruppert Stadium for $275,000 before it was torn down, and used it for a school sports center until 1961, when the board passed the site on to the City Housing Authority. Hanson & Hanson, developers of industrial properties, bought the stadium from the city in 1968 for $180,000. The developers built a 170,000 square foot facility on the site and leased it to Vita Foods for its use in packing and shipping cherries and olives. Glenn Fowler, the *New York Times* reporter, in recounting the stadium's past, mentioned the Bears and several players who attained fame with the Yankees, but did not say a word about the Eagles. Neither did Ester Blaustein in a nostalgic look-back piece on Newark in 1979. Of Ruppert Stadium, she said it was a place "where we joyfully flocked on Opening Day so that we could watch the old Newark Bears."[9]

Abe Manley died on December 9, 1952, at Effa's mother's home at 450 Mt. Pleasant Avenue in Germantown, Pennsylvania, a Philadelphia suburb. Two days before, Effa's stepsister Ruth, a registered nurse and Effa's mother and stepfather, had stopped by to see him at the Manleys' home following his operation for prostate problems. Ruth's care that day brought Abe to tears. Effa said Ruth "was a wonderful nurse who actually took her nursing seriously." During the visit, they decided to move him to her parents' home, where his heart gave out.

Effa speculated the demise of the Negro leagues might have hastened his death. "The breakdown of baseball irritated him. Whether that affected his physical being, I don't know, but he didn't live much longer." Father Howard Laughton conducted funeral services for the Quaker-raised Abe at a high mass in Saint Madeline-Sophie Catholic Church in Germantown. Monte Irvin and Larry Doby acted as honorary pallbearers. Effa's stepbrothers and sisters and their families attended the services, as did sixteen of Abe's nieces and nephews, many of whom had traveled from Hertford, North Carolina. Also in attendance were Percy Simon and two other Norfolk friends, Elijah Collins and George Harmon, plus another two hundred people. His burial took place in Newark's Fairmount Cemetery in a plot he and Effa had bought for themselves in 1949.

Effa's behavior at the burial offended many of Abe's friends and family. She made little effort to talk with them, talked to a man none of them knew as Abe's casket was lowered into the ground, and told the group at the end of the ceremony, "There's no reason for you to hang around. Abe left everything to me"—a brusque announcement of disappointing news for many Abe had promised would be taken care of after he died.[10]

Effa spent 1953 in Newark staying active with the Newark Chapter of the NAACP as a board member, joining ranks with several colleagues from her baseball days, including J. Mercer Burrell, James Curtis, and Jerry Kessler. She had relinquished her treasurer position at the end of 1949.

O

During her years with the Newark NAACP chapter she saw Irvin Rosenthal, his brother Jack, and another park official, Mrs. Anna Halpren, agree to implement a policy of nondiscrimination for the 1949 season at the Palisades Amusement Park. After five weeks of accepting all comers, Irvin Rosenthal told the Division Against Discrimination of the New Jersey Department of Education that he was completely satisfied with the new policy. His agreement represented a victory for CORE, which had been struggling for three years to eliminate discrimination at the park.

Their success was fleeting. By 1952 CORE had documented that Rosenthal had reneged on his promise and the committee activated the $270,000 damages suit, which had lain dormant for nearly three years. Effa also saw the Newark Housing Authority unanimously pass a resolution banning discrimination in the city's public housing projects. Challenges lay ahead in the implementation of the policy, but the legal precedent had at least been established.[11]

O

In Washington, D.C., on Christmas Day, 1953, Effa married New York City musician Henry Moton Clinton, onetime host at Atlantic City's Paradise Club. New York socialite and former Sugar Hill neighbor Elsie LaMoine was Effa's maid of honor. Judge Armond W. Scott officiated. FDR had appointed Scott as the third

African American to become a D.C. municipal court judge. Scott had been a fan of the Washington Homestead Grays and raised the flag in centerfield during the Grays' opening day ceremonies to start the 1943 season in Griffith Stadium. Columnist Lulu Jones Garrett of the *Baltimore Afro-American* described the newlyweds' relationship as "the re-flowering of a romance that began twenty-seven years ago that was interrupted by her marriage to the late baseball fancier."[12]

Twenty-seven years proved too long for the reflowering to take root; the marriage ended in August 1954. Effa left the marriage a poorer woman than she entered it because Clinton had made off with a sizeable chunk of her money. She took up residence at 333 West Queen Lane in Germantown to be near her parents. There she indulged her love for music and her business interest by opening a record shop across the street at 308. She stayed active in civic affairs as a member of several women's organizations in the Philadelphia area, including the Community Council for the Blind, the Junior Service League, the Concert Series Association, and Friends of Heritage House. A newspaper article describing the Heritage House's 1954 Christmas meeting, "where an array of games were leisurely enjoyed amid gay holiday chatter," described Effa as one of the "popular matrons who are members." Because many girls came to the Wissahickon Boys Club in nearby Wissahickon, New Jersey, to watch boys box and play basketball, Effa agreed to serve as an adviser to girls who wanted to form their own basketball league.[13]

Effa maintained her interest in male companionship, as can be seen in a poem called "Most Every Woman's Rhyme." She saved the poem in her scrapbook on the same page where she had reproduced a copy of a certificate, dated December 25, 1954, that made her an Honorary Citizen in Father Flanagan's Boys' Home in Omaha, Nebraska. She did not note the author of the poem, but she had put her feelings into verse at least once before and may have done so again here. The poem starts with the introduction:

> *This is most every woman's rhyme*
> *And will be 'till the end of time.*

And reads:

> *I'm looking for a man who weaves Black Magic*
> *That's what most every woman really seeks*

*He doesn't have to look so hot, just as long*

*as he has got*

*The charm to make me give my heart complete*

*The thing in life that really is most precious*

*Is the one you love, and know's your very own*

*Life is really mighty bare, there's just nothing*

*really there*

*Unless that man is living in a home with you*

*Unless the guy is truly all your own-true blue.*

She kept up her interest in Negro league baseball as well. In October 1956 Effa visited old friends Reverend John and Billie Harden, who, who in many ways, were much like herself and Abe. John had owned the Atlanta Black Crackers of the NAL and the Negro Southern League until the team folded in 1952. Abe made a point of playing the Crackers each spring that the Eagles journeyed north from spring training in Florida. John, like Abe, enjoyed traveling with the team more than tending to the business side, which was capably taken over by Billie, who sported the title of vice president, treasurer, and general manager of the Atlanta Black Cracker Baseball Corporation. Like Effa, whom the press often referred to as "Queen of the Negro Leagues," Billie was known among southern black sportswriters as "Queen of the Big Time Baseball Executives in Dixie." Unlike Effa, however, Billie shied away from generating headlines, choosing instead to operate effectively but quietly behind the scenes.

Eight years had passed since Abe sold the Eagles when Effa arrived at the Hardens' residence at 848 Hunter Street SW. She still lamented the loss of the Eagles but a wistful tone had replaced her earlier stridency. During her visit she regaled the press with accounts of the glory years of the Eagles before Robinson broke the color line. When talk turned to the demise of the Negro leagues, she said people were making a "tragic mistake by so quickly forgetting the Negro leagues and their long history of professionalized and entertaining baseball." She made the telling observation that only players went on to organized baseball. Those with managerial experience, she noted, were "shunted aside." Effa, no doubt, would have liked a shot at a general manager's position in organized baseball. When the baseball talk ceased, she joined with several hundred other friends of the Hardens for a buffet supper of turkey, ham, and a variety of salads.[14]

Romance drew her to Los Angeles in 1958. She had visited the city after the 1946 World Series, had friends there, and had heard good things about the City of Angels from Biz Mackey. But the main factor in her decision to move was "to marry an old boyfriend," Charles Wesley Alexander. Alexander, Effa said, "played the piano and sang for a living, and I've always been weak for music." At age sixty-six, Alexander was five years older than Effa. It was the fourth marriage for both. A Baptist minister, Whalen A. Jones, married the couple on December 2, 1956. They made their home at 4322 Kenwood Avenue.

During her brief marriage to Alexander, Effa wrote Walter O'Malley, owner of the recently transplanted Brooklyn Dodgers, now known as the Los Angeles Dodgers, a letter proposing that the Dodgers pay "a small but enough to help" sum to each NAL team in return for a first option on any player of interest to the Dodgers. Prior to writing O'Malley, Effa obtained support for the idea from J. B. Martin, still president of the NAL in its declining years. A penciled note at the top of her letter—"Buzzie [Bavasi, the Dodgers' general manager], please act. Your problem now"—signaled O'Malley's lack of interest. No record of Buzzie acting could be found.

The marriage lasted about a year, after which Effa purchased a four-unit bungalow complex at 451 North Occidental Boulevard, near Elysian Park, in hopes that some of her family from Philadelphia would join her. None did, but she made good use of the rent from the other three units. In light of her two brief marriages to musicians, a friend asked her if she was ready to settle for just playing records. She said that she was and that she kept records on in the house "all the time." She favored the Ink Spots, a popular black vocal group, and Bing Crosby's songs such as "I've Got the World on a String," "Down on the Old Road," and "My Honey's Loving Arms." She said about her last two marriages, "I've been married twice since Abe died—both of them very stupid."[15]

Stupid though they may have been, the failed marriages did not stop her from keeping up friendships with other male musicians whom she had known during her days with the Eagles. Andy Razaf, who had been a familiar sight at Ruppert Stadium, and who also had moved to Los Angeles, became alarmed when, in April 1959, he heard that Effa thought he was mad at her. "Anyone," Razaf wrote to her, "who would be so low as to give you such an impression is no friend of mine." He recalled "How down-to-earth and gracious you were to me" and assured her she was always welcome at his home. Eubie Blake, a composer, lyricist, and pianist of ragtime, jazz, and popular music, visited and corresponded with her. On her seventy-fifth birthday he sent greetings saying, "As I looked at you the last time, I saw you still looked good. Don't give up your love life. Look at me. I'm not thinking about giving up." Blake was eighty-five at the time.[16]

Effa disliked living alone. She often kept the lights on and stayed up all night, going to sleep only after sunrise. Yet she decided against marrying another, un-named, former boyfriend. After he came out for a visit, Effa realized the flame had gone out and "what's more," she said, "I just couldn't stand cooking all those meals for him." Still, she had not ruled out male companionship completely. "I've still got all my teeth and I've never had any of those operations most women have."[17]

Two failed marriages and anxiety about the dark could not deter her from her passion for keeping the memory of Negro league baseball alive. Chet Brewer, who pitched in the Negro leagues for twenty-three years and scouted and instruct-ed for the Pittsburgh Pirates, ran a boys baseball program in Los Angeles during the late '70s at a city-owned park. Effa helped in the effort to have the field named Chet Brewer Field in his honor. Danny Goodman, who had run the concessions at Ruppert Stadium for the Bears and was handling promotions for the major league Los Angeles Angels, chipped in $250 for the sign. Fran Mathews, the former Eagle, had settled in Los Angeles after a career in the Army and often visited with Effa at her home, as did Quincy Trouppe. Trouppe, a nineteen-year catcher with several Negro league teams and a scout for the St. Louis Cardinals for ten years, had opened a senior citizen home, the Queen Ann Manor, at 1111 3rd Avenue in Los Angeles.[18]

Effa took to writing about the Negro leagues. With Leon Hardwick, a longtime sportswriter for the *Baltimore Afro-American* who had moved to Los Angeles for a job with the black weekly *Los Angeles Sentinel*, she wrote *Negro Baseball . . . Before Integration.* Hardwick did the majority of the writing and drew heavily on Effa's memory and scrapbook for information. The book gives an accounting of the leagues, brief biographies of players she felt deserving of enshrinement in Cooperstown (seventy-three in number), and short pieces on players from the Negro leagues who made the majors. They could not find a publisher so they published it themselves with the help of Chicago-based Adams Press in 1976 at a cost of about $1,500 for the initial press run of five hundred copies, a few of which remain available today. It never achieved wide circulation, but the book did give Effa an outlet to put her views forth for perpetuity. (Saint Johann reprinted the book in 2006.) She also penned occasional articles for the *Sentinel* recounting the leagues' history and making the case for Baseball's Hall of Fame to induct more Negro leaguers. In one such article it's clear her articulate, edgy, "now-you-listen-here" style had not deserted her. After a summary of the league's accomplishments, and a poke at Rickey, she ends with a blast at the Hall of Fame's special committee (described below). "Whose idea," she wrote, "was it that they should function in such an insulting and irresponsible manner? I'd like to know." Her vision was still intact as well. She then proceeded to prophetically endorse an unnamed black sportswriter's proposal to form a committee composed of men who had covered and written about the leagues, whose membership "spanned the nation," who would, after extensive research, submit a list of twenty-five or thirty players to be inducted simultaneously.[19]

A year before the book appeared, Mrs. Jessie Carney Smith, a librarian at Fisk University, in Nashville, Tennessee, contacted Effa about establishing an exhibit on black baseball at Fisk. Over the next year and a half, Effa supplied newspaper clippings and photographs and asked others, notably Monte Irvin, Vic Harris (longtime outfielder with the Grays); Leon Hardwick; Clifford Kachline, the Hall of Fame's historian; and editors of black weeklies who had covered the games, to do the same.

In March 1976, in need of funds to purchase additional photographs, Effa asked Abe's family in Hertford for assistance through a letter to one of his nieces, Laura Lowe, an elementary school teacher whom the extended Manley family regarded as its spokesperson. Laura reminded Effa that she had been "quite rude and discourteous" at Abe's funeral twenty-four years earlier. Laura further wondered why Effa was asking for money since "Uncle Abe had plenty of money before he met you, and he told some of us that the two of you were sitting pretty for the rest of your lives. We are not concerned about the money he left you because you were his wife and you deserved it." Laura also wondered why the project was not being considered for Elizabeth City (North Carolina) State University, "just eighteen miles from here," which, she noted, "was in Uncle Abe's home state." Laura closed by saying, "I'm afraid that you may not be able to depend on hearing from us. Each contact I make among the family members, I get the same response." Effa subsequently sent Laura's letter to Jessie Carney Smith with the comment, "I felt she would give you a perfect picture of how the family feels. I do not think I was ever very popular with them, and now this letter proves it. HA." Smith did collect a number of articles and photographs but not enough to justify an exhibit. Those items and the correspondence relating to the proposed exhibit exist today at Fisk as the Effa Manley Collection.[20]

While helping to develop the Manley Collection, Effa also followed the progress of a special committee set up by baseball commissioner Bowie Kuhn in 1971 to select Negro leaguers for induction into the Hall of Fame. Based on talks with Roy Campanella, Monte Irvin, and other Negro league greats and drawing on his memory of games he saw in Griffith Stadium operating the scoreboard as a teenager, Kuhn believed many Negro leaguers deserved to be in the Hall. He thought the Hall's rule that every member had to have played ten years in the majors to be eligible for induction was a technicality that unfairly excluded many deserving black players whose only fault was being born too early.

Hall of Fame president Paul Kerr and Ford Frick, regarded as the father of the Hall of Fame during his tenure as National League president, believed that changing the ten-year rule would dilute the Hall's integrity. Kuhn understood their concerns. "In defense of Ford and Paul," Kuhn said, "they thought it was so important to have standards. If it didn't work out for somebody, that's too bad, but the authenticity and believability of the process needs to stay intact." Kuhn managed to persuade Kerr that inducting Negro leaguers would democratize the game without diminishing the Hall's reputation. They left undecided the questions of how the inductions would take place.[21]

Kuhn formed a committee consisting of former Negro league players and sportswriters and appointed his special assistant, Monte Irvin, to chair the committee. The group inducted nine players from 1971 to 1977. They chose Satchel Paige to lead the way because, as Irvin put it, "[H]e was pretty well known to the American public."[22]

Paige's election led to the next confrontation between Kuhn and Kerr. Kerr, while now agreeing that some Negro leaguers were worthy of the Hall, insisted their plaques be displayed in a separate wing and not be hung alongside those of major leaguers. Kuhn thought such an act would be a slap in the face to the Negro leagues and their inductees. Kuhn, however, needed Kerr's support to get Paige into the Hall, so Kuhn publicly agreed with Kerr while privately counting on cries of Jim Crow-ism from an incensed press and public to force Kerr to change his stand. Irvin publicly supported Kuhn's statement while also believing public pressure would force an about-face by Kerr and other Hall officials. "We knew that would happen," Irvin said, "but we couldn't just come out and say so."[23]

The outcry came fast and loud. Buck O'Neil said, "[T]he only change is that baseball has turned Paige from a second-class citizen into a second-class immortal." Jackie Robinson left no doubt about his feelings. "If it's a special kind of thing," Robinson said, "it's not worth a hill of beans. If it were me under those conditions, I'd prefer not to be in it." (Robinson was already in the Hall of Fame, having been inducted in 1962 for his play with the Brooklyn Dodgers.) Stan Isaacs wrote in *Newsday*, "It was not determined if a new wing will be built . . . that is apart from but just as large as the old wing. Or whether a black architect will design the new wing. Or whether black guides will direct the tourists." *Ebony* editorialized, "Satchel and other black stars do not belong in any anteroom. . . . If state and national constitutions can be rewritten and amended, surely something can be done to the rules governing something so mundane as a sports Hall of Fame." Something was done. The Hall mounted Paige's plaque in the existing gallery of plaques.[24]

Josh Gibson and Buck Leonard went in together in 1972; Monte Irvin, 1973; Cool Papa Bell, 1974; Judy Johnson, 1975; Oscar Charleston, 1976; Martin Dihigo and John Henry "Pop" Lloyd in 1977. "I can't over-emphasize to you," Irvin said about the inductions, "how important that was." The committee disbanded after Lloyd's induction.[25]

Important though it was, the outcome did not satisfy everyone. Sportswriter Bill Braucher, of the *Miami Herald*, noted that many deserving players had not been inducted and that few of the nine who were inducted were well known (probably meaning to whites). He added, "Centuries of fear and hatred and economic ostracism can't be smoothed over by popping busts of the victims in Cooperstown," and he concluded, "If the enshrinement serves some good purpose, fine. But in its incomplete and condescending sense, the gesture borders on travesty."[26]

Criticism of the committee was nothing new. Six days after Buck Leonard and Josh Gibson were inducted in 1972, Richard Powell, who had served the Baltimore Elite Giants in many capacities from reporter to executive, let it be known that the nine or ten players expected to be inducted by the special committee fell far short of the mark. "Thirty or forty would be closer to the truth," Powell said. "How can anyone believe that out of the thousands of players in over seventy-five years of play from the eighteen-seventies to 1950, that given an equal opportunity, only ten merit Hall of Fame inclusion?"[27]

Doc Young expressed similar sentiments in 1975, when he wrote, "I must say it is time to end this project, to relegate it to the attic where baseball keeps its other embarrassing mistakes. At best, this thing was no more than a left-handed compliment to Negro league baseball. At worst, it is an insult to the ten times more great Negro League players than it honors."[28]

John Holway, a Negro league historian, charged that cronyism among the committee members led to some Negro leaguers being inducted sooner than they should have been. "Of the nine greatest players in Negro league history, I do not think Irvin and Judy Johnson would qualify," Holway said. He noted that both were committee members and that they put themselves in ahead of players such as Oscar Charleston, Rube Foster, John Henry Lloyd, Bullet Joe Rogan, Turkey Stearns, and Biz Mackey. "Blacks," Holway continued, "can play the crony game as much as whites do. The whole rap on the whites was that they were electing their friends instead of deserving Negro leaguers. So the blacks did the same thing."[29]

Holway, however, was not the only one who questioned the order in which the committee made its selections. Former National League umpire Jocko Conlan was quoted shortly after Irvin's induction in 1973 as not being able to understand how Charleston, Foster, Rogan, and Bell had not been selected. "I don't know how," Conlan said without attributing a motive to the committee's selection, "Irvin could be selected over Oscar Charleston . . . he was no Charleston."[30]

Effa, of course, also weighed in. "Why in hell," she said, "did the Hall of Fame set that committee up, if they were going to do the lousy job they did?" Fearful that no more recognition of Negro leaguers would be forthcoming from the Hall, she fired off letters in 1977 to Kuhn and J. G. Taylor Spink, editor of *The Sporting News,* which had been, at best, lukewarm about integrating major league baseball. She wanted another committee to review the names of the best Negro leaguers. Her letter got Spink's attention. He wrote a column about her campaign and referred to her as a "furious woman." She liked that and saved the clipping. She was most irate at the omission of Rube Foster, the father of Negro league baseball, who was in her view "the all-time great." "Foster," she said, "was a great pitcher, great manager, great team operator, great league president, and great promoter. If he'd been white, he would have ranked right up there with Christy Mathewson, John McGraw, and Kenesaw Mountain Landis."[31]

While quick to criticize when she thought the Negro leagues were being slighted, she was equally quick to praise those who shone a positive light on the leagues. Joe Garagiola, former St. Louis Cardinals catcher turned NBC-TV pregame host, received a glowing letter from Effa in August 1974, thanking him for his interview of Cool Papa Bell. She closed her letter saying, "I will anxiously be waiting for next Monday's game—and your pregame show [when Monte Irvin would be Garagiola's guest]. Again, thanks a lot."[32]

Though real progress toward Effa's objective of inducting more Negro leaguers had to wait a quarter of a century, she did hear her coauthor, Leon Hardwick, refer to Abe at the 1978 Afro-American Sports Awards celebration at Southwest Sportsman's Park Auditorium in Los Angeles, "as ranking alongside the immortal Rube Foster as the two men who did the most in developing Negro baseball, organizationally and commercially." By way of acknowledging Effa's equal role with Abe, Hardwick awarded an Afro-American Sports Trophy to her "in honor of two of Negro baseball's most famous club executives." She received another honor a year later, when the Second Annual Negro Baseball League Reunion featured her as the special honoree during its June 22–23, 1978, gathering in Ashland, Kentucky. Among the returning players was Monte Irvin. He spied Effa sporting a mink stole. "Mrs. Manley," Irvin asked, "is that the stole, the one that you bought with half the money that should have been mine?" "Yes," she answered, "it still looks good and it keeps me warm."[33]

The trip to Ashland was one of her last. A loss of equilibrium bothered her and increasingly limited her public activities, including outings to Dodger Stadium, where the team that once stole Newcombe and tried to take Irvin from her now welcomed her at any game she desired to attend. She could no longer live by herself as 1980 drew to a close and moved into Trouppe's rest home. After she reported not feeling well one day in the spring of 1981, an ambulance took her to Queen of Angels Hospital, where she learned she had colon cancer. Peritonitis, an inflammation of the tissue that lines the wall of the abdomen and covers the abdominal organs, set in after surgery on March 8. A heart attack on March 16 took her life shortly after 6:00 p.m., three weeks short of her eighty-first birthday.

A funeral mass was held at Our Lady of Loretta Catholic Church. Internment took place at Holy Cross Cemetery in nearby Culver City in Section R, Tier 35, Grave 28. Her tombstone reads, "She loved baseball." Joe Louis, the individual icon of black sports, had died of a heart attack four days earlier at Desert Springs Hospital in Las Vegas, Nevada.[34]

# EPILOGUE

Had Effa lived a few months longer she would have had the satisfaction of seeing Rube Foster's plaque appear in Cooperstown in the summer of 1981. Only one other Negro leaguer, Ray Dandridge in 1987, joined the Cooperstown immortals. In 1995 the Hall's chairman of the board, Ed Stack, concluded, "It was becoming clear that Negro leaguers were not going to be elected using the existing process."[1]

The existing process consisted of the Hall's Veterans Committee, manned primarily by white major leaguer Hall of Famers and supplemented by Irvin, O'Neil, and Campanella for different periods during those years. Given the whites' well-founded skepticism of the records on the Negro leagues and their lack of experience with the leagues and its stars, Irvin and company were unable to muster the required number of votes for any Negro leaguer other than Foster and Dandridge. Stack charged an advisory group, known as the Blue Ribbon Committee, under the leadership of the Hall's vice president Bill Guilfoile, to come up with a short list of deserving Negro leaguers to be inducted at the rate of one a year.[2] This the committee did, with significant input from Irvin and O'Neil (Campanella died in 1993), bringing the total of Negro leaguers in the Hall to eighteen—progress to be sure but a far cry from the seventy-three Effa felt to be deserving of the honor.

A change in leadership at the Hall in 2001 brought about a new approach. Newly appointed president Dale Petroskey, with the support of the Hall's board of directors and a $250,000 grant from Major League Baseball, selected a team of researchers to review all Negro league players and executives in order to determine who among them deserved to be inducted. Officials at the Hall turned to well-respected Negro league baseball researchers and historians, Larry Hogan, Larry Lester, and Dick Clark, to lead the Negro Leagues Researchers/Authors Group. More than fifty other authors, researchers, and historians conducted the review. In justifying the study Petroskey said, "I wanted a transparent process that would let everyone know who the nominees were, what their records were, how they were nominated and by whom, and how many votes each nominee received."[3]

Following completion of the research, which produced the most complete Negro leagues player statistics to date, an eight-hundred-page footnoted history of black baseball in America, and the most complete bibliography of black base-ball books, articles, and other projects, the Hall asked a group of twelve Negro league historians to make the selections. The group nominated thirty-nine Ne-gro leaguers prior to holding the election. Fay Vincent, Major League Baseball commissioner from 1989 to 1992, chaired the group during its deliberations. The members elected seven Negro league players (Ray Brown, Willard Brown, Andy Cooper, Biz Mackey, Louis Santop, Mule Suttles, and Jud Wilson); five pre–Negro league players (Frank Grant, Pete Hill, Joe Mendez, Ben Taylor, and Cris-tobal Torriente); one pre–Negro league executive (Sol White); and four Negro league executives. In addition to Cum Posey, Alex Pompez, and J. L. Wilkinson, they chose Effa Manley—the first, only, and most likely the last woman to be enshrined in Cooperstown.[4] Her gender, according to James Overmyer, one of the electors and author of an earlier book on her, did not influence the outcome. "No one," Overmyer said, "in the room was salivating, as far as I could tell, to vote in the first woman member, and no one was aghast at the thought that a dame might get in among all the guys. That topic did not come up." Topics that the commit-tee members viewed favorably included her skillful management and promotion of the Eagles, her volunteer efforts in behalf of numerous social, civil rights, and World War II causes, and her lifelong commitment to preserving the memory of the Negro leagues.[5]

The election results were less transparent than Petroskey desired. Jeff Idel-son, the Hall's vice president, said, "We made the determination to not release the vote totals; our past experience led us to this format. We wanted to assure that the committee had open, frank, honest discussions about each and every one of the candidates. We also wanted the committee—comprised solely of academics and historians—to not be subject to individual criticism, which always comes after releasing vote totals from a small committee. We preferred that the focus be on who was elected, versus who was not elected. By not releasing vote totals, that story is only enhanced."[6]

In spite of the effort to keep the focus only on who was elected, the fact that Buck O'Neil was not among the elected continues to stir controversy. While most observers agree he was not a Hall of Fame caliber player, his efforts on behalf of the Negro leagues from the time of his retirement from Negro league baseball in 1955 to his death on October 6, 2006, just three months after the elections, have led many to believe he was deserving of induction. We'll never know how close he came.

That said, the Hall of Fame's efforts from 2001 to 2006 on behalf of the Negro leagues finally brought recognition, long deserved and long denied, to Negro league players and executives, including Effa, who personified the best of Negro league baseball and, by extension, the vital, if often forgotten, role of Negro league baseball in the life of many of America's African American communities during the first half of the twentieth century.

# APPENDIX

NEWARK EAGLES STANDINGS: 1936 TO 1948

NEGRO NATIONAL LEAGUE

1936

|  | 1ST HALF | 2ND HALF |
|---|---|---|
| Pittsburgh Crawfords | 16-15 | 20-9 |
| Newark Eagles | 15-18 | 15-11 |
| New York Cubans | 9-11 | 13-12 |
| Washington Elite Giants | 14-10 | 7-14 |
| Philadelphia Stars | 15-12 | 10-18 |
| Homestead Grays | 10-13 | 12-14 |
| New York Black Yankees |  | 7-14 |

1937

|  | 1ST HALF ONLY |
|---|---|
| Homestead Grays | 21-9 |
| Newark Eagles | 19-14 |
| Philadelphia Stars | 21-11 |
| Washington Elite Giants | 11-15 |
| Pittsburgh Crawfords | 11-16 |
| New York Black Yankees | 11-17 |

| 1938 | | 1ST HALF ONLY | |
|------|--|---------------|--|
| | Homestead Grays | 26-6 | |
| | Philadelphia Stars | 20-11 | |
| | Pittsburgh Crawfords | 14-14 | |
| | Newark Eagles | 1-11 | |
| | Baltimore Elite Giants | 12-14 | |
| | New York Black Yankees | 4-17 | |
| | Washington Black Senators | 1-20 | |

| 1939 | | TOTALS | |
|------|--|--------|--|
| | Homestead Grays | 33-14 | |
| | Newark Eagles | 29-20 | |
| | Baltimore Elite Giants | 25-21 | |
| | Philadelphia Stars | 31-32 | |
| | New York Black Yankees | 15-21 | |
| | New York Cubans | 5-22 | |

| 1940 | | TOTALS | |
|------|--|--------|--|
| | Homestead Grays | 28-13 | |
| | Baltimore Elite Giants | 25-14 | |
| | Newark Eagles | 25-17 | |
| | New York Cubans | 12-19 | |
| | Philadelphia Stars | 16-31 | |
| | New York Black Yankees | 10-22 | |

| 1941 | | 1ST HALF | 2ND HALF |
|------|--|----------|----------|
| | Homestead Grays | 17-9 | 8-8 |
| | Newark Eagles | 11-6 | 8-5 |
| | Baltimore Elite Giants | 13-10 | 9-8 |
| | New York Cubans | 7-10 | 4-2 |
| | New York Black Yankees | 7-13 | 5-5 |
| | Philadelphia Stars | 10-18 | 2-8 |

| 1942 | | Totals | |
|------|--|--------|--|
| | Baltimore Elite Giants | 37-15 | |
| | Homestead Grays | 26-17 | |
| | Philadelphia Stars | 21-17 | |
| | Newark Eagles | 19-17 | |
| | New York Black Yankees | 7-19 | |
| | New York Cubans | 6-19 | |

| 1943 | | Totals | |
|------|--|--------|--|
| | Homestead Grays | 31-9 | |
| | New York Cubans | 20-9 | |
| | Newark Eagles | 19-14 | |
| | Philadelphia Stars | 21-18 | |
| | Baltimore Elite Giants | 17-24 | |
| | New York Black Yankees | 2-21 | |

| 1944 | | 1st Half | 2nd Half |
|------|--|----------|----------|
| | Homestead Grays | 15-8 | 12-4 |
| | Baltimore Elite Giants | 12-11 | 12-9 |
| | New York Cubans | 12-10 | 4-4 |
| | Philadelphia Stars | 7-11 | 12-7 |
| | Newark Eagles | 13-9 | 6-13 |
| | New York Black Yankees | 2-13 | 2-11 |

| 1945 | | 1st Half | 2nd Half |
|------|--|----------|----------|
| | Homestead Grays | 18-7 | 14-6 |
| | Philadelphia Stars | 14-9 | 7-10 |
| | Baltimore Elite Giants | 13-9 | 12-8 |
| | Newark Eagles | 11-9 | 10-8 |
| | New York Cubans | 3-11 | 3-9 |
| | New York Black Yankees | 2-16 | 5-10 |

| 1946 | | 1ST HALF | 2ND HALF |
|---|---|---|---|
| | Newark Eagles | 25-9 | 22-7 |
| | New York Cubans | 13-13 | 15-8 |
| | Homestead Grays | 18-15 | 9-13 |
| | Philadelphia Stars | 17-12 | 10-17 |
| | Baltimore Elite Giants | 14-17 | 14-14 |
| | New York Black Yankees | 3-24 | 5-16 |

| 1947 | | 1ST HALF ONLY |
|---|---|---|
| | Newark Eagles | 27-15 |
| | New York Cubans | 20-12 |
| | Baltimore Elite Giants | 23-20 |
| | Homestead Grays | 19-20 |
| | Philadelphia Stars | 13-16 |
| | New York Black Yankees | 6-25 |

1948    No Standings Published

Source: Dick Clark and Larry Lester, eds., *The Negro Leagues Book* (Cleveland, OH: Society for American Baseball Research), 161–63. Used by permission.

# ACKNOWLEDGMENTS

Portions of chapters 10–13 appeared in my book *Willie Wells: "El Diablo" of the Negro Leagues*, published in 2007 by the University of Texas Press.

One of the pleasures of writing a book is meeting and working with knowledgeable and supportive people:

Paul Dickson, the author of fifty books and counting, has been a steadfast source of encouragement and advice in matters ranging from writing and research techniques to working with publishers, agents, and bookstores.

James Overmyer, who wrote the first book on Effa Manley, generously scoured this manuscript for errors of omission and commission and offered other valuable advice.

Robert "Skip" McAfee, a member of the Bibliography Committee of the Society for American Baseball Research lent his critical eye to the final draft and did a thorough job preparing the index.

Monte Irvin provided a wealth of information about growing up in the Newark area and his days playing for the Newark Eagles as did other former Eagles, Willie C. "Curly" Williams and James "Red" Moore.

Jerry Izenberg, sports columnist emeritus with the Newark-based *Star-Ledger*, contributed information on former Eagle Larry Doby's early major league experiences.

The staff at the Library of Congress has been unfailingly helpful and courteous. In particular I am indebted to Dave Kelly for his insightful and prompt response to questions; to Sibyl Moses, for her assistance on researching Newark's history; and to the staff of the Library's Manuscript Division and the Newspaper and Current Periodical Reading Room. People at the Manuscript Division of the Moorland-Spingarn Research Center at Howard University gave me easy access to Art Carter's papers. Members of the research staff at the National Baseball Hall of Fame and Museum in Cooperstown, New York, Jim Gates, Claudette Burke, Freddy Berowski, John Horne, and Pat Kelly, made my time there productive and pleasant.

The staff at the Charles F. Cummings New Jersey Information Center at the Newark Public Library helped me sort through Effa Manley's files.

Elizabeth Demers, Claire Noble, Kathryn Neubauer, Elizabeth Norris, and Sam Dorrance of Potomac Books, Inc., deserve much credit for turning the manuscript into a book and getting the word out about it.

Elena M. Cupingood with the Office of Facilities and School Operations in the Philadelphia Public School System provided a copy of Effa's high school transcripts.

Marla Katz at the Philadelphia office of the U.S. Census Department provided information on the 1900 and 1910 censuses.

Doug Boyd and William Marshall at the University of Kentucky provided transcripts of Marshall's interviews with Effa Manley, Larry Doby, Monte Irvin, and Bill Veeck.

My wife, Judy Wentworth, has given generously of support and encouragement.

I am grateful for the contributions made by one and all. Any errors are mine alone.

# NOTES

## INTRODUCTION

1. She gave her maiden name as Effa Louise Brooks on the marriage license for her marriage to Charles Wesley Alexander on December 2, 1956. Certificate of Registry of Marriage, Book 3955, Page 331, County of Los Angeles, Registrar/County Clerk.

2. "Ex-Newark Hurler Wins Salary Case," *Afro-American*, August 17, 1940; A. S. "Doc" Young, "Sport Show," *Los Angeles Sentinel*, January 14, 1951; W. Rollo Wilson, "Through the Eyes of W. Rollo Wilson," *Philadelphia Tribune*, July 24, 1943; Wendell Smith, "Sports Beat," *Pittsburgh Courier*, August 4, 1945.

3. Randy Dixon, "The Sports Bugle," *Pittsburgh Courier*, June 1, 1940.

4. Effa was the most flamboyant and the best known but not the only woman executive in black baseball. Mrs. Nathaniel Strong took over her husband Nate's booking operations, which extended from New York to Canada, after he died of a heart attack in 1938. By 1943 Mrs. Strong was reported to be managing the booking of fifty teams that generated revenues in the neighborhood of $350,000 a year. Rube Foster, Hall of Fame pitcher, manager, owner, and considered the father of Negro league baseball, was ably assisted by his wife in selecting players and managing the payroll for both the Leland and Chicago Giants until his death in 1930. Billie Harden performed many of the same duties for her husband John, owner of the Atlanta Black Crackers, that Effa did for Abe. These women performed their work competently but without Effa's vision and passion. Peter Suskind, "The Sportoscope," *Norfolk*

*Journal and Guide*, July 31, 1943; Spike Washington, "Atlantans Boast of Woman Boss of Big League Baseball Outfit," *Atlanta Daily World,* June 11, 1944.

5. Transcript for Effa Brooks supplied by the School District of Philadelphia, Office of Facilities and School Operations, May 30, 2008; Effa Manley, interview by William Marshall for the University of Kentucky Libraries A. B. Chandler Oral History Project, North Rutherford, NJ, October 26, 1977; Certificate of Registry of Marriage.

6. W. Rollo Wilson, "Through the Eyes of W. Rollo Wilson," *Pittsburgh Courier*, January 23, 1937.

7. Joel Manley DDS, great-nephew of Abe Manley, telephone interview by author. September 26, 2008; Monte Irvin, interview by the author, June 5, 2006.

8. Monte Irvin, interview by the author, February 21, 2008.

9. James Overmyer, *Effa Manley and the Newark Eagles* (Metuchen, NJ: Scarecrow Press, 1993), 5, 73; Larry Doby interview by William Marshall for the University of Kentucky Libraries A. B. Chandler Oral History Project, North Rutherford, NJ, November 15, 1979.

10. Allen Richardson, "A Retrospective Look at the Negro Leagues and Professional Negro Baseball Players" master's thesis, San Jose State University, San Jose, CA, 1980) 190.

11. Peter Genovese, "Where the Eagles Soared," *Star-Ledger* (Newark), February 13, 2009.

12. Amiri Baraka, *The Autobiography of Leroi Jones* (New York: Freundlich Books, 1984), 35.

13. Genovese, "Where the Eagles Soared."

14. Effa Manley, interview by William Marshall for the University of Kentucky Libraries A. B. Chandler Oral History Project, Los Angeles, CA, October 26, 1977.

## CHAPTER 1. THE LADY MAKES A SPLASH

1. Effa Manley and Leon Herbert Hardwick, *Negro Baseball . . . Before Integration* (Chicago: Adams Press, 1976), 37.

2. Manley interview.

3. Manley interview.

4. Overmyer, *Effa Manley*, 6.

5. Irvin interview, February 21, 2008.

6. *Measuring America: The Decennial Censuses from 1790 to 2000* (Washington, DC: U.S. Census Bureau, 2001), 27, 48.

7.  F. James Davis, *Who Is Black? One Nation's Definition*, 10th anniversary ed. (University Park: Pennsylvania State University Press, 2001), 5.

8.  Transcript for Effa Brooks supplied by The School District of Philadelphia.

9.  Donn Rogosin, *Invisible Men: Life in Baseball's Negro Leagues* (New York: Anthenum, 1983), 108; Effa Manley, letter to Miss Elizabeth Galbreath, April 23, 1942, Newark Eagles Files, Newark Public Library; "Society Women Display Fashions," *New York Amsterdam News*, May 5, 1926; http://www.nfo.net/usa/harlem.html (accessed on September 24, 2008); Cary D. Wintz and Paul Finkleman, *Encyclopedia of the Harlem Renaissance* (New York: Taylor and Francis Inc. 2004), 767. Overmyer, *Effa Manley*, 12.

10. 1910 U.S. Census; Joel Manley.

11. City directories for Norfolk, VA and Camden, NJ.

12. "Abe Manley of Newark Eagles Champions Dies," *New York Amsterdam News*, December 20, 1952; "Manley, Once Baseball Club Owner, Dies," *Norfolk Journal and Guide*, December 20, 1952; Joel Manley interview.

13. "Man Shot, 2 Break Legs in Holdup," *Philadelphia Tribune*, April 9, 1931. "Black Hooded Bandits Raid Swanky Club," the *Baltimore Afro-American*, April 11, 1931; "N.J. Buries Baron," *Baltimore Afro-American*, April 18, 1931; Joseph Rainey, "5 Guilty of Murder Charges in Camden Club Tragedy Where 1 Was Killed Easter," *Philadelphia Tribune*, July 9, 1931. Ray O. Light, "Camden Club House Bombed in Number Barons War," *Philadelphia Tribune*, September 15, 1932; "Aunt Clara Dead; Friend of Children," *Philadelphia Tribune*, September 23. 1937. The numbers business consisted of an illegal, all cash, gambling activity that resembled today's lotteries. A player placed a bet by writing three numbers on a piece of paper. A runner took the money and the paper to the banker's location, be it an office, club, or living room, under the protection of a lookout whose job was to scan the streets for police. Bankers chose a three-digit payoff number, which could be, for example, the last three numbers of the attendance figures for a sporting event. Payoffs were on the order of 600 to 1, allowing one who "hit his numbers" to realize a substantial payoff delivered to him by the same runner still under the lookout's protective gaze. A nickel wager could yield a $30 payoff, a substantial sum in times when $10 a week was considered a decent wage for many African Americans.

14. Henry Holt, "Women with a Mission," The *New York Post*, September 15, 1975.

15. Overmyer, *Effa Manley*, 8.

16. Richardson, "A Retrospective Look at the Negro Leagues, 158.

17. Manley interview; Lawrence D. Hogan, *Shades of Glory: The Negro Leagues and the Story of African American Baseball* (Washington, DC: National Geographic Press, 2006), 263; "Baseball Interest High in Camden," *Philadelphia Tribune*, September 12, 1929.

18. In her interview with Allen Richardson, Effa says she and Abe met at the ballpark (Yankee Stadium) but she did not specify the year. Lem Graves, a friend of the Manleys' and a sportswriter for the *New Journal and Guide* in Norfolk, Virginia, stated in his July 26, 1941, column that they met after a 1932 World Series game in Yankee Stadium. Perhaps they wanted to keep their Camden association quiet. "They Danced for Charity," "Grand March at Charity Ball," *Philadelphia Tribune.* February 4, 1932.

19. Overmyer, *Effa Manley*, 8; John Virtue, *South of the Color Barrier* (Jefferson, NC: McFarland Co., 2007), 46–47.

20. Marriage application, Effa Manley File, National Baseball Hall of Fame and Museum, Cooperstown, NY.

21. Overmyer, *Effa Manley*, 13.

22. Holt, "Women with a Mission."

23. Insurance payment receipts, Newark Eagles Files, Newark Public Library, Newark, NJ; Ronald E. Kisner, "White Widow of Black Baseball League Pioneer Writes Book about Saga," *Jet*, March 1977.

24. Joel Manley interview.

25. Ibid.; Glenda Manley Ashley, telephone interview by the author, October 2, 2008.

26. "Chicagoan Goes to Europe for Four Months Vacation," *New York Amsterdam News*, June 2, 1934; "Mrs. Cora Rollins Ends 3-Month Trip," *New York Amsterdam News*, August 18, 1934; "Parties," *Chicago Defender*, July 24, 1926; "Bride on Honeymoon," *Chicago Defender*, July 22, 1933; Effa Manley, letter to Mrs. Cora Rollins, May 1, 1940, Newark Public Library.

27. Manley interview; Note by Effa in Ashland File, National Baseball Hall of Fame and Museum.

28. Ludlow W. Werner, "Boycott Ends After Management Agrees to Hire 35 Negro Men and Women as Clerks by September 1 and More Thereafter as Business Warrants It," *New York Age*, August 4, 1934; Donald Hendricks, "Agreement With Store Reached After Several Meetings With League," the *New York Age*, August 4, 1934.

29. "Prominent Woman," newspaper clipping dated June 20, 1936 (name of newspaper cut away), Effa Manley File, National Baseball Hall of Fame and Museum.

## CHAPTER 2. THE MANLEYS COME TO BASEBALL

1. G. James Fleming, "Brooklyn and Cubans Give Body 9 Members; Rowdiness Is Rapped," *Afro-American*, January 19, 1935.
2. James A. Riley, *Biographical Encyclopedia of the Negro Baseball Leagues* (New York: Carroll & Graf Publishers, 1994), 875, 633–34, 637–38, 91–92, 338–39, 185; Brad R. Tuttle, *How Newark Became Newark* (New Brunswick, NJ: Rutgers University Press, 2009), 110.
3. "Negro Baseball Leaders in Enthusiastic Meeting," *New York Amsterdam News*, January 19, 1935; A. E. White, "Baseball Men Gather for Annual Assembly," *Atlanta Daily World*, January 23, 1935.
4. "Church City to Have a Team," *New York Amsterdam News*, December 8, 1934.
5. "Franchise to Brooklyn; Grays Get Bankhead," *Pittsburgh Courier*, November 17, 1934; Riley, *The Biographical Encyclopedia of the Negro Baseball Leagues*, 761–63.
6. Romeo Dougherty, "Sports," *New York Amsterdam News*, February 23, 1935.
7. Romeo Dougherty, "Sports," *New York Amsterdam News*, March 16, 1935.
8. "Brooklyn Team Ends Training This Week-End," *Chicago Defender*, April 27, 1935.
9. Kyle P. McNary, *Ted "Double Duty" Radcliffe* (Minneapolis, MN: McNary Publishing, 1994), 100.
10. Riley, *Biographical Encyclopedia*; 649, 317, 237; "Now It's the Size of the Adrenal Glands That Makes Our Stars So Proficient!" *New York Amsterdam News*, April 22, 1939.
11. Manley interview.
12. "Harlem Opera House," Cinema Treasures, http://cinematreasures.org/theater/533 (accessed on July 2, 2008) "Celebrities Will Greet Louis at Opera House," May 17, 1935, Undated clipping, Effa Manley File, National Baseball Hall of Fame and Museum.
13. Overmyer, *Effa Manley*, 34; "Harlem Opera House"; "Celebrities Will Greet Louis at Opera House."
14. Riley, *Biographical Encyclopedia*, 670.
15. John Johnson, letter to Mrs. Manley, May 8, 1935; George W. Harris letter to Abraham Manley, May 7, 1935, Effa Manley File, National Baseball Hall of Fame and Museum, Manley and Hardwick, *Negro Baseball . . .*, 43.
16. John Holway, *Voices From the Great Black Baseball Leagues* (New York: Dodd, Mead, 1975), 320.
17. Overmyer, *Effa Manley*, 34; "Grays Win 2, Lose 2 to Brooklyn," *Pittsburgh Courier*, May 25, 1935.

18. Romeo Dougherty, "Sports Whirl," *New York Amsterdam News*, June 1, 1935.

19. "Cuban Stars in Pair Win Over Brooklyn Team," *Chicago Defender*, June 8, 1935.

20. "Ben Taylor Enters Suit Against Manley's Brooklyn Team," *New York Amsterdam News*, July 6, 1935.

21. Romeo L. Dougherty, "Sports Whirl," *New York Amsterdam News*, November 30, 1935.

22. "Brooklyn Shows Giants How Easterners Play Baseball," *Chicago Defender*, July 6, 1935.

23. Riley, *Biographical Encyclopedia*, 388, 534–53; "Manley Plans to Continue at Ebbets Field," *New York Amsterdam News*, August 24, 1935, http://www.matrix.msu.edu/~expa/expa/hmarker.php?markerId=2 (accessed on March 2, 2009).

24. Running Romans XC/Track and Field, http://www.runningromans.com/Cornelius%20Johnson.htm (accessed on May 19, 2008).

25. Bessye Bearden, "New York Society," *Chicago Defender*, July 20, 1935.

26. "Manley Plans to Continue at Ebbets Field," *New York Amsterdam News*, 1935.

27. "Brooklyn Eagles Return to Ebbets Field Against Dodgers," *New York Amsterdam News*, August 31, 1935; "Manley's Eagles in Exhibitions," *New York Amsterdam News*. September 7, 1935.

28. "Brooklyn Eagles Return to Ebbets Field Against Dodgers," *New York Amsterdam News*, August 31, 1935; "Manley Plans to Continue at Ebbets Field," *New York Amsterdam News*, August 24,1935; Andrew Paul Mele, ed., *A Brooklyn Dodgers Reader* (Jefferson, NC: McFarland & Co., 2005), 42.

29. "Great Dihigo to Play Every Position in Charity Gamer Here," *New York Amsterdam News*, September 7, 1935.

30. "Eagles Split With Minor League Stars," *New York Amsterdam News*, September 21, 1935; "Manley's Eagles in Exhibitions," *New York Amsterdam News*, September 7, 1935.

31. "When the Baseball League Season Was Officially Closed," *New York Amsterdam News*, September 28, 1935.

32. Riley, *Biographical Encyclopedia*, 423, 745.

33. "Dance Will Aid Sanitarium," *New York Amsterdam News*, November 23, 1935.

## CHAPTER 3. ABE TRADES BROOKLYN FOR NEWARK

1. Neil Lanctot, *Negro League Baseball: The Rise and Ruin of a Black Institution* (Philadelphia: University of Pennsylvania Press 2004), 48.

2. Overmeyer, *Effa Manley*, 39.

3.  Ibid., 40.

4.  Charles O'Reilly, "Hinchliffe Staudium, Paterson, N.J.," 2001, http://mysite
    .verizon.net/charliesballparks/stadiums/hinchlif.htm (accessed on June 16,
    2009). While many amateur and semipro black teams played throughout New
    Jersey, the Eagles and the New York Black Yankees were the only teams in
    New Jersey that played under the auspices of the Negro leagues, the "major
    leagues" of black baseball. There were two Negro leagues at the time, the
    Negro National League and the Negro American League.

5.  Barbara J. Kukla, *Swing City: Newark Night Life, 1925–50* (New Brunswick,
    NJ: Rutgers University Press 2002), 5–6; "National Loop Has Big Meet in
    N.Y.C.," *Atlanta Daily World*, March 12, 1936. The Dodgers, incidentally,
    took their name, not from the Brooklyn Dodgers, but from the Dodgers' Bar
    and Grill, a club on 8 Bedford Street in Newark that, like similar clubs such
    as the Boston Plaza, the Nest Club, the Picadilly, and the Alcazar, featured
    singers, dancers, chorus girls, comedians, and emcees.

6.  Bob Golon, *No Minor Accomplishment: The Revival of New Jersey Profes-
    sional Baseball* (New Brunswick, NJ: Rutgers University Press 2008), 14;
    Philip J. Lowry, *Green Cathedrals: The Ultimate Celebration of Major
    League and Negro League Ball Parks* (New York: Walker and Co., 2006), 143.

7.  Kukla, *Swing City*, 3–4; 1930 Census.

8.  Kevin Mumford, *Newark: A History of Race, Rights, and Riots in America*
    (New York: New York University Press, 2007), 19; "Jersey Sheriff Com-
    mended for His Fairness," *Chicago Defender*, May 23, 1936; "Civil Rights
    Bill Signed," *New York Amsterdam News*, January 23, 1936; "Building Trades
    Groups Protest," *New York Amsterdam News*, June 13, 1936.

9.  Mumford, *Newark*, 24.

10. Kukla, *Swing City*, 7–10; Overmyer, *Effa Manley*, 15.

11. Overmyer, *Effa Manley*, 107.

12. Golon, *No Minor Accomplishment*, 13.

13. Overmyer, *Effa Manley*, 106; Alfred M. Martin and Alfred T. Martin, *The Ne-
    gro Leagues in New Jersey: A History* (Jefferson, NC: McFarland Co., 2008),
    20. From 1932 to 1960 Weiss worked in the New York Yankees organization,
    where he was best known for developing a twenty-team farm system; taking
    a no nonsense tack as the team's general manager; and convincing the Yan-
    kees brass that Casey Stengel, whom he hired in 1948 to manage the Yankees,
    was more of a baseball man than a clown. Stengel delivered ten pennants in
    twelve years. Weiss's plaque hangs among those of other baseball executives
    in Cooperstown.

14. Irvin interview, February 21, 2008; Martin and Martin, *The Negro Leagues,* 11; Baraka, *Leroi Jones*, 35.

15. http://www.ibhof.com/jhlewis.htm (accessed on March 4, 2009). Lewis lost the fight, one of only eight defeats he suffered while winning ninty-four bouts. Lewis reigned as light-heavyweight champion from October 1935 to January 1939, when he tried to step up to the heavyweight division only to be flattened by Joe Louis in the first round. That was Lewis's last fight.

16. Franklin Penn, "Giants to Join Western Ball Loop; Greenlee Out?" the *Chicago Defender*, February 8, 1936.

17. Cum Posey, "Cum Posey's Pointed Paragraphs" *Pittsburgh Courier*, February 8, 1936; Lanctot, *Negro League Baseball*, 51.

18. Manley interview.

19. "Eagles Leave For Warm-Up," *New York Amsterdam News*, April 4, 1936.

20. Ibid.

21. Irvin interview, February 20, 2008.

22. "Bolden Heads Negro League After Parley," *New York Amsterdam News*, March 14, 1936.

23. James Riley, *Dandy, Day, and the Devil* (Cocoa, FL: TK Publishers, 1987), 133–34.

24. Riley, *Biographical Encyclopedia*, 75.

25. Calvin Service, "Scribe Picks Newark to Win First Half in East," *Chicago Defender*, May 23, 1936; "Newark Opens With Giants," *Philadelphia Tribune*, May 7, 1936.

26. William B. Mead and Paul Dickson, *Baseball: The Presidents' Game* (Washington, DC: Farragut Publishing Co., 1993), 199.

27. Ibid., 76.

28. "Newark Drops 3 to Grays," *Pittsburgh Courier*, June 6, 1936.

29. "Future of Baseball Is Bright, Says Man Who Invested Most," the *Pittsburgh Courier*, June 6, 1936.

30. "Admit Black Yanks Into the League at N.Y. June Meeting," *Chicago Defender*, June 27, 1936.

31. "Louis at Ease Over Fite Date," *Norfolk Journal and Guide*, June 20, 1936.

32. James "Red" Moore, interview by the author, January 19, 2006.

33. "Eagles Home: Await Elites," *New York Amsterdam News*, August 1, 1936; "Eagles Await Night Session," *New York Amsterdam News*, August 15, 1936.

34. Cum Posey, "Naming of Loop President, Sec'y Set for Jan 19," *Pittsburgh Courier*, January 16, 1937.

35. Lanctot, *Negro League Baseball*, 58.

36. Ibid., "Code of Organized Baseball to Govern National League," *Pittsburgh Courier*, January 30, 1937; "Grays Get Gibson; Greenlee League Prexy," *Pittsburgh Courier*, March 27, 1937.

37. Riley, *Biographical Encyclopedia*, 170, 201, 706, 851; "Code of Organized Baseball to Govern National League."

38. "Newark Ball Club Gets Ready for Spring Tilt," *Chicago Defender*, April 24, 1937; "Winston-Salem Eagles Club to Be Operated as Farm by A. Manley," *Norfolk Journal and Guide*, March 27, 1937. "Rookie Shines as Senators Triumph," *Philadelphia Tribune*, April 3, 1937.

39. "Tough Amateur Card Ready," *New York Amsterdam News*, March 13, 1937.

40. "This Capable Matron Heads New Flood Aid Committee," *New York Amsterdam News*, February 13, 1937, http://tennesseeencyclopedia.net/imagegallery.php?EntryID=F022 (accessed on May 28, 2008)

41. "About the Savoy Ballroom," http://www.savoyplaque.org/about_savoy.htm (accessed on May 28, 2008).

42. "Friends Give Dinner for Bruce Wendell," *New York Amsterdam News*, May 1, 1937; "Eagles, Elites to Play Night Benefit," *Philadelphia Tribune*, June 3, 1937.

43. "McDuffie Has the Goods; Newark May Have Pennant," *Chicago Defender*, April 17, 1937; "Newark Ball Club Gets Ready for Spring Tilt," the *Chicago Defender*, April 24, 1937.

44. "Colored Nines Selected for All-Star Game," *Chicago Daily Tribune*, August 1, 1937.

45. "Grays Look Like Class of the League," *New York Amsterdam News*, June 26, 1937; "5-Game Series Yanks Vs. Eagles," *New York Amsterdam News*, July 31, 1937; Cum Posey, "Posey's Points," *Pittsburgh Courier*, August 21, 1937; "Colored Nines Meet Today in All-Star Game," *Chicago Daily Tribune*, August 8, 1937.

46. Lanctot, *Negro League Baseball*, 86.

47. "Greenlee Claims Proposed World Series Is Unsanctioned by League," *Pittsburgh Courier*, September 18, 1937.

48. John Holway, *The Complete Book of Baseball's Negro Leagues: The Other Half of Baseball History* (Fern Park, FL: Hasting House Publishers, 2001), 341, 346–47; "Chi Ready for Championship Series Opener," *Pittsburgh Courier*, September 18, 1937; "Homestead-Chicago Giants Split Twin Bill in Baltimore," *Afro-American*, October 2, 1937.

49. "To Fete Newark Eagles at Ball," *New York Amsterdam News*, September 4, 1937.

50. "Charges Chick Webb Failed to Play; to Sue," *New York Amsterdam News*, October 2, 1937.

51. "3-Pound Daughter of Dr. D. W. Holmes Dies," *Afro-American*, June 25, 1938.

52. "To Fete Newark Eagles at Ball," *New York Amsterdam News*, September 4, 1937.

53. "Teaches English to Russians," *Chicago Defender*, September 18, 1937; "Va. State Grad Doing Well in Russia," *Chicago Defender*, May 30, 1936.

## CHAPTER 4. EFFA STEPS UP

1. Thos. T. Wilson, letter to Mrs. Effa Manley, February 28, 1938, Newark Public Library.

2. "Eagles Not Likely to Trade Players," *New York Amsterdam News*, February 19, 1938.

3. "Baseball Mogul's Wife Denies That Airline Discriminated Against Him," *Pittsburgh Courier*, February 5, 1938.

4. Richardson, "A Retrospective Look at the Negro Leagues," 159.

5. Riley, *Biographical Encyclopedia*, 517. Cole, after leaving the NNL, had sold the team to Dr. John B. Martin, a dentist, funeral home owner, and real estate investor in Memphis, and his dentist brother, Dr. B. B. Martin.

6. "Moguls Revamp League," *New York Amsterdam News*, February 5, 1938.

7. Evans, an uncle of Douglas Wilder, the first African American to be elected governor of a state (Virginia), earned his nickname after a doctor replaced an eye he lost in a gang fight as a teenager with a glass orb.

8. "Eagles' Crack Moundsman, 3 Others, Balk, *New York Amsterdam News*, March 26, 1938; "Day, Evans, Dandridge, Stone Newark Holdouts," *Pittsburgh Courier*, March 26, 1938; Chico Renfro, "Sports of the World," *Atlanta Daily World*, April 30, 1991; Riley, *Biographical Encyclopedia*, 270.

9. Monte Irvin, interview by William Marshall for the University of Kentucky Library A. B. Chandler Oral History Project, New York, May 12, 1977.

10. Irvin interview, December 19, 2009.

11. Irvin interview, February 21, 2008. Fay Vincent, *The Only Game in Town: Baseball's Stars of the 1930's and 1940's* (New York: Simon and Schuster, 2006), 221.

12. Harry Webber, "Bell, Tomes Newark Pilot Is Released," *Chicago Defender*, April 2, 1938.

13. "Abe Manley in Powwow to Get Satchel Paige," *New York Amsterdam News*, April 9, 1938.

14. "'I'm Holding Out Because Joe DiMaggio Advised Me To.' Says Satchel Paige," *Pittsburgh Courier*, April 23, 1938. Whether the two men talked is not known. At the time of Satchel's comments DiMaggio was at his home in San Francisco, where he had been for two and a half months holding out on the New York Yankees. ("DiMaggio Ends Holdout Siege by Accepting $25,000 Offer," *Los Angeles Times*, April 21, 1938.)

15. "Satchel Paige Hauled Into Court by Manley," *New York Amsterdam News*, April 23, 1938.

16. "Satchel Paige Restrained From Going to S. America," *Pittsburgh Courier*, April 30, 1938; "Silence Envelops Satchel Paige–Newark Eagles Row," *New York Amsterdam News*, April 30, 1938.

17. "Newark Eagles Face Parkways," *New York Amsterdam News*, May 7, 1938; "Page Mr. Sherlock Holmes! Satchel Paige Has Disappeared!" *Pittsburgh Courier*, May 21, 1938; "Satchel Paige Confesses Fraud," *Pittsburgh Courier*, May 14, 1938.

18. "Newark Eagles Trounce Pittsburgh Crawfords to Open Official Season," *New York Amsterdam News*, May 21, 1938; Invoice from Burrell to Abe, January 29, 1938, Newark Eagles Files, Newark Public Library.

19. "Amateur Night at the Apollo: Ralph Cooper Presents Five Decades of Great Entertainment," Amazon.com, http://www.amazon.com/Amateur-Night-Apollo-Presents-Entertainment/dp/0060160373 (accessed on June 23, 2008); Louise Beavers IMD6, http://www.imdb.com/name/nm0064792/ (accessed on June 23, 2008); "Fans Glow Over Tan Filmfare," *Newark-Herald*, June 11, 1938.

20. "History of the Essex Mountain Sanatorium," http://www.mountainsanatorium.net/history.htm (accessed on June 24, 2008).

21. "Employment Sought for Local Negroes," *New Jersey Herald-News*, July 2, 1938; "Race Patients Refused Hospitalization in Many Cases," *Newark-Herald*, July 2, 1938; "Harrison, Tate, J. R. Rose Get Coveted Spots on Committee," *Newark Herald*, June 18, 1938; "Job-Picketing by Negro Groups Upheld in Jersey Court Verdict," *Pittsburgh Courier*, April 30, 1938; "Commission Is Charged With Bias," *New York Amsterdam News*, February 19, 1938; "Mass Meet in New Jersey to Fight Discrimination," *Chicago Defender*, March 26, 1938; "Set to Fight" (photograph caption) *Chicago Defender*, March 5, 1938; "Harold Lett on Newark Housing Authority Post," *New York Amsterdam News*, April 16, 1938.

22. "Abe Manley's Newark Eagles Move up in League Rating," *New York Amsterdam News*, July 2, 1938.

23. Effa Manley, letter to Mr. John L. Clark, July 22, 1938, Effa, letter to Abe, no date, Newark Public Library.

24. "Rain Wrecks Baseball in Eastern Loop," *Chicago Defender*, July 30, 1938.

25. The letter was in a file marked "Undated Correspondence, 1938" in the Eagles' papers at the Newark Public Library. Effa referenced the second letter in her 1977 interview with Marshall. "Satchel Paige Given Deadline," *New York Amsterdam News*, July 9, 1938; "Hint More NNL 'Raids,'" *New York Amsterdam News*, June 4, 1938.

26. "Rain Wrecks Baseball in Eastern Loop"; Riley, *Biographical Encyclopedia*, 498.

27. Riley, *Biographical Encyclopedia*, 536; James Overmyer, *Queen of the Negro Leagues: Effa Manley and the Newark Eagles* (Lanham, MD: Scarecrow Press, 1998), 81; "Manley Depending on Pitching Arm of Terry McDuffie to Win Pennant," *Newark Herald*, June 11, 1938; "McDuffie to Hurl Against Eagles," *Newark Herald*, August 27, 1938; "Eagles Trade McDuffie to Yanks for Rookie Hurler," *Philadelphia Tribune*, August 25, 1938.

28. Monte Irvin, *Nice Guys Finish First: The Autobiography of Monte Irvin,* with James A. Riley (New York: Carroll & Graf, 1996), 44.

29. W. W. Wolfe, letter to Mr. A. Manley, August 20, 1938, Newark Public Library; Wendell Smith, "Smitty's Sport Spurts," *Pittsburgh Courier*. August 27, 1938.

30. Manley interview.

31. Riley, *Biographical Encyclopedia*, 383; "Newark Eagles Face Bushwicks," *New York Amsterdam News*, September 3, 1938.

32. "Satchel Paige 'Not Wanted,'" *Chicago Defender*. December 17, 1938.

CHAPTER 5. EFFA COMES INTO HER OWN

1. Effa Manley, letter to Major R. R. Jackson, April 28, 1939, Newark Eagles Files, Newark Public Library.

2. Lanctot, *Negro League Baseball*, 59, 83.

3. Effa Manley, letter to Rufus Jackson and Cum Posey, May 5, 1939, Newark Eagles Files, Newark Public Library; Riley, *Biographical Encyclopedia*, 125.

4. Effa Manley, letter to Thos. T. Wilson, May 8, 1939, Newark Eagles Files, Newark Public Library.

5. Effa Manley, letter to Chester Washington, May 26, 1939, Newark Eagles Files, Newark Public Library.

6. Butts Brown, "In the Groove," *Newark Herald*, September 16, 1944.

7.  Wendell Smith, "Smitty's Sport Spurts," *Pittsburgh Courier*, June 3, 1939; Cum Posey, letter to Mrs. Effa Manley, Newark Eagles Files, Newark Public Library.

8.  Effa Manley, letter to Cum Posey, undated, and Cum Posey, letter to Mrs. Manley, April 29, 1939, Newark Eagles Files, Newark Public Library.

9.  Lanctot, *Negro League Baseball*, 81.

10. "Bury Slim Jones, Bolden's Philadelphia Star's Ace, *Chicago Defender*, December 10, 1938; Riley, *Biographical Encyclopedia*, 451.

11. Newark Eagles Files, Newark Public Library.

12. "D.C. Education Board Bars Marian Anderson," *Chicago Defender*, February 25, 1939; "Cite Law That Forbids Marian Anderson Recital," *Chicago Defender*, April 1, 1939; "Throng Honors Marian Anderson in Concert at Lincoln Memorial," *New York Times*, April 10,1939.

13. "Women of Three States Rally to Council After DAR Rebuff," newspaper clipping, Effa Manley's Scrapbook, National Baseball Hall of Fame and Museum. http://www.africanamericans.com/Achievers.htm (accessed on June 26, 2008.

14. "Negro Survey Report Cites Racial Discrimination," *Newark-Herald*, March 4,1939.

15. Stanley Glenn, interview by the author, January 12, 2006.

16. Effa Manley, letter to Mr. F. W. Martin, May 7, 1943, Newark Eagles Files, Newark Public Library.

17. J. Russell Lynn, letter to Mr. A. L. Manley, March 20, 1939, Newark Eagle Files, Newark Public Library; Irvin, Riley. *Nice Guys Finish First*, 53; Riley, *Biographical Encyclopedia*, 872.

18. Dick Lundy, letter to Mr. Abraham Manley, March 31, 1939, Newark Eagles Files, Newark Public Library; "Centerfield Recruit With the Newark Eagles Great With Stick," *New York Amsterdam News*, April 15,1939.

19. "Paige Wants to Get Back Into Organized Baseball," *Chicago Defender*, April 1, 1939; Riley, *Biographical Encyclopedia*, 598.

20. Effa Manley, letter to Mr. Murray Halpern, March 24, 1939, Effa Manley, letter to Prof. W. R. Valentine, May 1, 1939, Newark Eagles Files, Newark Public Library; "Institutional History: Manual Training and Industrial School for Colored Youth at Bordentown, NJ," Division of Archives and Records Management, State of New Jersey Department of State, http://www.state.nj.us/state/darm/links/guides/sedma000.html (accessed on June 27, 2008).

21. "John Borican," USA Track and Field—Hall of Fame, http://www.usatf.org/HallOfFame/TF/showBio.asp?HOFIDs=18 (accessed on June 29, 2008);

"Track Star Dolls Up," *Chicago Defender*, April 22, 1939. Effa Manley, letter to Mr. John Borican, April 24, 1939, Newark Eagles Files, Newark Public Library; "Newark Drops Loop Opener to Philadelphia," *New York Amsterdam News*, May 20. 1939; John Borican, letter to H. B. Webber, April 1, 1939, Newark Eagles Files, Newark Public Library.

22. "Nelson, Newark Third Sacker, Looms a Star," *Chicago Defender*, May 27, 1939. Confirmed in a telephone interview by the author with Irvin on July 3, 2008.

23. "Newark Wins 4 Straight on Home Lot," *New York Amsterdam News*, June 3, 1939.

24. "Newark Eagles Defeat Grays Twice," *Pittsburgh Courier*, June 10, 1939, Manely Interview, June 10, 1977.

25. "Newark Wins 4 Straight on Home Lot"; "Newark Eagles Defeat Grays Twice"; "15,000 See Black Yanks, Giants Win," *New York Amsterdam News*, June 10, 1939; "Second NNL 4-Team Twin Bill for July 2," *New York Amsterdam News*, June 17, 1939; "Newark, Black Yanks Go on Barnstorming Tour," *New York Amsterdam News*, July 1, 1939; "Newark, Baltimore Beat Philly Stars, Black Yanks," *Chicago Defender*, July 8, 1939; "Grays Win First Half in NNL Flag Chase," *New York Amsterdam News*, July 22, 1939.

26. Earl Sydnor, "Between the Acts," May 29, 1939, Effa Manley's Scrapbook, National Baseball Hall of Fame and Museum, "Geraldyn Dismond Says," *New York Amsterdam News*, November 20, 1943.

27. "Eagles Sign Biz Mackey," *Newark Herald*, July 2, 1939.

28. Fay Young, "The Stuff Is Here," *Chicago Defender*, September 9, 1939; Cum Posey, letter to Abe Manley, 1939, Newark Eagles Files, Newark Public Library.

29. Irvin interview, February 21, 2008; Craig A. Vail, letter to Mr. A. Manley, October 24, 1939, Newark Eagles Files, Newark Public Library.

30. Dr. Glenda Manley Ashley, Abe's great niece, telephone interview by the author, October 16, 2008; Joel Manley interview.

31. Effa Manley, letter to Alphonso Brooks, December 19, 1939, Effa Manley, letter to Jacob Brooks, December 19, 1939, Effa Manley, letter to Mr. Herman Natal, December 2, 1939, Newark Eagles Files, Newark Public Library.

32. "NNL Finances Shape Up Well," *New York Amsterdam News*, November 4, 1939; Effa Manley, letter to James Hill, October 30, 1939, Newark Eagles Files, Newark Public Library.

33. Effa Manley, letter to Mr. James Semler, November 25, 1939, Newark Eagles Files, Newark Public Library; Cum Posey, "Dr. Martin New A. L. President," *Pittsburgh Courier*, December 16, 1939; Lanctot, *Negro League Baseball*,

87; Sam E. Brown, "Birmingham Back in Negro American Loop," *Atlanta Daily World*, December 16, 1939.

## CHAPTER 6. FIREWORKS

1. Effa Manley, letter to Mrs. Thelma Wells, January 1940, Thelma Wells, letter to Mrs. Effa Manley, May 15, 1940, Newark Eagles Files, Newark Public Library.
2. Effa Manley, letter to Social Security Board, Newark, NJ, April 3, 1941, Newark Eagles Files, Newark Public Library; Overmyer, *Effa Manley*, 110–111; Form No. U.C. 24 Application for Exemption From Filing Reports, July 23, 1941, Newark Eagles Files, Newark Public Library.
3. "Satchel Paige Signs to Pitch for Newark Eagles," *Chicago Defender*, January 20, 1940.
4. Don Deleighbur, "Behind the Play," *Cleveland Call and Post*, August 21, 1943.
5. William H. Hastie, letter to Miss Effa Manley, February 1, 1940, Newark Eagles Files, Newark Public Library; Lanctot, *Negro League Baseball*, 88.
6. Cum Posey, "Posey's Points," *Pittsburgh Courier*, October 21, 1939.
7. "Posey Quits Eastern Baseball Meet," *Chicago Defender*, February 10, 1940; Cum Posey, "NNL Meeting Ends in Deadlock," *Pittsburgh Courier*, February 10, 1940; Lanctot, *Negro League Baseball*, 89; Art Carter, "Split Looms in Baseball League," *Afro-American*, February 10, 1940.
8. Art Carter, "From the Bench," *Afro American*, February 10, 1940.
9. Effa Manley, letter to Art Carter, February 17, 1940, New Jersey Public Library.
10. "Tom Wilson Defends Gottlieb in National League Deals," *Chicago Defender*, February 17, 1940; Effa Manley, letter to Cum Posey, February 14, 1940, New Jersey Public Library; Cum Posey, "Posey's Points," *Pittsburgh Courier*, February 17, 1940; Lanctot, *Negro League Baseball*, 413; Overmyer, *Effa Manley*, 113.
11. Lem Graves Jr., "From the Press Box," *Norfolk Journal and Guide*, July 26, 1941.
12. "National League Moguls Deadlock on Dr. C.B. Powell as Prex," copy of newspaper article, Effa Manley's Scrapbook, 1940, National Baseball Hall of Fame and Museum.
13. Oliva Mamie Rodolph, letter to "Stormy Petrel," February 12, 1940, New Jersey Public Library.
14. Effa Manley, letter to Cum Posey, March 1, 1940, Frank A. Young, letter to Mrs. Effa Manley, April 9, 1940, Newark Eagles Files, Newark Public Library; Dan Burley, "NNL Owners Go to Chi to Elect C. B. Powell," *New York*

*Amsterdam News*, February 24, 1940; Dan Burley, "Moguls Fight to Standstill," *New York Amsterdam News*, March 2, 1940, "NNL Retains Wilson as President," *Pittsburgh Courier*, March 2, 1940.

15. Ray Dandridge, interview by William Marshall, November 12, 1979; Manley interview.

16. "Savannah Gets Newark Eagles," *New York Amsterdam News*, April 20, 1940; Richardson, "A Retrospective Look at the Negro Leagues," 99. Effa Manley, letter to Dr. J. B. Martin, April 15, 1940, Richard E. Carey, letter to Department of State of the United States, May 8, 1940, and Edwin Gill, letter to Lemuel Hooker, May 17, 1940, Newark Eagles Files, Newark Public Library; Manley interview.

17. Effa Manley, letter to Mr. A. Phailstock, April 17, 1940, Ruth, letter to Dear Effa and Abe, April 15, 1940, Andy Razaf, letter to Hello There! May 2, 1940, Jocko Maxwell, letter to My dear Mrs. Manley, April 29, 1940, Effa Manley, letter to Mrs. Maggie Irvin, June 3, 1940, and Effa Manley, letter to Dear Mother, May 1, 1940, Newark Eagles Files, Newark Public Library; "Crowd of 12,000 Sees Newark Trim Black Yanks 5–2," *New York Amsterdam News*, May 11, 1940.

18. Dan Burley, "Backdoor Stuff," *New York Amsterdam News*, November 23, 1940; "Highlights of Game," *New York Amsterdam News*, May 11, 1940; "Reckless Driver," *New York Amsterdam News,* January 30, 1940.

19. Dan Burley, "Pitcher's Circuit Hit Stymies Gotham Gang," *New York Amsterdam News*, May 11, 1940; Dan Burley, "Black Yanks Leave for Spring Training Grind on March 30th," *New York Amsterdam News,* March 16, 1940.

20. "Satchel Paige to American League," *Chicago Defender*, June 29, 1940; Joe Blow, "Western League Gets Satchel Paige," *New York Amsterdam News*, June 29, 1940; Dan Burley, "Manleys Threaten 'Player War' Over Paige," *New York Amsterdam News*, June 15, 1940; Effa Manley, letter to Dr. B. B. Martin, June 2, 1940, and Satchel Paige, letter to Mrs. Manley, July 24, 1940, Newark Eagles Files, Newark Public Library.

21. Daniel, "Confidentially Yours," *New York Amsterdam News*, July 6, 1940.

22. "Umpire Kayoes Newark Pilot as Grays Win Night Game, 8 to 1," *Pittsburgh Courier*, June 22, 1940; Richardson, "A Retrospective Look at the Negro Leagues," 109.

23. "Newark Eagles to Battle Cubans Sun," *New York Amsterdam News*, August 22, 1940

24. Effa Manley, letter to Mr. F. Leon Harris, July 16, 1940, Newark Eagles Files, Newark Public Library.

25. "Gets Apology From Railway," *New York Amsterdam News*, February 15, 1940; Harry B. Webber, "Plan $15,000 Jim Crow Suit," *New York Amsterdam Star-News*, February 22, 1941; "Potato Pickers Win $9000 Verdict," *Philadelphia Tribune*, May 16, 1940.

26. "Eagles Revise Their Lineup," *New York Amsterdam News*, July 20, 1940; "Revamped Eagles Take 3 Games from Yankees." New York *Amsterdam News*, July 27, 1940. "Eagles Streak to 9 Straight," the *New York Amsterdam News*, August 10, 1940. "Homestead Grays Crowned 1940 Champions of Negro Organized Baseball," the *New York Amsterdam News*, September 14, 1940.

27. "Lundy Quits Newark," *Pittsburgh Courier*, August 10, 1940; "M'ley Seeks Charleston for Pilot," *Philadelphia Tribune*, August 29, 1940.

28. Cum Posey, "Posey's Points," *Pittsburgh Courier*, August 31, 1940; "Homestead Grays Take Double-Header," *Washington Post*, August 19, 1940; Cum Posey, letter to Mrs. Effa Manley, August 16, 1940; Effa Manley, letter to Mr. E. B. Eynon, February 8, 1941, Newark Eagles Files, Newark Public Library.

29. Wendell Smith, "Smitty's Sport Spurts," *Pittsburgh Courier*, August 24, 1940.

30. Irvin interview.

31. Effa Manley, letter to J. B. Martin, November 25, 1940, Effa Manley, letter to Mr. Cum Posey, December 16, 1940, Newark Eagles Files, Newark Public Library.

32. "Injured Ball Player Sues Newark Club," *Chicago Defender*, August 17, 1940; Effa Manley, letter to the Employers Group of Boston, MA, July 1, 1941, Newark Eagles Files, Newark Public Library.

33. Pearson, letter to Mr. and Mrs. Manley, November 25, 1940, Newark Eagles Files, Newark Public Library.

34. Iota Phi Lambda Sorority, letter to Mrs. Effa Manley, January 6, 1940, A.W. Hardy, letter to Mrs. Manley, May 25, 1940, Newark Eagles Files, Newark Public Library; Ruth Shipley, "Socially Speaking!" *Afro-American*, August 17, 1940.

## CHAPTER 7. COBBLING TOGETHER A LINEUP

1. "Baseball Magnates Squeeze Abe Manley out of Office at Baltimore Powwow," *New York Amsterdam Star-News*, January 11, 1941.

2. Effa Manley, letter to Mr. Raleigh Mackey, January 10, 1941, Raleigh Mackey, letter to Mrs. Manley, January 18, 1941, Newark Eagles Files, Newark Public Library.

3. James Hill, letter to Mrs. Manley, January 6, January 14, 1941, Effa Manley, letter to Mr. James Hill, April 12, 1941, Newark Eagles Files, Newark Public Library.

4.  Effa Manley, letter to Assemblyman Dan Burroughs, June 18, 1941, Raleigh Mackey, letter to Mrs. Manley, January 18, 1941, John H. Johnson, letter to Mrs. Effa Manley, May 1, 1941, Newark Eagles Files, Newark Public Library.

5.  Effa Manley, letter to Mr. Lenial Hooker, March 11, 1941, Maxwell Manning, letter to Mrs. Effa Manley, March 4, 1941, Effa Manley, letter to Mr. Maxwell Manning, March 5, 1941, Mr. Satchel Paige, letter to Dear Mrs. Manley, March 5, 1941, Effa Manley, letter to Mr. Terris McDuffie, February 28, 1941, Newark Eagles Files, Newark Public Library.

6.  "Newark Still League Club," *New York Amsterdam Star-News*, March 8. 1941; Dan Burley, "Confidentially Yours," *New York Amsterdam Star-News*, March 15, 1941; "Judgeship Coveted—Lost," *New York Amsterdam Star-News*, May 24, 1941.

7.  Ruth Marie Brown, letter to Mrs. Abraham Manley, April 7, 1941, Effa Manley, letter to Mrs. Ruth Marie Brown, April 16, 1941, Effa Manley, letter to Mr. John C. Keck & Co., May 22, 1941, Effa Manley, letter to The Philadelphia Electric Company, May 23, 1941, Newark Eagles Files, Newark Public Library.

8.  Monte Irvin, telephone interview by the author, June 15, 2009; Newark city directories.

9.  "Proclamation," Effa Manley's Scrapbook, National Baseball Hall of Fame and Museum, "2,500 Soldiers Invited to Newark's Opener," *New York Amsterdam News*, May 10, 1941; "Troops in N J. Turn Barracks Into a Morgue," *Chicago Daily Tribune*, September 9, 1934; Roy Wilkens, letter to Mrs. Effa Manley, March 26, 1941, Newark Eagles Files, Newark Public Library; "Newark Eagles Anticipate Big Opener," *New York Amsterdam News*, May 11, 1941.

10. "Newark Nine Discovers 2nd Satchel Paige," *Chicago Defender*, April 19, 1941; Jerry Kessler, "Newark Eagles, Cubans to Open Before Soldiers," *Chicago Defender,* May 10, 1941; Riley, *Biographical Encyclopedia*, 120, 170; "Newark Preps for Opener," *New York Amsterdam News*, May 3, 1941; "Leon Day Back With Newark," *Chicago Defender*, April 5 1941; "Now With Black Yankees," *Chicago Defender* (photo caption), June 7, 1941.

11. Carl Lawrence, "Your Man Lawrence Goes to Newark and Reports," *New York Amsterdam Star-News*, May 17, 1941; "Cubans in Win Over Newark," *Chicago Defender*, May 17, 1941.

12. Dan Burley, "Confidentially Yours," *New York Amsterdam Star-News*, June 7, 1941; Joe Blow, "Cubans Play Yanks Sunday," *New York Amsterdam Star-News*, June 7, 1941.

13. "Negro National League Results," *Pittsburgh Courier*, July 12, 1941.

14. Effa Manley, letter to Mr. S. H. Posey, August 1, 1941, Newark Eagles Files, Newark Public Library.

15. Effa Manley, letter to Cum Posey, October 15, 1941, Effa Manley, letter to Mr. Wm. G. Nunn, August 17, 1941, Newark Eagles Files, Newark Public Library.

16. Mrs. Effa Manley, "Negro League Owners Spend $480,000 Yearly," *Chicago Defender*, July 19, 1941.

17. http://ustfccca.cstv.com/sports/division2/spec-rel/121007aab.html (accessed on August 21, 2008); St. Clair Bourne, "Monarchs Trounce Eagles 6-1 Cubans Top Philadelphia, 4–3," *New York Amsterdam Star-News*, August 30, 1941; "Borican Guest of the Eagles," *New York Amsterdam Star-News*, August 23, 1941; "Eagles Lose Tilt, 7–2," *New York Amsterdam Star-News*, September 6, 1941.

18. "Double Bill at Polo Grounds," *New York Amsterdam Star-News*, August 30, 1941; Daniel, "Homestead Grays Blast Eagles 6–4 in Both Games at Polo Grounds," *New York Amsterdam Star-News*, September 20, 1941.

19. Lennie, letter to Mrs. Effa Manley, December 16, 1941, Newark Eagles Files, Newark Public Library.

20. Effa Manley, letter to Hon. Joseph Rainey, December 23, 1941, Newark Eagles Files, Newark Public Library; Lanctot, *Negro League Baseball*, 120.

CHAPTER 8. WAR COMES TO NEWARK

1. "Nation Needs Baseball, Say Congressmen," *Chicago Daily Tribune*, January 9, 1942.

2. "Manleys Bolt NNL Meeting in a Huff," *Pittsburgh Courier*, February 21, 1942; Dan Burley, "Tom Wilson Retained As NNL Prexy," *New York Amsterdam Star-News*, February 21, 1942.

3. Alvin Moses, letter to My dear Mrs. Manley, April 4, 1942; Dan Burley, "Confidentially Yours," *New York Amsterdam Star-News*, March 1, 1942.

4. Gus Greenlee, letter to Mr. Abe Manley, February 21, 1942, Newark Eagles Files, Newark Public Library. Their efforts to sell the team, suggests they still owned the team raising more questions about Simon's status with the team. Nothing further could be found about Simon's ownership role, if any, with the Eagles.

5. Effa Manley, letter to Art Carter, August 13, 1942, Newark Eagles Files, Newark Public Library.

6. Lanctot, *Negro League Baseball*, 121–122; Art Carter, "Newark Returns;

Pittsburgh Franchise Turned Down at NNL Schedule Meeting," *Afro-American*, March 7, 1942.

7. Effa Manley, letter to Mr. Leonard Pearson, January 9, 1942, Lenny, letter to Mrs. Manley, June 2, 1942, Effa Manley, letter to Essex County Draft Board #13, May 5, 1942, Newark Eagles Files, Newark Public Library.

8. Effa Manley, letter to Monty Irvin, January 22, 1942, Newark Eagles Files, Newark Public Library.

9. Effa Manley, letter to Raleigh Mackey, February 19, 1942, Raleigh Mackey, letter to Mr. Manley February 24, J. R. Mackey, letter to Mrs. Manley, March 10, Effa Manley, letter to Raleigh Mackey, March 14, Effa Manley, letter to J. Raleigh Mackey, May 6, James Raleigh Mackey, letter to Mrs. Manley, Newark Eagles Files, Newark Public Library.

10. Bob, Luke, *Willie Wells: "El Diablo" of the Negro Leagues* (Austin: University of Texas Press, 2007), 80–82.

11. James Hill, letter to Mrs. Manley, March 9, 1942, Effa Manley, letter to James Hill, March 19, 1942, James Hill, letter to Mrs. Manley, March 2, 1942, Effa Manley, letter to James Hill, March 6, 1942, Newark Eagles Files, Newark Public Library.

12. Francis Mathews, letter to Mrs. Manley, no date, Effa Manley, letter to Francis Mathews, March 16, Francis Mathews, letter to Mrs. Manley, no date, Newark Eagles Files, Newark Public Library.

13. "Willie Wells Newark Boss," *New York Amsterdam Star-News*, April 25, 1942; "Eagles Leave on Trip Soon," *Pittsburgh Courier*, February 28, 1942; "Diamond Stars in Puerto Rico May Be Victims of Axis Blockade," *Afro-American*," March 14, 1942; Art Carter, "Elites Get Kimbro for Griffith, Biot," *Afro-American*, February 28, 1942; "Newark Trades Spoon Carter and Clarkson," *Chicago Defender*, April 25, 1942; Riley, *Bibliographical Encyclopedia*, 78; "Effa Manley Demands Baseball Aid War Effort," *New York Amsterdam Star-News*, April 18, 1942.

14. "Grays Bow Twice to Newark Eagles," *Chicago Defender*, April 25, 1942.

15. Larry Schwartz, "'Brown Bomber' Was a Hero to All," ESPN.com, 2007, http://espn.go.com/sportscentury/features/00016109.html (accessed on August 30, 2008). Irvin interview, June 5, 2005; "Effa Manley Demands Baseball Aid War Effort"; "Fans Asking NNL to Help Uncle Samuel," *New York Amsterdam Star-News*, June 13, 1942; Effa Manley, letter to Mr. Julius J. Adams, June 23, 1942, Newark Eagles Files, Newark Public Library; Jocko Maxwell, letter to My dear Mrs. Manley, April 28, 1942, Newark Eagles Files, Newark Public Library; Carl Dunbar Lawrence, "18,000, Record Crowd, Sees

Grays Beat Eagles, 3-2," *New York Amsterdam Star-News*, May 2, 1942; "Dr. Cheney Is Host," *New York Amsterdam Star-News*, May 9, 1942; J. Mercer Burrell, letter to Mrs. Manley, March 13, 1942, Newark Eagles Files, Newark Public Library; Luke, *Willie Wells*, 25.

16. Irvin interview, February 21, 2008; Manley interview.

17. Irvin, *Nice Guys Finish First*, 90; Manley interview.

18. Robert S. Hartgrove; to Hon. Juan E. Richer, No date, Robert S. Hartgrove, letter to Mrs. Effa Manley, August 13, 1942, William H. Smathers U.S.S., letter to Dear Bob, August 19, 1942, Newark Eagles Files, Newark Public Library.

19. Dave Anderson, "Can Gwynn or Walker Hit.400?" *New York Times*. July 8, 1997; "Black Yanks Play Newark This Sunday," *Chicago Defender*, June 20, 1942; "Black Yanks Take Couple From Eagles," *Chicago Defender*, June 27, 1942; "Standing," *Chicago Defender*, June 20, 1942; "Eagles Take Three From Grays," *Pittsburgh Courier*, July 4, 1942; Paul Dickson, *The Dickson Baseball Dictionary*, 3rd ed. (New York: Norton, 2009), 90; "Baltimore Elites Capture First Half Flag in NNL," *Baltimore Afro-American*, July 11, 1942; Youth Director, letter to Mrs. Effa Manley, June 24, 1942, Newark Eagles Files, Newark Public Library.

20. "18,000, Record Crowd, Sees Grays Beat Eagles, 3–2."

21. "Results," *Chicago Defender*, May 23, 1942; "Baltimore in Two Victories Over Newark," *Chicago Defender*, May 30, 1942; "Willie Wells Revamps Newark Eagles Lineup," *Chicago Defender*, June 13; Doby interview.

22. Doby interview.

23. Fay Vincent, *The Only Game in Town: Baseball's Stars of the 1930's and 1940's*, Larry Doby DVD Disc 1, April 13, 2000, American Folklife Center, Library of Congress, Washington, DC.

24. Floyd G. Snelson, "Newark Booms With War Work; Negroes Fail to Get Their Share," *New York Amsterdam Star-News*, November 21, 1942.

25. "Plants Plead Ignorance of F.D.R. Job-Bias Order," *Pittsburgh Courier*, February 21, 1942; "Report Gains in War Employment," *New York Amsterdam Star-News*, March 7, 1942; "Tells 8 Concerns to Lift Racial Bars," *New York Times*, May 27, 1942; "Two Cleared of Job Bias," *New York Times*, August 9, 1942; "Newark Booms With War Work; Negroes Fail to Get Their Share," *New York Amsterdam Star-News*, November 21, 1942.

26. "Wm. Jackson Is on Board of Education," *Newark Herald*, July 4, 1942; "First Negro Named Member of Newark Education Board," *New York Amsterdam Star-News*, December 12, 1942; Mumford. *Newark*, 22.

27. "Segregation in Movies Calls for Technique," *Newark Herald*, July 11, 1942.

28. "Pirates' Chief Scout to Handle Epochal Try-Outs," *Pittsburgh Courier*, August 22, 1942.

29. Pvt Clarence C. Israel, letter to Mrs. Effa Manley, September 9, 1942, Newark Eagles Files, Newark Public Library.

30. "Newark Eagles Beat Baltimore," *New York Amsterdam Star-News*, July 18, 1942; "Eagles Streak to 9 Straight," *New York Amsterdam Star-News*, August 10, 1942; "Newark in 2 Wins Over Black Yanks," *Chicago Defender*, August 29, 1942; "Newark Eagles in Final Game on Home Soil," *Pittsburgh Courier*, September 5, 1942; "Grays Split With Newark in 4-2 Thrillers," *Pittsburgh Courier*, September 12, 1942.

31. "Grays Win, 4 to 1; Monarchs Protest," *Pittsburgh Courier*, September 26, 1942; "Protested Game Kicked Out," *Chicago Defender*, October 3, 1942; Holway, *The Complete Book*, 398–99.

32. Effa Manley, letter to Thomas A Edison Jr., October 31, November 18, 1942, Newark Eagles Files, Newark Public Library.

33. Manley interview; "Eagles Entertain Soldiers," *New York Amsterdam Star-News*, December 19, 1942; "Florence Mills," Sonny Watson's StreetSwing. com, http://www.streetswing.com/histmai2/d2flomills.htm (accessed on August 23, 2008); J. Mercer Burrell, letter to Mrs. Effa Manley, August 3, 1942, Newark Eagles Files, Newark Public Library.

34. Cum Posey, letter to Mrs. Effa Manley, November 24, 1942, Newark Eagles Files, Newark Public Library.

35. Irvin interview; June 4, 2005.

CHAPTER 9. THE EAGLES ADAPT TO THE WAR

1. Art Carter, "NNL Votes to 'Carry On,'" *Afro-American*, April 10, 1943; Holway, *The Complete Book,* 404; Lanctot, *Negro League Baseball*, 129; Jonathan White, "National League Owners Optimistic," *Pittsburgh Courier*, January 30, 1943.

2. "CIO Leader Raps Ban on Bus Drivers," *Chicago Defender*, March 20, 1943.

3. Abe Manley, letter to Cum Posey, February 10, 1943, Leon Ruffin, letter to Mrs. Manley. April 15, 1943, Newark Eagles Files, Newark Public Library; "Mexican Gold Lures Ball Stars," *New York Amsterdam Star-News*, 1943.

4. Cum Posey, "Posey's Points," *Pittsburgh Courier*, January 2, 1943; White, "National League Owners Optimistic" Wendell Smith, "Smitty's Sports-Spurts," *Pittsburgh Courier*, January 30, 1943; Effa Manley, letter to Dear Smitty, February 7, 1943.

5. Effa Manley, letter to Mr. Rufus Jackson, 1943, Newark Eagles Files, Newark Public Library.

6. Effa Manley, letter to Mr. Ed Gottlieb, February 20, 1943; Effa Manley, letter to Mr. J.B. Martin, February 20, 1943, P. E. Schwehm, letter to Emanuel Millman, Esquire, April 3, 1943, Newark Eagles Files, Newark Public Library.

7. "Eagles Begin Spring Grind on April 12," *New York Amsterdam News*, April 3, 1943; Dan Burley, "Confidentially Yours," *New York Amsterdam Star-News*, March 27, 1943; Wendell Smith, "Smitty's Sports-Spurts," *Pittsburgh Courier*, January 30, 1943; Andy Razaf, letter to Mrs. Effa Manley, undated, 1943, Effa Manley, letter to Lary Doby, April 8, 1943, Newark Eagles Files, Newark Public Library; http://www.virginiasportshalloffame.com/hall/induct_hucles.html (accessed on April 14, 2009).

8. Effa Manley, letter to Pvt. Maxwell Manning, April 28, 1943, Newark Eagles Files, Newark Public Library.

9. Andy Razaf, letter to Dear Mrs. Manley, April 8, 1942, Effa Manley, letter to Mrs. James Hill, April 16, 1943, A.B. Hermann, letter to Dear Mrs. Manley, April 17, 1943, Sidney Goldmann, letter to My dear Mrs. Manley, April, 19, 1943, Effa Manley, letter to Senator Albert W. Hawks, April 15, 1943, Effa Manley, letter to Hon. John B. Keenan, May 5, 1943, Newark Eagles Files, Newark Public Library; "Mule Suttles Replaces Wells as Newark Pilot," *Pittsburgh Courier*, April 10, 1943; http://www.georgiaencyclopedia.org/nge/Article.jsp?id=h-834 (accessed on September 30, 2008).

10. Carl Lawrence, "Eagles Trim Stars, in Slow Game at Newark Opening," *New York Amsterdam News*, May 22, 1943; James E. Overmyer, "The Negro Leagues at the Dawn of Civilization," in Alvin Hill, *The Cooperstown Symposium on Baseball and American Culture* (Cooperstown, NY: Baseball Hall of Fame and Museum, 1997), 69.

11. "Grays Prevail; Take Lead," *Washington Post*, May 21, 1943; "Philly Stars, Cubans Victors in Four Team Feature at Stadium," *Pittsburgh Courier*, June 5, 1943.

12. Effa Manley, letter to Mr. Tom Wilson, June 8, 1943, Newark Eagles Files, Newark Public Library.

13. "Grays Win East First Half Race," *Chicago Defender*, July 17, 1943.

14. Lem Graves Jr., "In Which the Sports Editor Does All Right as a Prophet," *New Journal and Guide*, July 17, 1943; "Eagles Take 6th in Row," *New York Times*, July 26, 1943; "Black Cracker Outfit Heading North in August," *New York Amsterdam News*, July 31, 1943; "Baseball," *Baltimore African American*, September 11, 1943; "Grays Snatch 2 From Philly," *New York Amster-*

*dam News*, September 18, 1943; Effa Manley, letter to Mr. Thomas T. Wilson, August 24, 1943, Newark Eagles Files, Newark Public Library.

15. "Lend-a-Hand Club Benefited by All-Star Baseball Game," *Philadelphia Tribune*, September 11, 1943; "South All-Stars Triumph 6-4," *Baltimore Afro-American*, September 11, 1943.

16. "Women Quit When Whites Just Hired, Get More Pay," *New Jersey Afro-American*, August 28, 1943; "Plan Housing in Newark for War Workers," *Newark Herald*, November 13, 1943; "Status of New 'Y. W.' Is Cleared," *Chicago Defender*, December 25, 1943; "Jersey C.I.O. Hits Army Segregation," *Chicago Defender*, December 18, 1943; Michael Carter, "Jersey Jives Colored People: An Interview With Governor Charles Edison of N.J.," *Baltimore Afro-American*, August 21, 1943.

17. "New Jersey Honor Roll," *Baltimore Afro-American*, February 19, 1944, in Effa Manley's Scrapbook, National Baseball Hall of Fame and Museum.

18. "Memphis Splits With St. Louis," *Chicago Defender*, September 18, 1943; "Negro National Leaguers Claim Agreement Broken," *Chicago Defender*, January 15, 1944.

19. "Former Co-Owner of Newark Eagles Shot at 'Chicken Shack,'" *New Jersey Afro-American*, February 12, 1944; "FBI Dragnet Catches N.J. Killer," *Afro-American*, March 11, 1944; "New Jersey Round-Up," *Afro-American*, June 3, 1944.

20. Effa Manley, letter to Mr. Raleigh Mackey, January 28, 1944, Raleigh Mackey, letter to Mrs Manley, February 21, 1944, Effa Manley, letter to Dear Mackey, March 4, 1944, Newark Eagles Files, Newark Public Library.

21. "Newark Signs Suttles as Team Pilot," *New York Amsterdam News*, April 1, 1944; "Newark Eagles Await Two New Outfielders From Canal Zone," *New York Amsterdam News*, June 10, 1944; Riley, *Biographical Encyclopedia*, 889; Manley interview; "Pearson to Play Wells' Position," *Chicago Defender*, April 29, 1944; Sam Lacy, "Crack on Checker Playing Started Big Don in Baseball," the *Washington Afro-American*, October 4, 1949.

22. Wendell Smith, "Wells to Succeed Hornsby," *Pittsburgh Courier*, May 6, 1944; "Smitty's Sports Spurts," *Pittsburgh Courier*, May 6, 1944.

23. "N. J. Establishes Unit to Enforce Civil Rights Law," *Chicago Defender*, March 25, 1944.

24. "Discrimination Exposed in 'It's Midnight Over Newark,'" *New York Amsterdam Star-News*, May 7, 1944; "N.J. Hospital Board Upholds Ban Against Negroes on Staff," *New York Amsterdam Star-News*, June 17, 1944.

25. Holway, *The Complete Book*, 413; Ollie Stewart, "Ex-Newark Hurler Drives DUWK [*sic*] in English Channel," *Baltimore Afro-American*, July, 15, 1944.

26. "Homers Plentiful as Eagles Win Two," *Philadelphia Tribune*, May 20,1944. "Negro League Opens Sunday in Brooklyn," the *New York Amsterdam News*, May 20, 1944; "Newark Eagles Await Two New Outfielders From Canal Zone," *New York Amsterdam News*, June 10, 1944; "NNL to Show Wares in Polo Grounds," *Norfolk Journal and Guide*, June 10, 1944; "War Bond Rally Features Newark Eagles-Cuban Tilt in Brooklyn," *Norfolk Journal and Guide*, June 24, 1944; "Tubman Ship Has Brooklyn Support," *Pittsburgh Courier*, July 22. 1944; "Grays Drub Eagles," *Chicago Defender*, May 27, 1944; "Newark Eagles and Grays Split," *Chicago Defender*, July 8, 1944; Carol Sears Botsch, "Mary McLeod Bethune," University of South Carolina-Aiken, June 10, 2002, http://www.usca.edu/aasc/bethune.htm (accessed on October1, 2008); "Harriet Tubman," America's Stories from America's Library, http://www.americaslibrary.gov/aa/tubman/aa-tubman-subj.html (accessed on October 10, 2008). Sculpted by Robert Berks and dedicated in 1974, the statue stands in Lincoln Park at East Capitol and 12th Streets NE.

27. Carl Dunbar Lawrence, "Homestead Grays Rally in 9th to Beat Eagles in Playoff, 8-4," *New York Amsterdam News*, August 26, 1944; W. Rollo Wilson, "Stars Win 2nd Half Opener as Eagles Meet 13-2 Defeat," *Philadelphia Tribune*, July 15, 1944.

28. "Stars Win 2nd Half Opener," *Chicago Defender*, July 8, 1944; "Baltimore Wins Two," *Norfolk Journal and Guide*, July 15. 1944; "Newark Defeats Baltimore 5-3," *Pittsburgh Courier*, August 5, 1944; "Grays Spank Newark Twice," *Pittsburgh Courier*, September 2, 1944.

29. Wendell Smith, "Smitty's Sports Spurts," *Pittsburgh Courier*, December 9, 1944; Wendell Smith, "Smitty's Sports Spurts," *Pittsburgh Courier*, December 16, 1944; "Baseball Seeks Capable Man for Commissioner," *Pittsburgh Courier*, December 23, 1944; Sam Lacy, "Baseball Owners Talk Much but Do Little," *Baltimore Afro-American*, December 23, 1944.

30. Holway, *The Complete Book*, 421; Monty, letter to Mr. and Mrs. Manley, January 12, 1945, Newark Eagles Files, Newark Public Library.

31. Effa Manley, letter to Mr. Raleigh Mackey, December 22, 1944, Effa Manley, letter to Mr. Raleigh Mackey, January 12, 1945, James R. Mackey, letter to Mrs. Manley, February 27, 1945, Effa Manley, letter to Mr. Nathaniel Brannon, February 27, 1945, Effa Manley to Mr. James R. Mackey, March 5, 1945. Raleigh Mackey, letter to Mr. Manley, March 14, 1945, Terris, letter to Dear Mrs. Manley, February 1945, Effa Manley, letter to Mr. Terris McDuffie, February 26, 1945, Effa Manley, letter to Mr. and Mrs. Newcombe, March 21, 1945, Effa Manley, letter to Mr. Terris McDuffie, March 21, 1945, Effa

Manley, letter to Mr. Murray Watkins, March 24, 1945, Newark Eagles Files, Newark Public Library; Manley interview.

32. Danny Peary, *We Played the Game: 65 Players Remember Baseball's Greatest Era. 1947–1964* (New York: Hyperion, 1994), 287.

33. H. B. Webber, letter to Dear Mrs. Manley, May 8, 1945, Effa Manley, letter to Mr. Harry Webber, May 12, 1945, Newark Eagles Files, Newark Public Library.

34. Effa, letter to Dear Baby, April 20, 1945, Newark Eagles Files, Newark Public Library.

35. Effa Manley, letter to Mr. Fred McClary, May 17, 1945, Effa Manley, letter to Mr. Brady Johnson, May 17, 1945. Effa Manley to Terris McDuffie, June 9, 1945, Effa Manley, letter to Mr. Percy Simon, June 10, 1945.

36. "National League Results," *Pittsburgh Courier*, May 12, 1945. "Cubans Face Crucial Doubleheader Series," *New York Amsterdam News*, May 26, 1945.

37. Buck Leonard, *Buck Leonard: The Black Lou Gehrig*, with James A. Riley (New York: Carroll & Graf Publishers, 1995), 184; John Holway, *Blackball Stars: Negro League Pioneers* (New York: Carroll & Graf Publishers), 228; Effa Manley, letter to Mr. Wm Leuschner, August 17, 1945, Newark Eagles Files, Newark Public Library.

38. "Grays Near First Half Pennant Title," *Norfolk Journal and Guide*, June 9, 1945; "Grays Down Newark 7–2, 3–2 to Widen National League Lead," *Norfolk Journal and Guide*, June 16, 1945; "Black Yanks Halt Stars Before 9000 at Stadium," *New York Amsterdam News*, July 7, 1945.

39. Effa Manley, letter to Mr. M. I. Stevens, June 26, 1945, Newark Eagles Files, Newark Public Library.

40. Cum Posey, "Posey's Points," *Pittsburgh Courier*, June 23, 1945; Lanctot, *Negro League Baseball*, 270–72; "Owners Pledge Crackdown on NNL 'Bad Boys.'" *Baltimore Afro-American*, July 14, 1945.

41. "Baltimore Takes 2 From Newark," *Norfolk Journal and Guide*, July 14, 1945; Lem Graves Jr., "Newark Eagles Take Lead in Team Batting," *Norfolk Journal and Guide*, September 1, 1945; Haskell Cohen, "Newark's Youthful Pitcher Defeats N.Y. Black Yanks," *Pittsburgh Courier,* July 28, 1945; "Newcombe Hurls 1-Hitter as Newark Takes Twin Bill," *Baltimore Afro-American*, August 11, 1945; Harold Jackson, "Race Tightens in NNL 2nd Half Pennant Scramble," *Baltimore Afro-American*, September 1, 1945; "Grays Halt Newark Eagles in Twin Bill, 5-2 and 4-3," *Baltimore Afro-American*, September 8, 1945, Effa Manley, letter to Mr. Oscar Charleston, July 28, 1945, Newark Eagles Files, Newark Public Library; "Biz Mackey Will Lead Newark Eagles

Against Homestead," *Daily Courier*, Connellsville, PA, August 30, 1945; Riley, *Biographical Encyclopedia*, 842.

42. Effa Manley, letter to The Newspapers of Newark NJ Sports Editor, September 16, 1945, Newark Eagles Files, Newark Public Library.

43. James A. Curtis, letter to Mrs. Effie Manley, October 8, 1945, Newark Eagles Files, Newark Public Library.

44. Lee Lowenfish, *Branch Rickey: Baseball's Ferocious Gentleman* (Lincoln: University of Nebraska Press, 2007), 375, 380.

CHAPTER 10. BRANCH RICKEY DROPS THE COLOR BAR

1. Wendell Smith, "Brooklyn Owner Guiding Light of New Circuit," *Pittsburgh Courier*, May 12, 1945; Riley, *Biographical Encyclopedia*, 536; "As McDuffie and Thomas Did Stuff for Rickey," *Norfolk Journal and Guide*, April 14, 1945; Letter to Henry J. Walsh, an attorney for the Dodgers, Branch Rickey Papers, Box 33, Folder 15, Manuscript Division, Library of Congress, Washington, DC.

2. Wendell Smith, "EXTRA-Courier Pressing Campaign for Negro Players in Major Leagues," *Pittsburgh Courier*, April 14. 1945; Irvin interview by Marshall, May 12. 1977.

3. "Rickey Admits Calling in Jackie Robinson," *Pittsburgh Courier*, September 1, 1945; Wendell Smith, "Major Leagues Baseball 'Color-Line' Smashed," *Pittsburgh Courier*, October 27, 1945; Manley interview; Lowenfish, *Branch Rickey*, 368.

4. "Eagle Owner Flays Rickey for Tactics in Player Deal," *Baltimore Afro-American*, November 3, 1945.

5. From Newark Eagles Team File, National Baseball Hall of Fame and Museum.

6. Effa Manley, letter to Dr. J. B. Martin, October 26, 1945, Newark Eagles Files, Newark Public Library; Letter signed by Posy and edited by Manley, dated November 1, 1945, Newark Eagles team file, National Baseball Hall of Fame and Museum.

7. Effa Manley, letter to Satchel Paige, September 13, 1945, Effa Manley, letter to Mr. T. Y. Baird, September 26, 1945, Newark Public Library.

8. Dan Burley, "Big Leaguers Play Negroes," *New York Amsterdam News*, October 6, 1945.

9. Effa Manley, letter to Mr. Vernon Green, October 21, 1945, T. Y. Baird, letter to Mrs. Effa Manley, September 21, 1945, Newark Eagles Files, Newark Public Library; Dan Burley. "Big Leaguers Make Negro Star Team Look Like Sand Lotters," *New York Amsterdam News*, October 20, 1945.

10. Harvey Frommer, *Rickey and Robinson* (New York: MacMillan, 1982), 110–11.

11. Rogosin, *Invisible Men*, 216.

12. Sam Lacy, "Rickey Signs Campanella for Nashua," *Baltimore Afro-American,* April 13, 1946; Dan Burley, "Dodgers Sign Campanella, Newcombe," *New York Amsterdam News*, April 13, 1946; Effa Manley, letter to Dear Abe, April 5, 1946, Newark Eagles Files, Newark Public Library.

13. Effa Manley, letter to Raleigh Mackey, January 19, 1946, Raleigh Mackey, letter to Mrs. Manley, February 10, 1946, Newark Eagles Files, Newark Public Library.

14. Gai Ingham Berlage, *Women in Baseball: The Forgotten History* (Westport, CT: Praeger, 1994), 124.

15. Effa Manley, letter to Mr. Pat Patterson, April 6, 1946, Newark Eagles Files, Newark Public Library.

CHAPTER 11. A REUNITED TEAM

1. "Chandler Sees Martin, Wilson," *Chicago Defender*, January 26, 1946. Lanctot, *Negro League Baseball*, 285.

2. Lanctot, *Negro League Baseball*, 284–85.

3. "Wilson Retained as President of N.N.L," *Pittsburgh Courier*, February 16, 1946; Effa Manley, letter to Cum Posey, January 12, 1946, Effa Manley, letter to Art Carter, February 23, 1946, Newark Eagles Files, Newark Public Library.

4. "Cum Posey's Death Brings Many Sports Testimonials," *New York Amsterdam News*, April 6, 1946; "Posey Leaves Half of Grays to His Widow," *Chicago Defender*, April 13, 1946; "Scope and Content Note—David L. Lawrence," PA State Archives, http://www.phmc.state.pa.us/BAH/dam/mg/mg191.htm (accessed on March 3, 2009); Riley, *Bibliographical Encyclopedia*, 638.

5. Effa Manley, letter to Raleigh Mackey, January 19, Newark Eagles Files, Newark Public Library; Riley, *Biographical Encyclopedia*, 383; Effa Manley, letter to Monte Irvin, February 9, 1946; Effa Manley, letter to Mr. Raleigh Mackey, February 18, 1946, Effa Manley, letter to Larry Doby, March 9 and 19, 1946, Eagles-Mackey Contract 1946–47, Eagles Salary Schedule, Newark Eagles Files, Newark Public Library; Irvin, *Nice Guys Finish First,* 90.

6. Manley interview; Effa Manley, letter to Mr. Pat Patterson, March 26, April 6, 1946, Newark Eagles Files, Newark Public Library.

7. "Eagles, Grays, Cubans Loom as Top NNL Teams," *Newark Herald*, April 20, 1946; Riley, *Biographical Encyclopedia*, 367, 609.

8. "Play That Caused Near Riot In Newark Eagle's No Hit Win From Philly," *New York Amsterdam News*, May 11, 1946; "Police Halt Philadelphia Stars-Newark Eagles Riot," *New York Amsterdam News*, May 11, 1946.

9. Effa Manley, letter to Mr. Ed Gottlieb, May 8, 1946, Newark Eagles Files, Newark Public Library.

10. Effa Manley, letter to Art Carter, May 9, 1946, Moorland-Spingarn Research Center, Howard University, Art Carter Papers, Box 170–16, Folder 9.

11. "8 Players Get 5-Year Suspensions, Elites Lose Star to Grays in NNL Action in Philly," *Baltimore Afro-American*, May 25, 1946.

12. Effa Manley, letter to Mr. Pat Patterson, May 28, 1946, Newark Eagles Files, Newark Public Library.

13. Reginald Simpson, letter to Mrs. Effa Manley, May 29, Effa Manley, letter to Mr. Reginald Simpson, June 6, 1946, Newark Eagles Files, Newark Public Library; "Cubans, Newark Tie for NNL Lead," *Chicago Defender*, May 25, 1946; "Biz Mackey Irked Over Slump; Cracks Whip Over Newark Eagles," *Philadelphia Tribune*, June 1, 1946.

14. "Eagles, Stars in Tie for NNL Lead; Newark Tops Cubans Twice," *Norfolk Journal and Guide*, June 15, 1946; "Eagles Lead Stars In Hot Pennant Race," *Philadelphia Tribune*, June 25, 1946; Dan Burley, "Back Door Stuff." *New York Amsterdam News*, June 15, 1946; "Cubans Beaten in 2 at Newark," *New York Amsterdam News*, June 29, 1946; "Newark Eagles Cinch Pennant for First Half," *New York Amsterdam News*, July 6.

15. "Newark Eagles Home in First Lap of NNL Chase," *Baltimore Afro-American*, July 6, 1946; "Grays Battle N.Y. Cubans, Newark Eagles," *Pittsburgh Courier*, July 6, 1946, Art Carter Papers, Box 170-16 File 9, Manuscript Division, Moorland-Spingarn Research Center, Howard University. Washington, DC. Irvin interview, January 17, 2007.

16. Effa Manley, letter to Dear Friend, July 19, 1946, Newark Eagles Files, Newark Public Library.

17. "Newark Eagles Heading West to Play Bucks," *New York Amsterdam News*, July 20, 1946; Wendell Smith, "The Sports Beat," *Pittsburgh Courier*, August 3, August 10, 1946; Effa Manley, letter to Mr. Ed. Gottlieb, June 25, 1946; Effa Manley, letter to Dear Friend, August 3, 1946; Newark Eagles Files, Newark Public Library; "Negro Baseball Vital Statistics," *New York Amsterdam* News, August 17, 1946.

18. "Newark Leads NNL; Cubans, Elites Second," *Pittsburgh Courier*, August 3, 1946; "Newark Wins East Pennant," *Chicago Defender*, September 7, 1946; "Monty Irvin Top Batter in Negro National League," *Chicago Defender*, October 5, 1946.

19. T. Y. Baird, letter to Mrs. Effa Manley, September 2, 1946, J. B. Martin, letter to Mrs. Effa Manley, September 6, 1946, Effa Manley, letter to Mr. T. Y. Baird, September 7, Newark Eagles Files, Newark Public Library.

20. Fay Young, "Through the Years," *Chicago Defender*, October 12, 1946; "Negro World Series Set," *New York Times*, September 11, 1949; J. B. Martin, letter to Mrs. Effa Manley, September 6, 1946, Newark Eagles Files, Newark Public Library.

21. Overmyer, *Effa Manley*, 204–207; "N.Y. Gets World Series Opener," *Baltimore Afro-American*, September 14, 1946; Sam Lacy, "19,423 Fans See Paige in Brilliant Performance," *Baltimore Afro-American*, September 21, 1946; "K.C. Monarchs Take 3-2 World Series Lead," *Baltimore Afro-American*, September 28, 1946; "Ike Permits Contract With Manager Expire," *Baltimore Afro-American*, October 5, 1946; Fay Young, "Newark Ties Kansas in World Series," *Baltimore Afro-American*, September 28, 1946; "Kansas City's 21 Hits Wallop Eagles, 15–5," *New York Amsterdam News*, September 28, 1946; "Newark Evens Series; Play in Newark Fri," September 28, 1946; "Kansas City Wins to Take One Game Lead in Negro World Series," *Pittsburgh Courier*, September 28, 1946; "Newark Eagles New Diamond Champs," *Pittsburgh Courier*, October 5, 1946; Amiri Baraka, *The Autobiography of Leroi Jones*, 34; Effa Manley, letter to Pat Patterson, October 4, 1946, Newark Eagles Files, Newark Public Library.

22. Luke, *Willie Wells,* 99.

23. Irvin interview, March 2, 2005.

24. Bob Feller, interview by the author, February 13, 2005.

25. "Important Sports Memorabilia and Cards at Public Auction," *Hunt Auction Catalogue*, March 7–8, 2008; Dan Burley, "Confidentially Yours," *New York Amsterdam News*, September 28, 1946; "Heavy Stickman Eye '47 Pennant For Champ Newark Club," *New York Amsterdam News*, April 5, 1947.

26. Irvin, *Nice Guys Finish First*, 68; Irvin Interview, March 2, 2005.

27. Melvin B. Johnson, "Discrimination in Jersey Jobs Seen on Increase," *New York Amsterdam News*, February 23, 1946; "YMCA Abolishes Separate Camps," *Newark Herald*, April 20, 1946; "Frequently Asked Questions," PalisadesPark.com, http://www.palisadespark.com/faqs.htm#locate (accessed on March 3, 2009), "Seeks End of Jim Crow in N.J. National Guard," *Chicago Defender*, April 27, 1946; "First Negro Medic at Newark Hosp. A Woman," *Chicago Defender*, January 26, 1947; "New Jersey Park Revives Former Anti-Negro Policies," *Chicago Defender*, August 24, 1947; "Won After All," *Afro-American*, December 7, 1946.

28. Martin and Martin, *The Negro Leagues in New Jersey*, 7; The Jackie Robinson Papers, Container 1, Folder 17, Manuscript Reading Room, Library of Congress, Washington, DC.

CHAPTER 12. STRIVING FOR RESPECTABILITY

1. Dan Burley, "NNL Names Rev. John Johnson as Prexy," *New York Amsterdam* News, January 11, 1947; "N.Y. Minister New N.L.L. Prexy," *Baltimore Afro-American*, January 11, 1947; "Minister Elected Head of Negro National League," *Chicago Defender,* January 11, 1947; Staff Correspondent. "Owners Oust Tom Wilson, Install First 'Independent' Administration," *Baltimore Afro-American*. January 11, 1947.

2. "Owners Bar Doubleduty Radcliffe," *New York Amsterdam News*, March 8, 1947; Dan Burley, "Confidentially Yours," *New York Amsterdam News*, January 18,1947; "Negro Loop List Rules," *New York Times*, March 1, 1947; Wendell Smith. "The Sports Beat," *Pittsburgh Courier*, January 6, 1947.

3. Wendell Smith, "Doby, Clarkson, Irvin Newest Brooklyn Farmhands," *Pittsburgh Courier*, February 1, 1947; "Newark Pilot Says Doby, Irvin, Clarkson Cinches," *Pittsburgh Courier*, February 15, 1947; "Partlow Fourth Race Tryout for Montreal Berth," *Pittsburgh Courier*, March 15, 1947; "Brooklyn's Rickey Signs Three More Negro Players," *Chicago Defender*, February 8, 1947.

4. "Leon Day, Ruffin Jump the Eagles," *New York Amsterdam News*, March 22, 1947.

5. "N.Y. Cubans on Top, 10-2," *New York Times*, April 28, 1947; "Johnson Fines Cubans-Eagles in PG Brawler," *New York Amsterdam News*, May 3, 1947.

6. "Black Yanks Open Sunday at Newark Against Eagles," *New York Amsterdam* News, May 3, 1947; "Newark Wins Two From Philly," *New York Amsterdam News,* May 17, 1947.

7. "Tom Wilson 'Strikes Out,'" *Chicago Defender*, May 24, 1947.

8. "Larry Doby Looms as Home Run King," *New Amsterdam News*, May 31, 1947; "Tops NNL at Bat," *New Amsterdam News*, June 14, 1947; "Newark vs. Cubans at Brooklyn," *New Amsterdam News*, June 21, 1947; 'MUST Stop Irvin and Doby to Win," *New Amsterdam News*, July 5, 1947.

9. Doby interview; Lem Graves Jr., "Press Box," *Norfolk Journal and Guide*, August 24, 1946; Wendell Smith, "The Sports Beat," *Pittsburgh Courier*, July 12, 1947; Bill Madden, "Hail Doby the Pioneer," *Daily News*, April 26, 1995; A. S. Doc Young, "Winning in the U.S.A.," *Los Angeles Sentinel*, January 28, 1993; Art Rust Jr., "Doby Talks Candidly About Baseball," *New York Amsterdam News*, July 15, 1978.

10. Joseph Thomas Moore, *Pride Against Prejudice: The Biography of Larry Doby* (New York: Praeger, 1988), 40, 43, 45; Sheep Jackson, "From the Sidelines," *The Cleveland Call and Post*, July 13, 1974.

11. Doby interview.

12. Jerry Izenberg telephone interview by the author. October 16, 2009. Doby was reluctant to name names, especially for publication, but Izenberg said he heard this story and the names directly from Doby.

13. Izenberg interview; Doby interview.

14. Wendell Smith, "The Sports Beat," *Pittsburgh Courier*, July 12, 1947; Al Dunmore, "Cleveland Owner Kept His Word," *Pittsburgh Courier*, July 12, 1947; "Larry Doby, Ace Negro Infielder, Signs Contract With Cleveland," *New York Times*, July 4, 1947.

15. Manley interview; Manley and Hardwick, *Negro Baseball*, 74–76.

16. Bill Veeck, interview by William Marshall, Chicago February 23, 1977. Seven weeks later Rickey signed Dan Bankhead of the Memphis Rex Sox to a contract but had to pay for the privilege. With the new player contracts containing a reserve clause and the deal coming in the middle of the season, there could be no question but that Bankhead was under contract to the Red Sox. Rickey paid B. B. Martin, general manager of the Memphis Red Sox, $15,000. The terms were exactly the same as those for Doby; $10,000 upon signing the contract in Memphis, Tennessee, on August 23, and another $5,000 if the Dodgers kept Bankhead for more than a month, which they did. (Branch Rickey Papers, Manuscript Division, Box 5, Folder 3, Library of Congress, Washington, DC.)

17. Moore, *Pride Against Prejudice*, 41; Irvin interview, February 21, 2008.

18. Wendell Smith, "The Sports Beat," *Pittsburgh Courier*, August 23, 1947; Stanley Williford, "Mrs. Effa Manley: She Owned the Greats," *Los Angeles Sentinel*, April 19, 1973.

19. Veeck interview; "Cubans Win Twice, Take Title," *New York Times*, September 12, 1947.

20. Wendell Smith, "The Sports Beat," *Pittsburgh Courier*, August 9, September 6. 1947; Dan Burley, "Confidentially Yours," *New York Amsterdam News*, December 27, 1947; "Expect 40,000 at 'Dream Game,'" *New York Amsterdam News*, July 26, 1947, "38,402 Crowd in PG Biggest Ever in East," *New York Amsterdam News*, August 2, 1947; Dick Clark and Larry Lester, eds., *The Negro Leagues Book* (Cleveland, OH: Society for American Baseball Research, 1994), 253.

21. "Named to High Post in Newark," *New York Amsterdam News*, July 19, 1947; "Plan Integration of Jersey Guard," *Chicago Defender*, October 8, 1947; "Woman Holds High Post With Housing Authority," *Chicago Defender*, October 4, 1947; "Jersey College Creates Sorority to Fight Bias," *Chicago Defender*, May 31, 1947; "Women Voters Urge Civil Rights Clause, *New*

*York Times,* June 21, 1947; "Labor Guarantee Urged," *Philadelphia Tribune,* July 6, 1947; Marion Thompson Wright, "Negro Suffrage in New Jersey, 1776–1875," *Journal of Negro History,* vol. 33, no. 2 (April, 1948); http://lawlibrary.rutgers.edu/news/newsletters/May07News&Events.pdf (accessed on November 14, 2008); "Job Gains in '46 Listed by League," *Pittsburgh Courier,* January 18. 1947.

22. "Arrest 29 Bias Fighters in NJ," *New York Amsterdam News,* September 6, 1947; "Charge 3 Chinese With Jim Crowing," *New York Amsterdam News,* August 23, 1947.

23. Jean O. Gibbs, "Mack Hoffler's Funeral Held at Hertford," *Norfolk Journal and Guide,* December 13, 1947.

24. Editorial, *New York Amsterdam News,* August 9, 1947; Manley interview, Sheep Jackson, "From the Sidelines," *Cleveland Call and Post,* July 13, 1974.

25. "Newark Fires Manager Biz Mackey," *New York Amsterdam News,* January 31, 1948; Dan Burley, "Confidentially Yours," *New York Amsterdam News,* April 3, 1948; "Newark Seen as Dark Horse Entry in NNL," *New York Amsterdam News,* May 22, 1948; "Bill Yancey Mentioned for Newark Post," *Philadelphia Inquirer,* February 3, 1948; "Manleys Sign Bill Bell to Pilot Newark," *Chicago Defender,* March 27, 1948.

26. Willie C. "Curley" Williams telephone interview by the author. October 7, 2009.

27. "Newark Eagles Nip Baltimore Elites by 2-1," *New York Amsterdam News,* May 8, 1948; "Buck Leonard Homers Nip Newark," *New York Amsterdam News,* May 15, 1948; "Newark Seen as Dark Horse Entry in NNL," *New York Amsterdam News,* May 22, 1948; "Newark Eagles Set Hot Pace for AL Nine," *New York Amsterdam News,* June 12, 1948; "Baltimore Won NNL's 1st Half," *Baltimore Afro-American,* July 24, 1948; "Bell Pleased With Pitching as Eagles Open Home Stand," *Chicago Defender,* June 5, 1948; "Baltimore vs. Newark Eagles Sunday June 20," *Washington Post,* June 19, 1948; "Grays, Newark Play Two Today," *Washington Post,* July 4.

28. "Would Have Quit NNL If Rickey Hadn't Signed Me Up—Robinson," *New York Amsterdam News,* November 1, 1947; Jackie Robinson, "What's Wrong With the Negro Leagues," *Ebony,* June 1948.

29. An article bearing the byline "By the Star's Sports Editors" and the title "Comments," Effa Manley's Scrapbook, Hall of Fame and Museum. "This Beef Is Spoiling, Jackie!" *Cleveland Call and Post,* May 29, 1948; "Mrs. Manley Calls Jackie Robinson 'Ungrateful,'" *Chicago Defender,* May 29, 1948.

30. Frank A. Young, "Through the Years," *Chicago Defender,* June 12, 1948.

31. "Mrs. Manley Sounds Off Again on Race in Majors," *Norfolk Journal and*

*Guide*, September 11, 1948; Lillian Scott, "Effa Manley 'Hotter Than Horse Radish,'" *Chicago Defender*, September 18, 1948.

32. Moore, *Pride Against Prejudice,* 21–22.
33. "Newark Beats Grays," *Chicago Defender*, August 21, 1948; Scott, "Effa Manley 'Hotter Than Horse Radish'"; "NJ Leader Says Eagles' Prexy Biased," *New York Amsterdam News,* October 2, 1948; Dan Burley "Confidentially Yours," *New York Amsterdam News,* September 29, 1945; Buck O'Neil, *I Was Right on Time,* with Steve Wulf and David Conrads (New York: Simon & Schuster 1996), 182; "Denies Kansas City Had Robinson Under Contract," *Sporting News*, October 27, 1948.
34. "N.J. Herald Elects 42 Distinguished Citizens to Hall of Fame," *Norfolk Journal and Guide*, November 13, 1948.
35. "Manleys Disbanding Club in Negro National Leagues," *Sporting News*, November 17, 1948; A.S. Doc Young, "Long Subjects, Short Comments," *Los Angeles Sentinel*, April 30, 1981.
36. Russ Cowans, "Down Dixie Way," *Chicago Defender*, March 19, 1949; "Memphis Fete Rivals Famed Mardi Gras," *Chicago Defender*, May 22, 1949; "Mitchell Is Bus. Manager Houston Team," *Chicago Defender*, January 22, 1949.
37. Overmyer, *Effa Manley*, 241.
38. Ibid., 242–43; "Monty Irvin Joins the St. Paul Saints," *New York Amsterdam News*, January 1, 1949; "Brooklyn Gives up Monte Irvin," *Pittsburgh Courier*, January 22, 1949.
39. Wendell Smith, "Sports Beat," *Pittsburgh Courier*, January 22, 1949; Irvin, *Nice Guys Finish First*, 119–120; Chris Perry, "Mrs. Manley Lowers the Boom on Rickey, Monte Irvin Better Off," *Philadelphia Tribune*, January 18, 1949.
40. Williford, "Mrs. Effa Manley: She Owned the Greats" Irvin interview, February 21, 2008.
41. "Larry Doby Signed to Play ABL Ball on Paterson '5,'" *New York Amsterdam News*, January 10, 1948; "Black Yanks, Newark Eagles Break Rochester Color Line," *New York Amsterdam News*, May 22, 1948. The National Basketball League had been integrated in 1942.

CHAPTER 13. EFFA'S LIFE AFTER THE EAGLES
1. Mary McLeod Bethune Papers: The Bethune Foundation Collection, Part Correspondence Files, 1914–1955, Reel 14, File Folder Frame No. 0924, Manuscript Division, Library of Congress.

2.  Overmyer, *Effa Manley*, 2–3; George Lyle Jr., "On the Limb," *Norfolk Journal and Guide*, August 20, 1949; Sam Lacy, "From A to Z," *Baltimore Afro-American*, June 25, 1949; Lanctot, *Negro League Baseball*, 260–61. Lacy had won permission from organized baseball in 1945 to form a committee consisting of Yankees owner Larry MacPhail; Branch Rickey, himself; and another of Lacy's choosing. He chose Joe Rainey, former unsuccessful candidate for NNL president. The committee was to seek ways to admit the colored leagues into organized baseball. Martin and Wilson declined Lacy's invitation for an owner of each league to join the committee. The moguls' lack of interest and foot-dragging by MacPhail killed the effort. Lacy no doubt felt his initiative had gone unappreciated as well as unheeded. Effa kept a copy of Lacy's column in her scrapbook and wrote in the margin, "More brickbats by Sam."

3.  Sam Lacy, letter to Dear Friend, Effa Manley File, National Baseball Hall of Fame and Museum. Lacy admitted in his autobiography to having an addiction to betting the horses that almost made a jailbird out of him after he wrote bad checks. He claimed his addiction lasted into his late twenties, but he would have been in his early forties when he wrote the letter to Effa. (Sam Lacy *Fighting for Fairness: The Life Story of Hall of Fame Sportswriter Sam Lacy*, with Moses J Newson [Centreville, MD: Tidewater Publishers, 1998], 17).

4.  "Fay Says," *Chicago Defender*, July 30, 1949.

5.  Wendell Smith, "The Sports Beat," *Pittsburgh Courier*, November 26, 1948.

6.  Irvin interview, February 21, 2008.

7.  Overmyer, *Effa Manley*, 248–49.

8.  "Basketball Ability Opened O.B. Door to Torgy's Rival," *Sporting News*, March 26, 1952; Gai Berlage, *Women in Baseball: The Forgotten History* (Westport CT: Praeger, 1994), 122.

9.  "Ed Bolden, Philadelphia Stars Owner, Dies," *Chicago Defender*, October 7, 1950; Riley, *Biographical Encyclopedia*, 91, 625; "Yankees Tearing Down Historical Ruppert Stadium," *Christian Science Monitor*, October 11, 1952; "Newark Buys Ruppert Stadium," *New York Times*, November 26. 1952; "Newark Plot Sold for Industry Plant," *New York Times*, August 25, 1961; Glenn Fowler, "Ex-Stadium to Become Food Plant," *New York Times*, November 3, 1968; Esther Blaustein, "The Newark of Old: It Continues to Live," *New York Times*, October 14, 1979.

10. Manley interview; Samuel Hoskins, "Abe Manley, Baseball Founder, Buried," *Baltimore Afro-American*, December 20, 1952; Joel Manley interview, October 14, 2008; Laura, letter to Dear Effa, March 9, 1976, Effa Manley

Collection, Box 1, Fisk University Archives, Nashville, TN; "Doby, Irvin Pallbearers for Manley," *Philadelphia Tribune*, December 16, 1952; Overmyer, *Effa* Manley, 248.

11. "Win Fight Against Park Segregation," *Philadelphia Tribune*, July 19, 1949; "Ban Segregation in Newark, N.J. Public Housing," *New York Amsterdam News*, September 23, 1952; "Palisades Trial in 2nd Week," *New York Amsterdam News*, March 1, 1953.

12. Lulu Jones Garrett, "Gadabouting in the U.S.A," *Baltimore Afro-American*, January 9, 1954; Harry Hazelwood Jr., letter to Mr. Madison Jones, November 3, 1950; NAACP Papers, Part II, Box C-110, Folder 5, Manuscript Division, Library of Congress; Application for License No. 381975, December 22, 1953, Washington, DC Municipal Court Archives; Eve Lynn, "Exclusive!" *Pittsburgh Courier*, January 9, 1954; "Gibson Big Gun as Elites Bow to Grays," *Baltimore Afro-American*, May 22, 1943.

13. Monte Irvin interview, February 21, 2008; Jack Saunders, "I Love a Parade," *Philadelphia Tribune*, August 10, 1954; Mrs. Julia Jordan, "Germantown Gems," *Philadelphia Tribune,* January 11, 1955; *Philadelphia Tribune,* November 13, 1955; "Plan Tea for Home for Blind," "Concert Series Association Chairmen Make Plans," *Philadelphia Tribune,* December 14, 1955; Barbara Prigmore, "Here and There in Philly," *Philadelphia Tribune,* December 18, 1955; "Wissahickon Boys Club," *Philadelphia Tribune* December 21, 1955

14. Marion E. Jackson, "Sports of the World," *Atlanta Daily World*, September 5, 1956; Spike Washington, "Atlantans Boast of Woman Boss of Big League Baseball Outfit," *Atlanta Daily World*, June 11, 1944; Ozeil Pryer Woolcock, "Social Swirl," *Atlanta Daily World*, September 5, 1956.

15. Overmyer, *Effa Manley*, 249; Manley interview; J. B. Martin, letter to Mrs. Effa Alexander Manley, August 11, 1958, J. B. Martin, letter to Mrs. Effa Manley Alexander, September 16, 1958, Effa Manley Alexander, letter to Mr. Walter O'Malley, January 17, 1959, courtesy of Robert Edward Auctions.

16. Andy Razaf, letter to Dear Friend Effa, April 3, 1959, Eubie Blake, letter to Dear Effa, undated, Eubie Blake, letter to Dear Mrs. Manley, January 13, 1975, Effa Manley Scrapbook, National Baseball Hall of Fame and Museum.

17. A. S. Doc Young, "Long Subjects, Short Comments," *Los Angeles Sentinel*, April 30, 1981.

18. Overmyer, *Effa Manley*, 250–51;. Riley, *Biographical Encyclopedia*, 105–7, 792; Larry Lester, "The Gentleman Quincy Trouppe, as I Knew Him," in Quincy Trouppe, *20 Years Too Soon: Prelude to Major League Integrated Baseball* (St. Louis: Missouri Historical Society Press, 1995), 5.

19. Ronald E. Kisner, "White Widow of Black Baseball League Pioneer Writes Book About Saga," *Jet*, March 1977. St. Johann Press reprinted the book in 2006 under the editorship of Robert Cvornyek. Two of the *Sentinel* articles are: "Negro League Owner Blasts Baseball," July 7, 1977, and "Fame Overlooks Great Rube Foster," August 18, 1977.

20. Correspondence between Effa Manley and Mrs. Jessie Carney Smith from 1975 to 1976, Effa Manley Collection on Negro Baseball, John Hope and Aurelia E. Franklin Library, Fisk University, Nashville, TN; Laura, letter to Dear Effa, March 9, 1976, Effa Manley Collection.

21. Bowie Kuhn, *The Education of a Baseball Commissioner* (New York: Times Books), 110–11; Bowie Kuhn, telephone interview by the author, January 26, 2006. The committee consisted of Judy Johnson (Negro league player for twenty years, eventual Hall of Famer, and scout for the Philadelphia Phillies); Bill Yancey (Negro league shortstop for over twenty years and former scout for the Yankees and Phillies); Roy Campanella; black sportswriters Wendell Smith and Sam Lacy (both longtime advocates for inducting Negro leaguers); Ed Gottlieb (former owner of the Philadelphia Stars and one of the first to schedule games in major league parks); Alex Pompez (a scout for the New York Giants and former owner of the Negro leagues' Cuban Stars); Frank Forbes (senior judge with the New York Boxing Commission, former scout for the New York Giants, and former Negro League player); and Everett D. (Eppie) Barnes (athletic director at Colgate University, former president of the National Collegiate Athletic Association, a first baseman for the Pittsburgh Pirates for four games during the 1923–24 seasons, and the only white voting member of the committee). Barnes had managed the semipro team—the East Orange Base Ball Club, a frequent opponent of the Eagles and other Negro League teams. As a result, Barnes had personal knowledge of many Negro league stars.

22. Irvin interview, June 4, 2005. For a detailed discussion of the cumbersome process it took to induct the nine players, see Luke, *Willie Wells*, 104–33.

23. Kuhn, *The Education*, 111; Irvin interview, June 4, 2005.

24. O'Neil, *I Was Right on Time*, 222; Milton Gross, "Robinson Speaks Out," *New York Post*, February 4, 1971; Stan Issacs, "Why Doesn't Baseball Put Paige in Front of the Hall?" *Newsday*, February 5, 1971, National Baseball Hall of Fame and Museum; "Ebony Photo-Editorial: A Hollow Ring to Fame," *Ebony*, April 1971, 124.

25. Irvin interview, June 4, 2005.

26. Baucher, Bill, "Baseball's Black Nine," *The Miami Herald*, February 7, 1977.

27. "Too Few Black Baseball Greats in Hall: Powell," *Chicago Daily Defender*, August 12, 1972.

28. A. S. (Doc) Young, "Junk Negro Shrine Vote, Says Young," *Sporting News*, March 15, 1975.

29. Irvin interview, January 26, 2006.

30. John M. Coates II, "Ex-umpire tabs blacks for hall of fame," *Chicago Defender*, September 29, 1973.

31. Overmyer, *Effa Manley*, 255.

32. Effa Manley, letter to Dear Mr. Garagiola, August 13, 1974, courtesy of Robert Edwards Auction.

33. "Awards Show Honors Oldtimers," *Los Angeles Sentinel*, February 16, 1978; Brad Pye Jr., "Prying Pye," *New Pittsburgh Courier*, March 2, 1981; "Negro League Reunion to Honor 'Cool Papa,' Satchel," *New Pittsburgh Courier*, June 6, 1981; Irvin interview, February 21, 2008.

34. Overmyer, *Effa Manley*, 256.

EPILOGUE

1.   Ed Stack, telephone interview by the author, July 22, 2005.

2.   *Silhouette: The Official Newsletter of the Negro Leagues Baseball Museum*, vol. 4. no. 1 (Spring 1995): 1. Those inducted between 1995 and 2001 were Leon Day (1995), Bill Foster (1996), Willie Wells (1997), Joe Rogan (1998), Joe Williams (1999), Turkey Stearns (2000), and Hilton Smith (2001).

3.   Dale Petroskey, interview by the author, February 21, 2006.

4.   The historians and their areas of expertise were Todd Bolton, Latin America; Greg Bond, nineteenth-century history; Adrian Burgos, Latin America; Dick Clark, Negro leagues; Ray Doswell, overall knowledge and Negro leagues; Leslie Heaphy, overall knowledge and Negro leagues; Larry Lester, Negro leagues; Sammy Miller, eastern and western teams; Jim Overmyer, eastern teams and nineteenth century; Robert Peterson, overall knowledge; and Rob Ruck, eastern teams. Peterson died before the process was completed.

5.   James Overmyer, e-mail to the author, June 28, 2009.

6.   Jeff Idelson, e-mail to the author, March 14, 2008.

# INDEX

admission prices, xi, 20, 79
African Americans
  contracting tuberculosis, 37
  housing for, 37, 45, 100, 104, 153
  jobs for, 7–8, 19–20, 37, 45, 76, 90,
  96, 100, 113, 131, 140
Aitken, Bertram R., 77–78
Alexander, Charles Wesley, 150
Anderson, Marian, 44–45
Argentina, 35
Armstrong, Henry, 61
Arnold, T. Hill, 75
Atkins, Leroy, 4–5
Atlanta Black Crackers, 43, 155
Austin, Frank, 118

Baird, Thomas, 92, 107, 117–18, 127–
  28, 138
Baltimore Elite Giants, 27, 135
  1939 season, 48–49, 51
  1941 season, 77
  1942 season, 88
  1944 season, 106
  1945 season, 112
  1946 season, 125–26
  1947 season, 135

1948 season, 142
Bankhead, Sam, 43, 91, 105, 118
bans on players, 32, 66–67, 71, 73,
  112–13, 124, 134
Baraka, Amiri, xi–xii, 21
Barnhill, Dave, 17
barnstorming, 62–63, 127, 130, 131
Battle, Samuel J., 77, 121–22
Bavasi, Buzzie, 156
Bell, Butch, 39
Bell, "Cool Papa", 16, 160–62
Bell, William, Sr., 23, 26, 34, 141
benefit games, 16, 27, 64, 78, 100, 142
Benson, Eugene "Spider", 83, 85
Benswanger, William, 91
Bethune, Mary McLeod, 106, 149–50
Bishop, John Marcus, 1
Black, Joe, 142
Black, Julian, 72, 74
Blake, Eubie, 157
Blaustein, Ester, 152
Blumstein, William, 7–8
Bolden, Edward "Chief", 10–11, 22, 25,
  57, 59, 69, 71, 96, 102, 133, 151–52
booking agents, 17, 21, 56–59, 76, 82,
  105, 110, 121, 134

Borican, John, 48, 61, 77–78
Bostic, Joe, 115
Boston Red Sox, 115
Boudreau, Lou, 137
boycotts, 7–8
Bradford, Bill, 99
Braithwaite, 103
Braucher, Bill, 160
Brewer, Chet, 157
Brewer, Obadiah, 46
Brice, Carol, 45
Brooklyn Brown Dodgers, 115–17
Brooklyn Dodgers, 11, 15, 115–16,
    118, 134
Brooklyn Eagles, 9, 11–16, 22, 56
Brooks, Benjamin, 1
Brooks, Bertha Ford, 1–2
Brooks, Jacob, 52
Brooks, Ruth, 61–62, 152
Brown, Barney, 83–84, 112, 124
Brown, James, 47–48, 50, 73, 84
Brown, Jesse, 48
Brown, Raymond, 42, 85, 105, 166
Brown, Ruth Marie, 71–72
Brown, Willard, 77, 127, 129, 166
Bumbrey, Clara, 4
Bumbrey, Robert, 4–5
Burley, Dan, 71, 81, 133
Burnett, Tex, 27
Burnett, Victor, 103
Burrell, J. Mercer, 18, 36–37, 48, 61,
    92, 140, 145, 153
Burroughs, Dan, 70
Bush, Charles, 3
Bushwicks, 17, 40
Byrd, Bill, 88, 118

Camden Leafs, 5
Campanella, Roy, 118–19, 130, 136,
    139, 149, 159, 165
Carey, Addison, 13

Carey, Richard, 61
Carter, Art, 57–58, 69, 82, 85, 95, 124
Carter, Ernest "Spoon", 63
Carter, Eunice, 15
Cash, Bill, 124
ceremonial first ball, 13, 23, 24, 36, 48,
    61, 74, 98, 105
Chainey, Dr., 110
Chandler, A. B. "Happy", 113, 117,
    121, 137
Charleston, Oscar, 16, 66, 112, 119,
    160–61
Cheeks, Bob, 124
Cherry, Hugh, 145, 147
Chicago American Giants, 14, 23, 28
Christopher, Thadist, 26, 73, 83
Church, Robert, 111
civil rights, xii, 104, 106, 131
Clark, Dick, 166
Clark, John, 21, 26, 38
Clarkson, Buzz, 63, 83–85, 91–92, 134
Cleveland Buckeyes, 126
Cleveland Indians, 136–38
Clinton, Henry Moton, 153–54
Cole, Benjamin A., 1
Cole, Cecil, 124
Cole, Robert, 10–11, 23
Collins, Elijah, 153
color bar, 132, 147
Comiskey Park, Chicago, 129
Conlan, Jocko, 161
Conlon, Joseph E., 95–96
contract jumping, 12, 25, 32, 55, 57,
    60–61, 67, 71, 124, 134
Cooper, Al, 92
Cooper, Andy, 166
Cooper, Anthony, 35
Cooper, Darltie, 67–68
Craig, Homer, 36
Crocker, Claude, 115
Crosby, Bing, 156

Crowe, George, 151
Crutchfield, Jimmy, 26, 47
Cuba, 108
Cuban Giants, 128
Curry, Homer, 124
Curtis, James A., 113, 153

Dabney, John M., 29
Dandridge, Ray, 23, 26, 28–29, 33, 47,
    56, 60, 73, 87, 96–97, 103, 124, 165
Darden, W. T., 24, 27
Daughters of the American Revolution,
    44–45
Davis, John Howard "Johnny", 70, 101,
    103, 105–6, 118, 123, 125, 127–28
Davis, Spencer "Babe", 26
Davis, William, 7
Day, Leon, 12, 15–16, 28, 33, 36, 40,
    47–48, 50, 60, 73–74, 77, 85–86,
    88, 91–92, 99–100, 101, 105, 122,
    124–29, 134–35, 142
Dihigo, Martin, 16, 47, 160
discrimination, 7, 19, 31, 37, 45, 65,
    75–76, 90, 95–96, 100–101, 104,
    113, 131, 140, 153
Doby, Larry, xi, 98, 122, 124–25, 130,
    134–36, 145, 147, 151–52
    Brooklyn Dodgers, scouted by, 136
    Cleveland Indians, signed by,
        136–38
    drafted in army, 101
    high school years, 89
    Newark Eagles, joins, 89
    1946 Negro World Series, 127–29
    pseudonym, 89
Dougherty, Romeo, 12–13, 15
Douglass, Bob, 68
Dressen, Chuck, 118
Durocher, Leo, 115

Eastman, Joseph P., 95

East-West Classic, 9, 16, 28, 50, 55, 63,
    76, 86, 140
Edison, Thomas, 98, 101
Ellenstein, Meyer, 73–74
Ellidge, Eric, 12, 39
Enyon, Edward B., 66
Evans, Bob "Glasseye", 33, 36

Fair Employment Practices Committee
    (FEPC), 76, 90, 100
fans, xi–xii, 45–46, 62, 74, 90, 106, 130,
    135, 141, 144
Felder, William, 125
Feller, Bob, 127, 130
Feller All–Stars, 127, 130–31
fines, 10, 32, 65–66, 71, 73, 113, 124
Fitzgerald, Ella, 29
Forrest, Percy, 105
Foster, Rube, 161–62, 165
Fox, William, 36
Foxx, Jimmie, 33
Frick, Ford, 117, 121, 159

Garagiola, Joe, 160
Garcia, Silvio, 135
Garrett, Lulu Jones, 154
Gehrig, Lou, 33, 74
Gibson, Josh, 16, 27, 34, 66–67, 86, 91,
    105–6, 118, 160
Giles, George, 12, 13–14, 16, 23
girlfriends of players, xi
Glenn, Stanley, 45–46
Goldsmith, Leonard H., 95–96
Goodman, Danny, 157
Gordon, Joe, 137
Gottlieb, Ed, 11, 42, 56–59, 76–77, 83,
    97, 102, 105, 124, 133–34
Grant, Frank, 166
Graves, Lem, Jr., 58–59
Green, Bobbie, 92
Green, Vernon, 44, 119, 135

Greenlee, W. A. "Gus", 10–12, 16, 21–22, 25, 28, 32, 34–36, 38, 40, 41, 43, 57, 59, 82, 115–16
Griffith, Clark, 66
Griffith Stadium, Washington, DC, 66, 85, 99, 100, 111–12
Grove, Lefty, 33
Guilfoile, Bill, 165

Hall, Horace Greeley, 21
Hall of Fame. *See* National Baseball Hall of Fame
Halpern, Murray, 47
Halpren, Anna, 153
Hannegan, Robert, 149
Harden, Billie, 155, 177n4
Harden, John, 155
Hardwick, Leon, 157–58, 162
Harmon, George, 153
Harridge, Will, 121
Harris, George W., 13
Harris, Vic, 158
Hartgrove, Robert S., 67, 87
Harvey, Bob, 103, 118, 123–24
Hastie, William, 53, 56, 97
Hayes, Thomas, 107
Hegan, Jim, 137
Height, Dorothy, 45
Hendrickson, Robert C., 61
Hill, James O., 113
Hill, Jimmy, 40, 48, 52, 61–62, 65, 69–70, 77, 83–86, 88, 97, 99, 103–6, 108, 111, 123, 141
Hill, Pete, 166
Hoffman, Harold G., 29, 61
Hogan, Larry, 166
holdouts, 32–33, 35
Holler, Buddy, 103
Holloway, Christopher "Crush", 14
Holmes, Ben, 128
Holway, John, 161

Homestead Grays, 22, 40, 76, 96, 134, 145, 154
    1935 season, 13
    1936 season, 24
    1937 season, 27–29
    1939 season, 43, 48–51
    1940 season, 63–66
    1941 season, 75, 78
    1942 season, 85–86, 88, 91–92
    1943 season, 99–100
    1944 season, 42, 105–7
    1945 season, 111–12
    1946 season, 125, 127
    1947 season, 135
    1948 season, 142
Hooker, Lenial, 61, 70, 77, 85, 88, 99–100, 103, 105, 111–12, 118, 129
House of David, 16
Houston Eagles, 146
Hucles, Henry, 98
Hueston, William, 93, 111

Idelson, Jeff, 166–67
Indianapolis Clowns, 82
Ink Spots, The, 156
Irvin, Maggie, 62
Irvin, Mary, 62
Irvin, Monte, xi, 2, 21, 34, 46–49, 51–52, 61, 65–67, 73, 77, 82–83, 85, 93, 108, 112, 118, 123, 125, 130, 131, 134–36, 139, 141–42, 151–52, 158, 162, 165
    Brooklyn Dodgers, contract with, 116, 134, 146
    drafted in Army, 99
    Mexico, playing in, 86–87
    National Baseball Hall of Fame, 159–61
    Newark Eagles, signed by, 33
    New York Giants, signed by, 146–47
    1946 Negro World Series, 127–29
    pseudonym, 34, 48

Isaacs, Stan, 160
Israel, Clarence "Pint", 61, 65, 73, 84, 91

Jack, Beau, 98
Jackman, Bill "Cannonball", 15
Jackson, R. R., 41
Jackson, Rufus "Sonneyman", 11, 42, 97, 133
Jackson, William R., 90
Jacobs, Carrie, 12
Jacobs, Eddie, 105
Jenkins, Clarence "Fats", 16
Jethroe, Sam, 115
Johnson, Brady, 110
Johnson, Cornelius, 14–15
Johnson, Jimmy "Slim", 39
Johnson, Rev. John H., 7–8, 13, 16, 49, 70, 117, 133, 140
Johnson, Judy, 160–61
Johnson, Leaman, 73, 83
Jones, A. J., 145
Jones, Ham, 39
Jones, Louis, 136–37
Jones, Mel, 134
Jones, Stuart "Slim", 44
Jones, Whalen A., 156

Kachline, Clifford, 158
Kansas City Monarchs, 1, 28, 63, 77, 92, 127–30
Keenan, John B., 98
Kerr, Paul, 159–60
Kessler, Jerry, 47, 68, 74, 146–47, 153
Kite, Alban, 70
Kuhn, Bowie, 159–61

Lacy, J. Russell, 46
Lacy, Sam, 43, 103–4, 107, 128, 150, 210–11n2
LaGuardia, Fiorello, 13, 78
LaMoine, Elsie, 61, 153
Landis, Kenesaw Mountain, 22, 58, 81

Laughton, Father Howard, 152
Lawrence, Carl, 74, 106
Leak, Curtis, 115
Lemon, Bob, 137
Leonard, Buck, 34, 105–6, 111, 118, 142, 160
Lester, Larry, 165
Lett, Harold, 37, 98
Leuschne, Bill, 76
Lewis, Ira, 25
Lewis, Rufus, 1, 124–29, 135
Lloyd, John Henry "Pop", 160–61
Los Angeles Dodgers, 156
Louis, Joe, 7, 13, 24, 37, 56, 72–73, 78, 85, 128, 163
Lowe, Laura, 158
Lundy, Dick "King Richard", 39, 47, 64–65
Lyle, George, 150

Mackey, Raleigh, "Biz", 5, 52, 61, 69, 96, 102, 108–9, 111–13, 118, 120, 122, 125–26, 131, 134, 156, 161, 166
    Newark Eagles, becomes manager of, 66, 110
    Newark Eagles, replaced as manager of, 83, 141
    Newark Eagles, sold to, 50
MacPhail, Larry, 134, 144
Malloy, James, 132
Manley, Abe, x–xi, 4–5, 11, 19, 24, 139, 141, 158, 162
    Brooklyn Eagles, operation of, 9, 11–16
    Camden Leafs, purchased, 5
    death of, 152–53
    family relations, 51–52
    formative years, 3–4
    Negro National League, administration of, 10, 21–22, 24, 32, 57, 81–82

Negro National League, threaten
to quit, 81–82
Negro National League, treasurer
of, 25, 31, 38, 58, 69, 96, 102
Newark Eagles, formation of, 17
poker player, x–xi
real estate endeavors, 71–72
signing players, 12, 14, 16, 23,
25–26, 33, 40, 50, 56, 60–61,
103, 141–42
thrifty nature, 51
trades, 26, 39, 73, 85, 96, 105,
110, 123
wealth of, 6, 9, 51–52, 153
Manley, Effa
birth date, x
Brooklyn Eagles business manager, 12
charitable events, 5–6, 24, 26–27,
85–86, 92
civic activities, 16, 101, 106, 154,
166
civil rights, passion for, xii, 7–8,
75, 166
entertainers, support of, 126
ethical behavior, 41–42
Father Flanagan's Boys' Home,
honorary citizen of, 154
Fisk University, 158–59
formative years, 3
fur coats, 6, 147, 162
game results, reporting on, 42
gender issues, 57–59, 81–82,
96–97, 166
good looks, ix, 151, 157
honors received, 68, 101, 145,
154, 162
marriages, 6, 153–54, 156
Mexican League, 86–87
millinery job, 3
musicians, friendships with, 153,
156–57

NAACP, treasurer of Newark
Chapter, 140, 153
National Baseball Hall of Fame,
elected to, 166
Negro leaguers, compensation for
signing, 117, 138, 146
Negro leagues, defending, 77, 143,
149–50, 157–58, 161–62, 166
Negro National League, administration of, 25, 28, 32, 41–42,
50, 57–60, 67, 76, 96, 122
Negro National League, non-
baseball persons as president,
32, 43–44, 56, 58, 78, 81, 93,
96, 121–22, 133
Negro National League, threaten-
ing to quit, 63, 81–82
Newark Eagles, administration of,
31–32, 38, 60, 67–68, 86–87,
93, 109–10, 112–13, 139, 166
New Jersey Afro Honor Roll,
name added to, 101
*New Jersey Herald Tribune* Hall
of Fame, inducted in, 145
opening day galas, 13, 47, 61–62,
72–73, 98
Organized Baseball, desired position in, 155
Paige, Satchel, relationship with,
35–36, 39, 61–63, 71
racial identification, 2
racial pride, 73
real estate endeavors, 52, 71–72
Rickey, Branch, relationship with,
116–20, 144–46, 149, 158
Robinson, Jackie, criticism of, 143
romantic relationships, x, 14, 39
signing players, 60, 69–70, 82–87,
97, 122–23
social activities, 27, 29

sportswriters, relationships with, 31, 42–43, 50, 57–58, 60, 86, 109, 144–46, 150–51, 161
trades, 83–84
war relief activities, 85–86, 92, 96, 101, 106, 166
YMCA honor, 68
Manley, Ivory, 51
Manley, Joel, 6
Manley, Langston, 51
Manley, Nathan, 4, 51
Manley, Rebecca, 3
Manley, William, 3
Manning, Max, 49, 52, 61, 65, 70, 77, 88, 96, 98, 108, 122, 126–27, 129–30, 135, 142
Marshall, Thurgood, 6
Martin, B. B., 102, 145–46
Martin, Clarence, 102
Martin, F. W., 46
Martin, J. B., 61, 63, 67, 97, 102, 107, 116–17, 121, 127–28, 143, 145, 156
Mathews, Francis, 60, 64, 72–74, 84–85, 157
Maxwell, Jocko, 61, 86
McDuffie, Terris, 14, 24, 27, 29, 36, 39–40, 49, 51, 71, 78, 105, 108, 110, 112, 115, 124
McHenry, Henry, 124
McKechnie, Bill, 137
McKeever, Steven W., 15
Memphis Red Sox, 102
Mendez, Joe, 166
Mexican League, 55, 60, 67, 73, 86–87, 96–97, 113, 124, 134, 141
Mexico, 66–67
Mills, Florence, 92
Mills, Maude, 92
Moore, Henry, 99
Moore, James "Red", 25–26
Morris, Leroy, 70

Morton, Ferdinand, 21, 24
Morton, Sherman, 23, 26
Moses, Al, 81–82
movie theaters, 36–37, 90–91
Murphy, Newark Mayor, 129

National Association for the Advancement of Colored People (NAACP), xii, 56, 73, 75–76, 140
National Baseball Hall of Fame, African Americans in, 157–62, 165–67
Negro American League (NAL), 28, 32, 41–42, 52–53, 63, 71, 95, 102, 107, 111, 116–17, 127, 145
Negro leaguers
compensation for signing, 117, 119–20, 138–39, 146, 156
tryouts for, 91, 115, 134
Negro leagues
constitution of, 121
criticism of, 116, 126, 138, 142–44
demise of, 149–52, 155
proposed commissioner of, 56, 107, 111
World Series, 1, 28–29, 91–92, 127–30
Negro National League (NNL), 9, 16
administration of, 9–10, 42, 57, 67, 116, 140
constitution of, 10, 133–34
end of, 145
finances of, 10, 28, 32
governance of, 21–22, 32
meetings of, 21–22, 24–26, 32, 42–44, 50–51, 56–57, 59, 69, 81–82, 95–96, 112, 122, 124, 133
umpires, 10, 44, 99, 124
Nelson, Jimmy "Cracker", 34, 48
Newark, NJ, 18–20, 65, 90, 104, 126
Newark Bears, 18, 20, 22, 64
Newark Dodgers, 15, 17–18

Newark Eagles
    bus (team), 75, 95, 126, 131
    finances of, 51, 120, 131, 141
    formation of, 17
    insurance coverage, 68, 75
    name change, 56
    1936 season, 23–25
    1937 season, 27–28
    1938 season, 36, 38
    1939 season, 47–51
    1940 season, 61–66
    1941 season, 73–75, 77–78
    1942 season, 85–86, 88, 91, 93
    1943 season, 98–100
    1944 season, 104–7
    1945 season, 110–13
    1946 season, 1, 124–30
    1947 season, 135–36, 139
    1948 season, 142sale of, 145
    standings (1936–1948), 169–72
Newcombe, Don, 2, 103, 105–9, 112, 118–20, 139, 149
New York Black Yankees, 17, 21, 73, 110, 145
    1938 season, 38
    1939 season, 49–50
    1940 season, 61–62, 65
    1941 season, 74, 77
    1942 season, 88
    1943 season, 99, 100
    1944 season, 105
    1945 season, 111–12
    1946 season, 124
    1947 season, 135–36
    1948 season, 142
New York Cubans, 17
    1935 season, 15
    1941 season, 74
    1942 season, 88
    1943 season, 99
    1944 season, 106

    1945 season, 110–11
    1946 season, 125
    1947 season, 135, 139
New York Giants, 146–47
New York Renaissance Five, 68
New York Yankees, 152
no-hit game, 99
numbers, 10, 179n13
Nunn, William, 25

O'Malley, Walter, 156
O'Neil, John "Buck", 77, 127, 129–30, 160, 165, 167
Overmyer, James, 166
Owens, Jesse, 14

Paige, Miles A., 105
Paige, Satchel, 16, 27, 32, 47, 64, 67, 71, 77, 92, 118, 130
    contract jumping, 60–63
    National Baseball Hall of Fame, inducted in, 159–60
    Newark Eagles, recruited by, 34–36, 38–40
    Newark Eagles, signed by, 56
    1946 Negro World Series, 127–30
Paige All-Stars, 127, 130–31
Parker, Tom, 142
Parks, Charlie, 77, 85, 96, 101
Partlow, Roy, 106, 118, 123, 125, 129–30, 142
Pasquel, Jorge, 60, 67, 86–87
Patterson, Pat, 84, 120
Peace, Warren, 135–36
Peacock, Eulace, 14
Pearson, Lennie, 1, 36, 61–62, 65, 68, 73, 75, 78, 82, 88, 91–92, 100, 103, 111, 118, 125, 128–29, 131, 135, 151
Petroskey, Dale, 165–66
Phailstock, A., 62
Philadelphia Stars, 83–85
    1935 season, 14

1936 season, 24
1938 season, 38
1939 season, 48–49, 51
1940 season, 62, 64
1941 season, 74, 77
1943 season, 98–100
1944 season, 104–6
1945 season, 111
1946 season, 124–26
1947 season, 135–36
Pittsburgh Crawfords, 36, 38, 41–42
Pittsburgh Pirates, 91
Pollock, Syd, 82, 107
Pompez, Alejandro "Alex", 10, 16, 53, 56–57, 59–60, 93, 107, 133, 166
Posey, Cumberland Willis "Cum", 10–11, 25, 28, 42–43, 50, 57–60, 66–67, 69, 76, 92–93, 96, 102, 117, 121–122, 166
Posey, Ethel, 122, 133
Posey, Seward "See", 76, 122
Powell, Rev. Adam Clayton, Jr., 15
Powell, Rev. Adam Clayton, Sr., 74
Powell, Clilan Betnany "C. B.", 56–57
Powell, Richard, 160
Powers, Jimmy, 13
prostitution, 67, 72, 104
Puerto Rico, 67, 78, 85
Puerto Rico Winter League, 22, 60, 68

Radcliffe, Ted "Double Duty", 12, 134
Rainey, Joseph 78, 81–82, 210n2
Randolph, A. Philip, 75
Randolph, Oliver, 140
Razaf, Andy, 61, 98, 156–57
Richer, Juan E., 87
Rickey, Branch, 144, 149, 207–8n16
    Brooklyn Brown Dodgers, founder of, 115
    Campanella, Roy, signing of, 119, 149
    Doby, Larry, scouting of, 136
    Irvin, Monte, attempted signing of, 116, 134, 146
    Negro leagues, contempt for, 116, 126, 138
    Newcombe, Don, signing of, 119, 149
    Robinson, Jackie, signing of, 113–17, 137–38, 149
Riddick, Vernon, 60–61
Roan, Joseph, 29
Roberts, Spec, 110
Robinson, Bill "Bojangles", 45, 49
Robinson, Jackie, 113–18, 130, 132, 137–39, 142–43, 149, 160
Rodolph, Oliva Mamie, 59
Rogan, "Bullet Joe", 161
Rollins, Cora, 7, 59, 61
Roosevelt, Franklin Delano, 23–24, 75–76, 81, 100
Rosen, Al, 137
Rosenthal, Irvin, 153
Rosenthal, Jack, 153
Ruffin, Leon, 85, 96, 101, 129, 134–35, 142
Ruppert, Jacob R., 20
Ruppert Stadium, Newark, N.J., xi–xii, 1, 17, 20–21, 45–46, 62, 75, 90, 130, 152
Ruth, Babe, 5

Saigh, Fred, 149
St. Louis Stars, 102
salaries of players, 32, 33, 35, 60, 63, 66, 86, 93, 96, 103, 108, 122–23, 142–43
Santop, Louis, 166
Saperstein, Abe, 76, 82
schedule problems, 100
Schmeling, Max, 24
Schultz, Dutch, 10

Schwehm, P. E., 97
Scott, Armond W., 153–54
Seay, Dick, 26, 28, 61
segregation, 6, 18–19, 44–45, 88–91, 100, 104, 113, 132, 144
Semler, James "Soldier Boy", 22, 24, 38, 53, 56–57, 59–60, 133–34
Service, Calvin, 23
Shackelford, John G., 107, 116
Shipley, Ruth, 68
Simon, Percy, 55–56, 88, 110, 153
Simpson, Reginald, 125
Smathers, William H., 87
Smith, Ford, 128–29, 146–47
Smith, Hilton, 77, 127–30
Smith, Howard Alexander, 113
Smith, Jessie Carney, 158–59
Smith, Wendell, 10, 40, 43, 91, 96, 107, 115, 126–27, 134, 140, 145, 151
Snow, Felton, 126
Sowell, Herb, 1, 128
Spink, J. G. Taylor, 161–62
Springfield Grays, 23
Stack, Ed, 165
Stearns, "Turkey", 161
Stone, Ed, 16, 28, 33, 49, 61, 73, 91, 99
Stoneham, Horace, 146
Strauch, Peter, 124
Strong, Nat, 17, 76
Strong, Ted, 77
Sukeforth, Clyde, 115–16, 136
Suttles, George "Mule", xi, 23, 25–26, 28, 43, 48–50, 61–62, 73–74, 88, 97, 103, 166
Sydnor, Earl, 49–50

Taylor, Ben, 11–14, 166
Thomas, Dave "Showboat", 115, 118
Thomas, Edison, 12, 66
Thomas, Lowell, 13
Thomas, Nelson, 136

Thomason, Charles, 74
Thompson, Charlie, 96, 101
Torriente, Cristobal, 166
Trautman, George, 150
Trouppe, Quincy, 157
Turner, "Bulldog", 64–65
Tyler, Carrie, 102
Tyler, Charles H., 11, 17, 102

umpires, 10, 44, 64, 99, 112, 124, 126–27
United States League, 115–17

Vail, Craig, 51
Veeck, Bill, 136–39, 144
Vincent, Fay, 166

Walker, Larry, 89
Washington, Chester, 42
Washington Elite Giants, 23–24
Watkins, Murray, 103, 109, 118–19, 123
Webb, Chick, 29
Webber, H. B., 109
Weiss, George, 20, 22, 183n13
Wells, Thelma, 55
Wells, Willie, 26, 28–29, 46, 49–50, 86, 91, 110–11, 118
    batting helmet, 88
    beaning, 88
    Mexico, playing in, 55, 60, 73, 96–97, 103–4
    Newark Eagles, became manager of, 83–84, 109
    Newark Eagles, signed by, 23
White, Sol, 166
Wigden, Hazel M., 63–64
Wilkes, Jimmy "Sea Biscuit", 112
Wilkins, Roy, 15, 73
Wilkinson, James Leslie "J. L.", 10, 61–63, 76, 92, 117, 166
Williams, Bill "Cotton", 129, 135–36
Williams, Harry, 26, 43

Williams, Lemuel, 25
Williams, Leonard "Big Bill", 25
Williams, Marvin, 112, 115
Williams, Willie C. "Curly", 141–42
Wilson, Fred "Sardo", 46–47
Wilson, Jud, 166
Wilson, Thomas "Smiling Tom", 10, 25, 31–32, 39, 42–44, 56–59, 61, 63, 67, 81, 96, 99–100, 102, 106–7, 116–17, 127–28, 133–35
    NNL, efforts to remove as president of, 56, 76, 93, 121–22, 133
Wilson, W. Rollo, 10
Winston-Salem Eagles, 26
Wolfe, W. W., 40
women (white), adulating black players, 144
workman's compensation, 67–68
World War II, 78, 85, 95, 105
    defense industry employment, 75–76, 96, 98–100, 113
    draft effects, 91–92, 96–97, 101, 103, 111
    gasoline rationing, 95–96
    green light letter, 81
    war relief activities, 85–86, 92, 96, 101, 106
Wright, Ernest, 107
Wright, John, 36, 43, 99, 118, 149
Wurm, Frank, 115

Yancey, Bill, 103
Yankee Stadium, New York City, 38, 49, 56–58, 74, 76–77, 88, 111, 130, 134, 139
Young, A. S. "Doc", ix, 161
Young, Fay, 128
Young, Frank A., 50, 60, 75, 143, 150–51
Young, W. H., 145, 147

,

# SUGGESTED READINGS

Robert W. Peterson's *Only the Ball Was White* (New York: Prentice Hall, 1970) offers a classic, well-written synthesis of library research and interviews with many stars from the Negro leagues. Other books of interviews with Negro league players are John B. Holway's *Voices from the Great Black Baseball Leagues* (New York: Dodd Meade & Co., 1975); Brent Kelley's *Voices from the Negro Leagues: Conversations with 52 Baseball Standouts of the Period, 1924–1960* (Jefferson, North Carolina: McFarland & Co., 1997) and *The Negro Leagues Revisited: Conversations with 66 More Baseball Heroes* (Jefferson, NC: McFarland & Co., 2000).

For biographical information on players, umpires, and executives see James A. Riley's *The Biographical Encyclopedia of the Negro Baseball Leagues* (New York: Carroll & Graf Publishers, Inc., 1994). For comprehensive statistics by team, seasons, and players see Dick Clark and Larry Lester's *The Negro Leagues Book* (Cleveland, OH: Society for American Baseball Research, 1994) and John B. Holway's *The Complete Book of Baseball's Negro Leagues: The Other Half of Baseball History* (Fern Park, FL: Hastings House Publishers, 2001). A number of Negro league players' life stories are available, including Joe Black's *Ain't Nobody Better Than You* (Scottsdale, AZ: Ironwood Lithographs, Inc., 1983); Roy Campanella's *It's Good to Be Alive* (Boston: Little, Brown and Company, 1959); Monte Irvin's *Nice Guys Finish First: The Autobiography of Monte Irvin* (with James A. Riley, New York: Carroll & Graf, 1996); Buck Leonard's *Buck Leonard: The Black Lou Gehrig* (with James A. Riley, New York: Carroll and Graf, 1995); Bob Luke's *Willie Wells: "El Diablo" of the Negro Leagues* (Austin, TX: University of Texas Press, 2007); Bob Luke's *The Baltimore Elite Giants: Sport and Society in the Age of Negro League Baseball* (Baltimore, MD: Johns Hopkins University Press, 2009); Leroy (Satchel) Paige's *Maybe I'll Pitch Forever: A Great Baseball Player Tells the Hilarious Story Behind the Legend* (Lincoln: University of Nebraska Press, 1993); Murray Polner's *Branch Rickey: A Biography* (New York: Antheneum, 1982); Lee Lowenfish's *Branch Rickey: Baseball's Ferocious Gentleman* (Lincoln: University of Nebraska Press, 2007); Bob Motley's *Ruling Over Monarchs, Giants and Stars: Umpiring in the Negro Leagues and Beyond* (New York: Sports Publishing, 2007); James Overmyer's *Effa Manley and the Newark Eagles* (Metuchen, NJ: Scarecrow Press, 1993); Jackie Robinson's *I Never Had It Made* (New York: Putnam. 1972); Phil S. Dixon's *John "Buck" O'Neil: The Rookie, The Man, The Legacy 1938* (Bloomington, IN: Author Solutions, 2009).

For in-depth treatment of the history of the Negro leagues see Leslie A. Heaphy's *The Negro Leagues: 1869–1960* (Jefferson City, MO: McFarland & Co, 2002); Neil Lanctot's *Negro League Baseball: The Rise and Ruin of a Black Institution* (Philadelphia: University of Pennsylvania Press, 2004); Donn Rogosin's *Invisible Men: Life in Baseball's Negro Leagues* (New York: Atheneum, 1983); and Lawrence D. Hogan's *Shades of Glory: The Negro Leagues and the Story of African American Baseball* (Washington, DC: National Geographic, 2006).

Brad Snyder's *Beyond the Shadow of the Senators: The Untold Story of the Homestead Grays and the Integration of Baseball* (Chicago: Contemporary Books, 2003) offers an insightful history of one of the Eagles' nemesis, the Washington Homestead Grays. For the other nemesis see Janet Bruce's *The Kansas City Monarchs: Champions of Black Baseball* (Lawrence: University of Kansas Press, 1987) in which she gives the history of the team many consider to have been the best in the Negro leagues.

For accounts of Newark's history, see Brad R. Tuttle's *How Newark Became Newark: The Rise, Fall, and Rebirth of an American City* (New Brunswick, NJ: Rutgers University Press, 2009); and Barbara J. Kukla's *Swing City: Newark Night Life*, 1925–50 (New Brunswick, NJ: Rutgers University Press, 2002).

# ABOUT THE AUTHOR

BOB LUKE has published three previous books: *Dean of Umpires: The Biography of Bill McGowan, 1896–1954* (2005); *Willie Wells: 'El Diablo' of the Negro Leagues* (2007), which won the 2008 Robert Peterson Recognition Award; and *The Baltimore Elite Giants: Sport and Society in the Age of the Negro Leagues* (2009), which won the 2009 Robert Peterson Recognition Award. He lives in Garrett Park, Maryland, with his wife Judy Wentworth.